Experiment Perilous

Experiment Perilous

Physicians and Patients Facing the Unknown

Renée C. Fox

With a new epilogue by the author

Transaction Publishers

New Brunswick (U.S.A.) and London (U.K.)

This book is printed on acid-free paper that meets the American National Standard for Permanence of Paper for Printed Library Materials.

Library of Congress Catalog Number: 97–9857
ISBN: 1–56000–949-7
Printed in the United States of America

Library of Congress Cataloging-in-Publication Data
Fox, Renée C. (Renée Claire), 1928–
    Experiment perilous : physicians and patients facing the unknown /
Renée C. Fox : with a new epilogue by the author.
        p.   cm.
    Previously published: Glencoe, Ill. : Free Press, 1959.
    Includes bibliographical references and index.
    ISBN 1–56000–949–7 (pbk. : alk. paper)
    1. Human experimentation in medicine—Moral and ethical aspects.
2. Clinical medicine—Research—Moral and ethical aspects. 3. Human
experimentation in medicine—Social aspects. 4. Clinical medicine—
Research—Social aspects. 5. Physician and patient. 6. Peter Bent
Brigham Hospital—Research—History. I. Title
R853.H8F68   1997
619—dc21   97–9857
                                                              CIP

For the physicians of the Metabolic Group

and the patients of Ward F-Second

. . . and for Joe

Contents

Acknowledgments

THE FOLLOWING persons made it possible for me to undertake and realize the writing of this book: P. Fred and Henrietta Fox, my parents; Talcott Parsons, Bernard and Elinor G. Barber, Dr. Paul D. McGehee, Joseph A. Precker, Dr. Roy C. Swan, Toinette Balkema, Dahla Larson, Jennie Pecevich, Bridget Gellert, Elisabeth G. Humez, the physicians of the Metabolic Group, and the patients of Ward F-Second. My debt to these friends, teachers, and participants in the *Experiment Perilous* is beyond words.

Renée C. Fox

New York, N. Y.

Introduction to the 1974 Edition

IN THE EARLY 1950s, when I undertook the research on which *Experiment Perilous* is based, the sociology of medicine, though in its infancy, had begun to flourish. I was one of a number of social scientists, for example, who were engaged in what were then pioneering, participant-observation-based studies of hospitals or hospital wards as social systems. Out of these inquiries eventually came William Caudill's *The Psychiatric Hospital as a Small Society*, Rose Laub Coser's *Life in the Ward*, Erving Goffman's *Asylums*, Julius Roth's *Timetables*, and *The Mental Hospital* by Alfred H. Stanton and Morris S. Schwartz, among others.[1]

However, my own field experiences differed from those of my colleagues in at least one significant respect. I had become involved in studying a hospital community, known as F-Second, that was a metabolic research ward. The men who were hospitalized here were ill with diseases that had not yielded to the diagnostic and therapeutic capacities of modern medicine. Partly as a consequence, they were patients who were willing, and in many instances zealous, research subjects for the physicians of the Metabolic Group, a team of clinical investigators with the dual and often conflicting responsibility of caring for the patients of F-Second and conducting research upon them in order to advance medical knowledge and technique.

Ward F-Second plunged me into a world of extreme stress that turned around inexorable illness, human experimentation, uncertainty, suffering, and death. In this shared predicament, along with the patients and physicians, I had to find ways of coming to terms with the existential implications of that "perilous experiment," the anguished emotions it aroused and the ethical dilemmas it posed. My professional obligation was to navigate sufficiently well in that situation to make good, objective, but feeling sociology out of it. The ways that I developed for coping with the tragicomedy of the ward were explicitly and implicitly taught to me by the patients and physicians of F-Second. The shared stresses and the common modes of dealing with them that these two groups of men had evolved gradually became the focus of my study.

The major intellectual challenge with which Ward F-Second confronted me was that, to my knowledge, no first-hand sociological study of terminal illness, medical experimentation with human subjects, or the psychosocial dynamics of therapeutic innovation had ever been made. Not only was there no precedent for such an inquiry, but its legitimacy was questionable. Neither the moral justification for this type of study nor its social scientific meaningfulness was established. If anything, the academic medical and social scientific climate of the 1950s ran counter to it. A strong commitment to "being scientific" prevailed, with a heavy emphasis on achieving the highest possible standards of rationality, objectivity, and rigor. Even in medical settings conducive to it, for example, serious, outright discussions about death, dying, or terminal illness were generally considered too philosophical and too emotional to conform to this image of science. Among social scientists, these topics were not proscribed; they simply fell outside the orbit of what was then defined as an appropriate and fruitful topic to pursue. Both medical and social scientific milieus had been sufficiently influenced by psychoanalytic thinking to be wary about the implications of getting "over-involved" in the human situations with which they dealt as professionals, or of becoming "overly identified" with them. This was regarded as not only unscientific and unprofessional, but also as a symptom of deeper personality problems that ought to be "worked through." The predominant ideology of rationality and detachment inhibited the development of a sociology of suffering or of death. And it contributed to widespread skepticism about the findings of participant-observation field studies on the grounds that however "real" they might seem to be, and however sensitively and compassionately they might be rendered, they were inherently subjective. Finally, the early 1950s was a time of great enthusiasm about clinical medical research. World War II seemed to have brought in its wake a new, very promising era of biomedical advance. Expectation about imminent breakthroughs in medical knowledge and healing capacities ran high. Especially in the United States, clinical investigation enjoyed prestige as well as approval, and was being handsomely supported by private foundations and the young National Institutes of Health. Memories of the Nazi medical war crimes were still hauntingly present. But the renaissance of medical research was incompatible with sustained brooding about the ethicality of human experimentation under various conditions, or about the social and cultural questions that it raised.

Twenty years later, the orientation and ambience both in medicine and social science are markedly different. Although the canon of scientific objectivity still guides medical and social research, criticism of the "dehumanization" that an overly detached approach can effect is more frequently heard. There is also less of a tendency to view "involvement" exclusively as a methodological aberration. Concerned interest in ethical and existential issues related to biomedical advance, the delivery of medical care, and medical decision-making in general is now more salient in medicine and social science. Such issues have become proper, even fashionable, subjects of study in these fields, and in the fields of philosophy, theology, and law, as well. Two substantive areas on which this interest has come to focus are death and dying, and medical research with human subjects. The attention now being devoted to these subjects is one of numerous signs that a serious re-examination of certain values and beliefs on which modern medicine is premised may be taking place. These developments in medicine are part of a broader and deeper process of cultural reflection, reorientation, and change currently taking place in American society.[2]

Experiment Perilous deals with phenomena that are matters of widespread concern in the 1970s. And it does so in a way that tries to infuse objectivity with compassion. In both these senses, the work is more contemporaneous now than it was at the time of its initial publication. Furthermore, some of the biomedical developments that it treats are still in the forefront, notably steroid and immunosuppressive therapy, cardiac surgery, the use of the artificial kidney machine to effect hemodialysis, and the transplantation of human organs. In fact, these are among the therapeutic innovations most often invoked when social, moral, or metaphysical questions about the consequences of biomedical advance are discussed. Yet, despite the florescence of interest in the kinds of experiences that were lived out by the patients and physicians of Ward F-Second, no comparable study of a medical research unit has appeared since the publication of *Experiment Perilous*. Thus, the reissuance of this book in a paperback edition seems fitting as well as timely.

The Hippocratic aphorism that inspired the book's title was etched in stone on a building of the medical school with which Ward F-Second was affiliated. During the period in which I conducted my participant observation, I passed that building every day. Each time I did, I was confronted with the perspective on the human condition expressed by Hippocrates' maxim. In the final pages of the book I implied that I shared this cosmic view, in suggesting that what F-Second's patients and physicians underwent, and how they responded to it linked them with "other experiments perilous of which men are a living and dying part." After more than twenty years of first-hand medical sociological research and of all the personal life experience that two decades can bring, I would still claim that this is "the most basic and general significance" of Ward F-Second and of *Experiment Perilous*.

RENÉE C. FOX
Philadelphia, 1973

NOTES

1. The full references to these works are: William Caudill, *The Psychiatric Hospital as a Small Society*. Cambridge, Mass.: Harvard University Press, 1958; Rose Laub Coser, *Life in the Ward*. East Lansing, Mich.: Michigan State University Press, 1962; Erving Goffman, *Asylums*. Garden City, N.Y.: Doubleday and Co., Anchor Books, 1961; Julius Roth, *Timetables: Structuring the Passage of Time in Hospital Treatment and Other Careers*. Indianapolis, Ind.: Bobbs-Merrill Co., 1963; Alfred H. Stanton and Morris S. Schwartz, *The Mental Hospital*. New York: Basic Books, 1954.

2. The analysis on which these statements are based is too complex to present adequately here. It is further developed in: the introductory and concluding chapters of *The Courage To Fail: A Social View of Organ Transplants and Dialysis* (co-authored with Judith P. Swazey; forthcoming from the University of Chicago Press); "The 'Gift of Life' and its Reciprocation" (co-authored with Talcott Parsons and Victor M. Lidz), *Social Research,* Vol. 39, No. 3, Autumn 1972, pp. 367-415; and in a still unpublished paper, entitled "Ethical and Existential Developments in Contemporaneous American Medicine," prepared for presentation at the Conference on Medical Sociology held in Warsaw (Jablonna), Poland, August 20-August 25, 1973.

CHAPTER 1 — Introduction to the Metabolic Research Group and Ward F-Second

Life is short
And the art long
The occasion instant
Experiment perilous
Decision difficult
           —Hippocrates, "Aphorisms"

IN A TIME-SEASONED red brick building, set back a few hundred yards from a maze of trolley-car tracks and a big-city traffic circle, bounded and illumined by the famous medical school that flanks it, and situated at the end of a long hospital corridor—there existed a special community known as Ward F-Second. The windows of F-Second overlooked the laboratory:

There's not much else to see, except the rest of the building [a patient hospitalized on the ward explained]. Only in the evening, if I sort of get back by the door and look out, sometimes I can see the sunset . . .

F-Second was an all-male, fifteen-bed metabolic research ward in a small but renowned teaching hospital, affiliated with a prominent medical school, located in one of the major cities of New England. A considerable number of the patients hospitalized on Ward F-Second were ill with diseases that are still not well understood and cannot be effectively controlled by present-day medical science. Partly as a consequence, many of these patients had agreed to act as research subjects for the so-called Metabolic Group of the hospital. This was a team of eleven young physicians: clinical investigators, whose dual responsibility was to care for the patients of F-Second and also to conduct research upon them.

13

Experiment Perilous is a study of the physicians of the Metabolic Group and the patients of Ward F-Second.[1] It focuses particularly on various problems these physicians and patients encountered in this setting; some of the stresses they experienced as a consequence; their ways of trying to cope with these problems and stresses; and some observed consequences of the ways of coming to terms they evolved.

The point of view of this study is predominantly sociological. By this we mean that it deals with these physicians and patients chiefly in terms of the ways their common predicament and roles as members of the Metabolic Group and the Metabolic Ward respectively affected their reactions and behavior. Attention is primarily concentrated on the *shared* difficulties of physicians and patients in this context, and on their *socially patterned* ways of meeting these difficulties. Less emphasis is given to those more individualized reactions of particular physicians and patients which are assumed to be largely personality-determined.

Although in this respect the study is more sociological than psychological in its analytic focus, a good deal of the material to follow represents something like a middle-ground fusion between these two sorts of orientation. To cite a specific example: as will be seen, some of the forms of behavior designated "ways of coming to terms" or "ways of coping" with the stresses of Ward F-Second are in a sense what psychologists would call "defenses" and indications of "transference," "countertransference," and "secondary gain." This study deals with such mechanisms and modes of adjustment in considerable detail. However, this is done more from the point of view of some of the circumstances on Ward F-Second out of which they seemed to originate, the social processes by which they appeared to be learned and enforced, and the social functions and dysfunctions which seemed to ensue from the kinds of behavior they governed, than from the standpoint of their relevance to the personalities of individual patients and physicians.

The primary materials on which this book is based are the actual words I heard these physicians and patients speak and the concrete ways in which, from the vantage point of a participant observer on Ward F-Second, and in the laboratory and conference room of the Metabolic Group, I saw them behave. Most of this observing was done in two concentrated periods of five months each. From September, 1951, through January, 1952, and again, from September, 1952, through January, 1953, I spent every day, from early morning to late evening, in continuous, direct, intimate contact with the physicians and patients of F-Second, taking part in their activities in order to observe systematically and to try to understand their problems and ways of coming to terms. In the periods between these intervals of intensive observation, significant happenings on the ward and in the laboratory were followed through correspondence, occasional telephone calls, and a number of visits to the Hospital. Since 1953, contact with physicians and patients has been maintained in the same ways. Most recently, in the summer of 1957, I spent several weeks at the hospital reviewing past events and catching up on new developments, by talking to the physicians currently affiliated with the Metabolic Group as well as to several "veteran" patients from Ward F-Second, and by studying the charts of many of the patients who were hospitalized on the ward during the era in which direct observations were originally made.

Participant observation was the chief, but not the sole, method of research for *Experiment Perilous*. Two auxiliary methods have already been mentioned: focused interviews with physicians and patients, and a survey of hospital charts. I had access to several other rich sources of clinical material. The Metabolic Group allowed me to read and draw upon a vast file of letters which they had written to and received from patients who had been hospitalized on Ward F-Second. In addition, the Psychiatric Group of the Hospital gave me typed verbatim copies of all the interviews that they conducted with patients from this ward. I also reviewed the professional publications of the Metabolic Group over the past ten years, the descriptive essays about their work published in the annual reports of the Hospital, and as many of the numerous lay-press accounts of their research activities as could be located. Each of the physicians of the Metabolic Group was asked to fill out a questionnaire about certain aspects of his personal background and his professional training interests and plans. Finally, there is a sense in which the research in which I have been engaged during the past five years (1952-1958) can be regarded as supplementary to what I learned directly from and about the physicians and patients of Ward F-Second. In connection with studies of medical education which are now being conducted by the Bureau of Applied Social Research of Columbia University,[2] I have been a participant observer in a medical school, witnessing at first hand some of the events, experiences, and processes by which medical students become physicians. This has given me an opportunity to enlarge and deepen my understanding of physicians, patients, and hospital wards, and, above all, to learn a good deal about the knowledge, skills, attitudes, values, and behavior patterns that enter into the growth and development of physicians.

This study of Ward F-Second and the Metabolic Group is a single part of a larger research undertaking still in progress. It was carried out under the auspices of a long-term investigation of the biochemical and psychological effects of stress on man, which was organized in 1951 by the Metabolic and Psychiatric Groups of the Hospital as a collaborative enterprise.[3] In turn, these research activities were a direct consequence of medical scientific developments that made it possible to isolate and synthesize ACTH, cortisone, and a number of other compounds of steroid structure produced by the pituitary and adrenal glands. Since "the pituitary-adrenal system is an essential factor in the response of the human organisms to life stress,"[4] the Metabolic and Psychiatric Groups felt that these developments gave them an "opportunity which had never previously existed for studying the intimate psychological and biochemical repercussions of certain crucial human experiences,"[5] as well as of physiologically- and pharmacologically-induced stress.

In many respects, the period during which the observations of the Metabolic Group and Ward F-Second were made was an exciting, forward-going time of progress in the history of this clinical research unit. After a half-century of intensive investigation by the medical profession at large, a number of the hormones produced by the adrenal cortex had been discovered and synthesized, and were being tried on a host of diseases, in some instances with what appeared to be dramatic therapeutic effects. Within the framework of these medical-scientific advances, the Metabolic Group itself was engaged in assaying the activity of newly-synthesized steroids that had shown potential usefulness as therapeutic agents when tried on laboratory animals. They were administering these compounds to patients with a wide variety of clinical conditions (primarily metabolic, endocrinological, cardiovascular, renal, and malignant diseases);

experimenting with various modes (intravenous, intramuscular, and oral) of administering them; and studying their biochemical, biological, and clinical effects. At the same time, in the laboratory, the Group was making steady progress in developing standardized methods for the quantitative measurement of adrenal response in man.

Perhaps the most heartening events which the Metabolic Group experienced during this period were those connected with the diagnosis and treatment of Addison's disease (adrenal cortical insufficiency). The advent of ACTH and cortisone had opened a new chapter in the clinical management of this condition, which until this time had been incapacitating and, in many instances, fatal. The Group had done pioneer work in developing an ACTH test for rapidly and accurately diagnosing this disease, and in evolving a regimen for treating it with cortisone. Largely as a result of their research and experimentation, it had become possible to maintain the majority of such patients in good health, and to restore many of them to an active, normal life.

The synthesis of cortisone and other adrenal cortical steroids had also made it possible to remove completely the adrenal glands of patients, and to maintain them postoperatively on substitution therapy. Thus, in collaboration with the Surgery and Renal Groups of the Hospital, the Metabolic Group was investigating the effect of total adrenalectomy on patients with advanced hypertensive vascular disease, reactivated cancer of the prostate, and hyperadrenalism. In conjunction with the Surgery Group, the Metabolic Group was also studying the body water and electrolyte problems of patients who had undergone cardiac surgery (mitral valvuloplasty) for mitral stenosis. With the Renal Group, they were conducting studies on patients in acute renal failure and with chronic renal disease—particularly those with severe edema and those in renal shutdown who underwent hemodialysis on the artificial kidney machine. Finally, the Metabolic, Renal, and Surgery Groups were experimenting with surgically transplanting an apparently healthy kidney into the bodies of a few patients dying of renal failure.

The work of the Metabolic Group with total bilateral adrenalectomy, hemodialysis,[6] and kidney transplants was connected with some of the more somber and discouraging aspects of their endeavors. For the period during which the physicians of the Metabolic Group were observed was not simply a time when they were enjoying the triumphs of significant advances in knowledge of adrenal cortical steroids and evidence of their beneficial clinical effects. Quite to the contrary, there were certain respects in which these two years (in the words of one physician) were among the most "grim" and "frustrating" in the history of the Group.

Because procedures like adrenalectomy, hemodialysis, and renal transplant were radical and still largely untried, they were attempted only on patients who were acutely, seriously, and often terminally ill. (Many of these were patients, as one physician put it, "who could very well be dead the next day.") In fact, at the time when I began observing the Group they had recently lost a number of patients with advanced hypertension on whom they had conducted adrenalectomies—including the patient for whom they had previously held the most hope. As yet, no transplanted kidney had survived for more than a matter of weeks. Adrenalectomies for hyperadrenalism and reactivated carcinoma of the prostate seemed to offer more promise, but the results were still very unpredictable. Furthermore, because of the severe illnesses of the patients on whom these procedures had been tried and the tentative state of the Group's relevant knowledge at the time, the clinical problems that the postoperative management of these patients presented were "formidable" ones.

It was also becoming increasingly apparent to the Group at this time that ACTH, cortisone, and related compounds were less effective and more dangerous in some ways than had been originally suspected. Beginning with the report of Hench and his associates in 1949, which pointed out that ACTH and cortisone produced remarkable improvement in patients with rheumatoid arthritis, many dramatic descriptions of the therapeutic effects of these substances on a number of apparently unrelated illnesses had appeared in the medical literature. However, in 1951, the Metabolic Group was finding that in many cases these beneficial effects were "more apparent than real." That is, rather than curing the underlying cause of the disease to which they were applied, these hormones only temporarily relieved some of its symptoms. The Group was also discovering that under certain circumstances these agents had undesirable and even hazardous side-effects. Patients to whom they administered these drugs sometimes developed edema, glycosuria, an ulcer, or symptoms like those of Cushing's syndrome, such as acne, hirsutism, buffalo hump, rounding of the face, and osteoporosis. The Group had begun to realize that in bacterial infections, ACTH and cortisone could mask the symptoms while the invasion of tissues by pathological organisms progressed more rapidly. In some cases administering these hormones to patients precipitated psychotic episodes; in others, their withdrawal after a prolonged period of therapy left patients in a temporary state of adrenal insufficiency until their adrenal and pituitary glands resumed normal function.

The fact that the hormones with which the Metabolic Group was experimenting had unanticipated negative side effects on patients, and that they were proving to be ameliorative rather than curative, along with their difficulties in keeping alive and managing the clinical course of patients who had undergone radical experimental surgery, account for many of the stressful problems which these research physicians faced at the time this study was made.

"Viewed from a few years later, we seem rather sophomoric," a member of the Metabolic Group commented when he read this book in manuscript. "In fact, we *were* young," he went on to say, "relatively inexperienced and enthusiastic, with less good judgment and more immediate goals than are probably ideal for clinical investigation." As a lay person, I am not qualified to judge whether or not this physician's retrospective appraisal of the outlook and performance of the Metabolic Group was justified. However, what he said does suggest that the way in which the members of the Group thought, felt, and acted in the face of the problems and stresses they shared may have been significantly influenced by certain personal and professional characteristics that they had in common. I shall not attempt systematically to relate such background characteristics to my analysis of the problems, stresses, and ways of coming to terms of these physicians. However, because it may be pertinent, and enlightening to the reader, I shall simply present certain factual information about the members of the Group here.

As the physician quoted indicated, the members of the Group were young. The oldest among them was thirty-four years of age, the youngest twenty-eight, and the majority (seven) between the ages of thirty and thirty-one.

The members of the Group were not only young chronologically.

They were also in a relatively early phase of their professional careers. All had completed their internships and served as residents. Two members of the Group had Ph.D. degrees (one in Pharmacology, the other in Biochemistry). All had done some teaching, some research (for the most part, basic rather than clinical research), and (with the exception of one physician) each had published several articles before joining the Group. (Eight members of the Group had published two articles; one had published four; and the physician with a Ph.D. in Pharmacology had published twelve articles). Only one member of the Group had spent any time in practice (one and a half years).

These physicians were all seriously interested in having a career in academic medicine which would combine "work with patients, teaching and clinical research." However, although committed to an academic career in this general sense, they were less decisive about some of its more specific aspects. They did not know exactly what kind of balance between caring for patients, teaching, and research they wished to strike permanently; and they were not yet sure about the kinds of metabolic-endocrine problems they would most like to investigate. In fact, without exception, these young physicians looked upon their affiliation with the Group as an opportunity to "get excellent fundamental training, in a very stimulating environment, in the field of metabolic-endocrine disease . . . to learn how to do clinical research in this area . . . to see how [they] would like this sort of research . . . [and] on that basis to definitely decide how much of [their] professional career [they] would devote to it."

One final distinguishing characteristic of the Group as a whole was that they were exceptionally competent, select young physicians who had been carefully chosen by the Professor of Medicine who was their Chief on the basis of their demonstrated and potential abilities as clinicians and investigators.

In the chapters to follow, after the physicians of the Metabolic Group have spoken about the problems and stresses which they faced, and their ways of dealing with them, their patients on Ward F-Second will talk about their own related difficulties and characteristic ways of coming to terms. It has already been stated that many of these patients were seriously ill with inexorable or progressively debilitating diseases; and it will soon become apparent that they were very articulate about the situation they shared and the tragicomic ward community they created about it. In certain respects, as one patient put it, Ward F-Second was a "very different sort of world." However, its inherent poignancy and the expressiveness of the patients who comprised it might make it seem to the reader more "different" than it actually was, unless he knows the following descriptive facts about the men of Ward F-Second.

To begin with, the amount of formal education represented by the patients on F-Second was probably not unusual. For example, if we consider the first one hundred patients encountered on Ward F-Second, we find that 3 had less than an elementary school education; 26 had graduated from an elementary school; 32 were high-school graduates; 26 were college graduates; and 13 were young enough still to be classified as students. At first glance, it might appear that these patients had a better-than-average education. However, as we shall see, the patients on Ward F-Second were relatively young in age; and it is a well-established fact that persons in the younger age groups in our society have a higher average level of education than those in older age groups.

Furthermore, our close-to-verbatim records of what we heard patients say as we moved about the ward do not suggest that the better-educated patients were always the more eloquent. For example, in Chapter V, which is devoted to case studies of several patients, we shall have occasion to meet two of the more articulate members of the ward community (Paul O'Brian and Leo Angelico) and to hear them speak at considerable length. Neither of these patients had an outstanding amount of formal education. Leo Angelico never completed high school; and Paul O'Brian was a high-school graduate who had taken a few college-level courses. Thus, the articulateness of patients on Ward F-Second was not necessarily connected with a high level of education. (As a well-known novelist has pointed out, if you listen intently to how people talk you discover that "so many persons say things poetically."[7] However, to some degree, the nature and magnitude of the problems F-Seconders faced may have enhanced their ability to say things feelingly and well.)

Looked at in the very broadest diagnostic and prognostic terms, the cross-section of cases on Ward F-Second probably did not differ too greatly from those found on medical wards of many general hospitals. The majority of patients on F-Second were ill with chronic or degenerative conditions—particularly endocrine, metabolic, renal, cardiovascular, and malignant diseases.

However, when we look at the age distribution of patients on F-Second, this picture of a ward comprised mainly of patients with chronic conditions, often progressive in nature, becomes less typical. If once again we consider the first one hundred patients hospitalized on F-Second during the period of our observations, we find that 53 of these patients were between the ages of fifteen and forty-four; 40 were between forty-five and sixty-four years of age; and only 7 were sixty-five years of age or older. Such evidence as we have available suggests that adults at mid-life and beyond (forty-five to sixty-four and sixty-five and over) now constitute larger proportions of the typical general-hospital population than they did twenty years ago, and that the sixty-five-and-over group has been increasing the most rapidly of all. The fact that there seems to be a much larger proportion of older people in hospitals now than formerly, along with the relatively high degree of control over infectious diseases which the development of chemotherapy has effected, accounts for the fact that today hospitals admit many more patients with underlying conditions that are chronic than they did in previous eras.[8]

Seen against the backdrop of what would appear to be the general trend in hospital populations at large, the patients of F-Second were probably atypical in several respects. They were concentrated in the younger rather than the older age brackets. Furthermore, one might say that despite their relative youth, many of them had irreversible chronic conditions. And, if we consider the illnesses of F-Seconders in greater particularity, we find that the array of chronic diseases represented on the ward were "rather out of the ordinary." As one member of the Group put it, many F-Seconders had "unusual conditions" or "usual conditions with unusual or very serious manifestations."

To be more specific, there were always at least a few patients with Addison's disease (hypofunction of the adrenal cortex) and Cushing's disease (hyperfunction of the adrenal cortex) hospitalized on F-Second. A considerable proportion of patients were in advanced stages of the kidney disease known as chronic glomerular nephritis. It has already been pointed out that Ward F-Second had a significant number of patients in the terminal phases of malignant hypertensive cardiovascular disease and of carcinoma of the prostate. Individual cases of rare endocrine and metabolic conditions were generally present on the ward—for example, hypoparathyroidism (insufficiency of the parathyroid glands), hypopituitarism (insufficiency of the pituitary glands), hemochromatosis (a disease characterized by pigmentation of the skin and viscera producing interstitial fibrosis, sclerosis of the tissues, severe diabetes, impotency, and loss of axillary hair), gout (a condition characterized by perversion of the purine metabolism, excess of uric acid in the blood, attacks of acute arthritis, and chalky deposits in the cartileges of the joints), myoglobinuria (a condition in which myoglobin, the hemoglobin of muscle, is found in the urine), myopathic atrophy (muscular atrophy due to a disuse of the muscle tissue), Hodgkin's disease (a progressive and fatal enlargement of the lymph nodes, spleen, and general lymphoid tissues), sarcoma (a highly malignant form of tumor made up of a substance like the embryonic connective tissue), lupus erythematosus (a systemic, fulminating sepsis or poisoning associated with visceral lesions and characterized by skin eruptions, prolonged fever, and other constitutional symptoms), and sarcoidosis (a chronic infectious disease of unknown cause marked by granulomatous lesions on the skin, lymph nodes, salivary glands, eyes, lungs, and bones).

As already indicated, patients who were afflicted with common disorders were likely to have more intricate, severe forms of these diseases than could be considered typical, or to have them in combination with other conditions not ordinarily associated with them. For example, a number of the diabetic patients on Ward F-Second had that form of the disease accompanied by severe renal complications, which is known as the Kimmelstiel-Wilson syndrome; and in the course of my periods of observation on the ward, although it is a very rare phenomenon, I saw three patients who had both diabetes and Addison's disease.

In short, the range of diseases found on Ward F-Second reflected the rather specialized research interests of the Metabolic Group (and other research units in the Hospital with whom they collaborated). In addition, many of the cases on the ward were unusually complicated and serious in nature. This was both because some of the radical procedures with which the Metabolic Group was experimenting were justifiable only if attempted on patients whose conditions had failed to respond to orthodox therapy, and because the Group had a profession-wide reputation for being more competent than most other physicians to handle some of the diseases mentioned.

These, then, are some of the basic facts about the two groups of men who comprised the "experiment perilous": the talented, young, academically-inclined physicians who undertook the experiment, and the articulate, relatively young patients, ill with serious, chronic, often unusual conditions who underwent it.

With this as introduction, we will first enter the laboratory and conference room of the Metabolic Group in order to learn about the problems these physicians faced, the ways they felt about their difficulties, and the manner in which they dealt with them. We shall then move on to Ward F-Second, where we will observe the shared problems, stresses, and ways of coming to terms of patients. After that, we will meet three patients who the ward community regarded as living symbols of their common predicament and alternative modes of adjusting to it. This will be followed by a chapter on the relationships between Ward F-Second, the Metabolic Group, and the sociological observer. The last chapter will be devoted to a discussion of the general significance of this study. Its implications for conceptualized knowledge about the social aspects of illness, medical practice, and research; the actual as well as "ideal" attitudes, values, and behavior patterns of scientists; and the socially structured ways in which groups of individuals react to situations of stress, will be considered.

But first, we will hear what the physicians of the Metabolic Group said about the problems and stresses of their "laboratory life."

NOTES FOR CHAPTER I

1. Throughout this book arbitrary initials have been assigned to the physicians of the Metabolic Group and pseudonyms to the patients of Ward F-Second. Such letters, hospital charts, and other documents as are used in this book are, of course, reproduced as they originally appeared, without editorial retouching.

2. With a grant-in-aid of research from the Commonwealth Fund, the Bureau of Applied Social Research of Columbia University is engaged in studying the processes and experiences through which students in three medical schools become physicians. I have been the chief field worker in one of these medical schools. In this capacity I have observed and interviewed students, faculty, patients, and medical staff in the teaching hospital, as well as in the medical school itself. I have also supervised the journals kept by several students in each of the four years of medical school. For the first published set of reports from this study see, Robert K. Merton, George G. Reader, M.D., and Patricia L. Kendall, eds., *The Student-Physician: Introductory Studies in the Sociology of Medical Education* (Cambridge, Massachusetts: Harvard University Press, 1957).

3. This investigation was supported in part by the Medical Research and Development Board, Office of the Surgeon General, Department of the Army, under Contract No. DA-49-007-MD-213, and in part by a grant from the Ford Foundation.

4. "Report of the Physician-in-Chief" in *Thirty-Ninth Annual Report of the ———— Hospital* (1952), p. 30.

5. *Ibid.*

6. The first successful use of the artificial kidney for hemodialysis on a human patient was carried out by Kolff in Holland in 1943. In the few years which have ensued since the observations for this book were made, the artificial kidney has come into increasing use, and is no longer only considered a "final desperate measure" to be applied when a patient is moribund or comatose. An editorial which appeared in a February, 1958, issue of the *Journal of the American Medical Association*, for example, advocates that it be used "whenever temporary relief of uremia may help the patient," providing that it is "fitted into a definite plan of medical treatment." See "The Artificial Kidney" (Editorial), *Journal of the American Medical Association*, Vol. 166, No. 6 (February 8, 1958), p. 642.

7. See the interview with Nelson Algren in *Writers at Work: The Paris Review Interviews*, ed. by Malcolm Cowley (New York: The Viking Press, 1958), p. 246.

8. See "The General Hospital in Transition," *Progress in Health Services* (New York: Health Information Foundation), Vol. VI, No. 7 (September, 1957). The findings in this bulletin primarily stem from a recent survey of the records of the Beth Israel Hospital of Boston for the calendar years 1932 and 1952. The survey was conducted by Cecil G. Sheps, M.D., M.P.H., and Mark G. Field, Ph.D., under a grant from the Health Information Foundation.

CHAPTER II — The Physicians of the Metabolic Group: Some of Their Problems and Stresses

> He deals not with insensate matter like the stone-mason or bricklayer, who can choose their materials and adjust them along mathematical lines . . .
> (McCandles vs. Mc. Wha., 22 Pas. St., 261)

> For it is impossible to make all the sick well . . .
> —Hippocrates

> What was the role in this patient's clinical course played by the bilateral adrenalectomy? There is no evidence that the surgical procedure did anything to alter the progressive relentless downhill course exhibited by a patient suffering from chronic glomerular nephritis . . . Certainly the patient was never able to return to a socially or economically productive individual. He became physically and psychically dependent on the hospital for his very life, which was inevitably short. This is not an indictment of his management, his physicians, or medical research. It should be construed as an indication of how little the medical profession knows about a common disease . . .
> (From the final summary of autopsy findings by a pathologist, in the chart of one of the Metabolic Group's patients.)

IF YOU LISTEN for it, you'll hear one or another of us saying, 'How long can I live this laboratory life anyway?' " a physician who was a member of the Metabolic Research Group commented to the sociological observer one day. In a sense, this chapter is a product of such "listening." Its primary data are the actual words that the physicians of the Metabolic Group spoke and wrote. It focuses especially on thoughts and feelings they expressed about some of their problems as clinical investigators. The chapter will deal primarily with problems of the Group connected with the fact that many of their patients were ill with diseases not well understood or not within the easy therapeutic control of modern medicine; and that these patients, for whom they were clinically responsible, were also their research subjects.

Although I shall concentrate on these problems, I do not mean to imply that they were the only kinds of difficulties that contributed to some of the stresses the physicians of the Metabolic Group experienced in carrying out their professional duties. Career problems, financial difficulties, family troubles, and the like were probably also relevant. However, such problems fall outside the orbit of this study and the selective attention on which it is based.

Furthermore, I do not want to convey the impression that the so-called laboratory life of these physicians was exclusively, or even predominantly, problematic and stressful. On the contrary, all of them maintained that the gratifications and rewards they enjoyed as members of the Metabolic Research Group "strongly confirmed" or "reinforced" their "wish to have a career of clinical investigation." In the words of one of these physicians, affiliation with this Group provided them with a "gratifying dress rehearsal" for what they chose to do subsequently.[1] During the few years that have elapsed since this study was made, all these physicians have moved on to more responsible positions elsewhere. However, every one of them is connected in some way with a metabolic-endocrine clinical research unit similar to that of the Metabolic Group. Thus, each continues to do a certain amount of investigative work comparable to that of the Group or logically connected with it.

Despite the over-all cogency of their experiences with the Metabolic Group, as we shall see, there were times when these physicians felt that the problems and stresses of clinical investigation with which they were grappling were greater than the satisfactions it provided.

If you listen for it, you'll hear one or another of us saying, "How long can I live this laboratory life anyway? I've just got to get back to *real* medicine!"

We turn now to a consideration of some of the problems that evoked such statements from the physicians of the Metabolic Group: problems of uncertainty, of therapeutic limitation, of finding and motivating patients to serve as research subjects, and of resolving points of conflict between research and therapy.

Problems of Uncertainty

All physicians are confronted with problems of uncertainty. Some of these result from their own incomplete or imperfect mastery of available medical knowledge and skills; others derive from limitations in current medical knowledge; and still others grow out of difficulties in distinguishing between personal ignorance or ineptitude and the limitations of medical science.[2]

In a sense, the physicians of the Metabolic Group can be thought of as specialists in problems of uncertainty—particularly those uncertainties related to limits of present medical knowledge. As clinical investigators, it was their special role to work on the periphery of what is medically known: to concern themselves with ill-understood basic mechanisms underlying the normal and abnormal functioning of the human body, and with unresolved problems in the diagnosis, treatment, and prognosis of human disease. Chiefly by means of experimentation, their task was to devise, explore, and appraise new ideas, methods, procedures, and drugs that might possibly contribute to medical knowledge, skill, and clinical prowess.

Because they worked "close to the growing edge of things"[3] in the capacity of researchers, the physicians of the Metabolic Group were confronted with uncertainties of the medically unknown in a variety of forms. These included uncertainties regarding fundamental biochemical and physiological mechanisms underlying the phenomena and conditions they studied; uncertainties connected with the experimental compounds and procedures with which they worked—their basic properties and potential clinical effects; methodological uncertainties, related to the laboratory techniques they were developing; and finally, clinical uncertainties that were nonexperimental in nature, which had to do with the diagnosis, treatment and prognosis of their patients' illnesses.

As research pioneers or trail-blazers, who often worked outside the terrain of well-established medical knowledge, the physicians of the Metabolic Group were perhaps more continuously and immediately exposed to problems of uncertainty that result from limits of the field than were many of their nonresearch colleagues.[4] The advances in knowledge and skill which their work effected helped to clarify and occasionally even dispel some of these uncertainties.[5] But at the same time, as in all research, these gains in knowledge frequently uncovered new problems of uncertainty to be explored.

Things multiply. You solve one problem, and you're faced with two others. Things you didn't know once become obvious. But then other things you didn't even know existed arise . . .

As we shall see, "chance" factors, which the physicians of the Metabolic Group did not necessarily plan or anticipate, played a considerable role in bringing various uncertainties to the attention of these physicians, and in determining the direction of their experimental work.[6] The greater part of their research, of course, consisted of rationally-organized experimental attempts to learn more about various problems of uncertainty, or, hopefully, to resolve them. For the purpose of experimentation, one might say that the physicians of the Metabolic Group intentionally sought out problems of uncertainty, and, to some extent, deliberately induced them. In this sense, they were actively responsible for creating some of the uncertainties with which they worked. As we shall see, this affected the way that they felt about the consequences of these uncertainties for their research subjects, who were also their patients.

Some statements about various of the problems with which the physicians of the Metabolic Group worked—abstracted from their publications, their entries in patients' charts, and their discussions with one another—will provide concrete examples of such problems, and also demonstrate that there were many occasions on which these physicians experienced as stressful the uncertainties they faced.

As indicated earlier, the major share of the Metabolic Group's investigative and clinical activities centered around problems related to the normal and abnormal functioning of the adrenal glands. A considerable number of their studies involved estimating the metabolic activity of newly synthesized adrenal steroids and related compounds that had been tested on animals and had shown promising evidence of being useful as therapeutic agents. (Primary among these substances were desoxycorticosterone, ACTH, cortisone, hydrocortisone, and, later, aldosterone.) The Group "hoped that through long-term studies extensive correlations might be made between modifications of steroid structures and modifications of their biological activity in man."[7] However, in spite of the intensive investigative work they devoted to this problem and some empirical success in the treatment of various clinical syndromes with these adrenocortical hormones, the physicians of the Metabolic Group were "still largely in the dark as to their exact nature and basic mechanisms of action."[8]

The Metabolic Group received the steroid preparations which they assayed directly from the laboratories of the pharmaceutical firms that manufactured them. Since methods for synthesizing steroid compounds are still "far from foolproof," these preparations sometimes contained impurities that could adversely affect patients who received them. However, the Group had no sure way of detecting these impurities before administering the steroids to patients; nor could they always explain the reactions that such impure compounds evoked. "We have had five reactions of the type you had to Lot No. 2179," a member of the Group wrote to a patient,

but we must admit that we are not certain why this particular lot has caused these reactions. It is essentially no different from previous lots in any way we have so far been able to determine, except for the obvious important fact that no reactions have occurred with other batches . . .

The laboratory methods which the group had developed for investigating the nature and quantities of steroids secreted by the adrenal cortex were still characterized by a considerable degree of error, and were not yet refined enough to separate steroids originating from the adrenal cortex from those originating from other tissues:

We can't say that he *doesn't* have something wrong with his adrenals; and yet we can't really say that he *does*. Histologically, his glands are normal. But that doesn't tell you a damn thing about what comes out of them chemically!

Actually, you're measuring urine that has God-only-knows-what in it! A little E, a little F, a little hydro-this, a little hydro-that, some crud from the testes, and eighteen other things you don't know about. You're not even sure that the same pattern of stuff is coming out in the urine each time you measure it!

These chemistries look awfully strange to me. Just the opposite of the way we thought they'd come out . . .

The fact that the medical sciences have not yet developed a "broad, over-all theory of drug action"[9] also contributed to the many elements of uncertainty which characterized the Group's investigative work with steroids.

In spite of an enormous amount of experimentation by chemists in making new substances and pharmacologists in testing them on animals and on men [writes Dr. James B. Conant], one can say that it is almost impossible to predict the action of a chemical substance of a given structure on a human being . . .[10]

Partly as a consequence, many of the experiments conceived by the Group were highly empirical in nature: "trial-and-error shots in the dark" of which the outcome was very uncertain and unpredictable:

We need all the information we can get on low-dosage steroids given to Addisonians and adrenalectomized patients . . . Now, what I'd like to do is give Mr. Flynn an around-the-clock infusion of thirty-seven-and-a-half milligrams of cortisone (the same amount he gets by mouth), and compare the effects of the two methods of administration. If the contention we've been making all along is correct—that steroids given over a longer period of time are enhanced in their effectiveness—then we should get more of a response to the continuous I.V. than from the oral dose . . . This is just casting in the dark, of course. But this seems like a fair zero start. Shall we give it a fling?

The fact that the Group conducted most of its research on patients—individuals who were afflicted with some form of illness—rather than on healthy subjects, added to the elements of uncertainty which so often complicated the course of their experiments, or "clouded" their interpretation:

Joe obligingly entered the hospital for a study of the pattern of 17-hydroxycorticoid excretion in patients with Addison's disease receiving a constant dose of cortisone . . . Despite the fact that no detectable urinary corticoids could be measured twenty-four hours after the beginning of intravenous cortisone at a dosage level of 12.5 mgms. per 24 hours, eosinophils were zero and remained zero throughout the infusion. This is not particularly gratifying since our past experience (based largely on ACTH infusions in normal subjects) has suggested that eosinopenia due to adrenal cortical steroids should be accompanied by detectable urinary

levels of 17-hydroxycorticoids. However, at 8 A.M. on the second day of
the infusion, the patient exhibited a fever of 100 to 101 degrees, possibly
due to the continuous infusion of glucose without adequate cortisone
coverage. Therefore, the interpretation of eosinopenia is somewhat clouded
since illness in patients receiving cortisone has previously, on rare occasions, been associated with significant falls in the number of eosinophils.
The latter explanation in this case may, it is admitted, be somewhat whimsical . . .

Gradually, out of experimental "casting in the dark,"[11] the
Metabolic Group (and other research units like it) have been able
to advance understanding of the adrenal glands and its secretions,
develop programs for the treatment of patients suffering from disorders of adrenal function, and modify certain generalized disease
processes of nonadrenal origin by manipulation of the type and
quantity of adrenal steroid secretion, or by surgical removal of
adrenal tissue. But "the problem is never finally solved; the last
word is never said."[12] For, as we have indicated, the advance in
knowledge and clinical efficacy which the Group's research brought
about led to the detection and, in a sense, to the creation of problems of uncertainty not previously encountered, recognized, or
explored:[13]

Before cortisone, the treatment of diabetes and Addison's disease combined was frightful—just hopeless. Jim Hayes, for example, was in the
hospital fifty-five times—most of those admissions because he was hypoglycemic. But cortisone has really changed this whole disease picture. In
the last two or three years, he hasn't had to come in at all . . . *Now* the
trouble is that when Addisonians *do* arrive, they come in with "crisis *sine*
crisis." According to the textbook definitions, they're not actually in crisis.
It's a different sort of picture. How would you classify Ed Murray's symptoms, for example? And how do you treat them? Well, in the past three
or four years, we've had only one case come in with the classic symptoms.
All the rest arrive the way he did . . . What's more, Addisonians live
longer now. So they are developing neoplastic and degenerative diseases.
Last year, for instance, we had three hypertensive Addisonians; and we
can expect to have more diabetic Addisonians as time goes on . . .

As stated earlier, in collaboration with the surgical service, the
Metabolic Group was also engaged in studying the effects of several
types of experimental surgery on patients: the effects of bilateral
complete adrenalectomy on patients with severe advanced hypertensive vascular disease, reactivated cancer of the prostate, and hyper-

adrenalism; the effects of transplanting a healthy kidney into the bodies of patients with terminal renal disease; and to a lesser extent, the effects of cardiac surgery on patients with serious heart disease.

Were such procedures "justified as an experimental approach in man"? Could they be "carried out with reasonable safety" in patients? How should patients be prepared for such surgery? What kind of anesthesia ought to be chosen? What kind of surgical approach ought to be used? How should patients be maintained post operatively? What kinds of operative complications would be forthcoming? What therapeutic benefits, if any, could be derived from these procedures?[14]

In the words of the Surgeon-in-Chief of the Hospital, this kind of research "could not have been undertaken by the faint of heart."[15] For the only way that such questions could be answered and problems resolved was by actually performing these procedures on a certain number of patients and studying their results. Medical ethics required the Group to try this radical experimental surgery on patients who were beyond help by conventional means, before attempting to carry it out on patients less gravely ill. The magnitude of the uncertainties with which the Group was faced in undertaking these procedures on patients this seriously ill, and the human consequences of these uncertainties which they had to withstand, are suggested by an excerpt from a speech made by the surgeon in this hospital who was primarily responsible for developing and performing surgery on the mitral valve of the heart:

That the work during the war in connection with the removal of foreign bodies [from the heart] should have led us to think we knew something about the rules of the game—what makes the heart work, and what makes it fail to work—was natural . . . The success led us to try out another kind of foreign material, namely, the barrier. Experimental work in the laboratory showed us conclusively that there was a great difference in the two leaflets, and now, further investigation has shown us that there are more than two leaflets. In fact, there are four leaflets in the mitral. We learned more about the anatomy and pathology of the mitral valve. We learned more about its physiology. And the people at Cox and Lindsey have worked diligently to get instruments of good quality into our hands promptly. They made instrument after instrument from eleven successive valvulotomes before I found out that I couldn't do an operation with that instrument and have the patient survive in a substantial number of cases. In fact, six of my first nine patients succumbed . . .

However, again we learned more about the rules of the game, and as is so often the case, simplicity replaces the complicated . . . Well, so much for that. I just want to point out that this operation is simple enough so that we can do it—which is, after all, an important landmark in the surgery of mitral valvuloplasty . . .

Now let's look at some of the results . . . Here are some statistics presented last June . . . The mortality in Group I was zero because there were no operations performed. In Group II, we had the same remarkable record because no operations were performed. In Group III there were 43 patients and 4 deaths . . . That was less than 10%. We just squeaked under . . . Now, let's look at the next group in red—and properly so. It's of the order of 80 and there have been 29 deaths—25 of those surgical deaths — a 35% mortality rate . . . Why do we keep operating in that situation, with such an overwhelming mortality rate? Because if we don't, we think these people would die in the normal course of their disease. And if we do, people look like some of the patients you see here . . .

The fact that radical experimental surgery had been superimposed on the "very severe and complicated forms" of illness with which the patients who underwent these procedures were already afflicted compounded the uncertainties with which the Group was faced in dealing with the problems of their postoperative clinical management:

The patient's hospital course was long and stormy and was characterized mainly by the problem of advancing uremia, which was complicated by the fact that the patient had undergone an adrenalectomy. The variations in the therapeutic regimen were many, and these variations were necessitated by the fact that it was necessary to balance fluid intake and salt intake against the three deranged physiological states of decreased renal function, congestive heart failure, and hypoadrenalism . . .

Mr. Vaughn is now six weeks post-operative. His course, as previously noted, during the first two weeks was excellent. Since that time, numerous difficulties have continued to appear. At this writing, the major concerns are: (1) severe headaches and (2) nausea . . . The pathogenesis of these symptoms is not clear. It is to be noted that such post operative doldrums, beginning the second or third week and continuing from four to twelve weeks thereafter, have been previously encountered in these patients, both here and elsewhere. It is possible that this unfortunate period represents a state of relative (not absolute) adrenal insufficiency in that, having been used to a high level of corticoids, he may simply be unable to adjust so rapidly to relative steroid depletion. If this is true, this patient should be helped by temporarily raising the dose of cortisone. Undesirable metabolic effects thereby induced could be partially offset by the simultaneous administration of testosterone. Other causes for the present difficulties are possible. The patient is to be redigitalized, using digitoxin. He will be allowed to diurese sodium chloride and water to reduce edema, including possible cerebral edema. We doubt that these difficulties have a primary emotional basis, but it would be interesting to know current psychiatric opinion.

The complex and serious condition of patients selected for such procedures, and the high mortality rate involved, also made it difficult for the Metabolic Group to learn what they had hoped to through their studies, and in this way, resolve some of the attendant uncertainties:

The study of total adrenalectomy and hypertensive disease was begun with the concept of gaining more information about this crippling and highly fatal ailment. Only patients with advanced disease and with co-existent renal disease were selected for study . . . [16]

Because of the nature of the very severe and complicated form of hypertensive vascular disease presented by the majority of the group of patients selected for this initial study, many desirable and critical procedures either were not feasible because of the precarious clinical condition of the patients, or significant follow-up, postoperative comparative studies were precluded by the relatively early death of several of the patients.[17]

The uncertainties involved in undertaking this kind of research were so pervasive that apparent successes were sometimes as hard to explain as relative failures:

On the eighteenth hospital day, the patient was subjected to bilateral adrenalectomy. He was prepared for the procedure by receiving 200 mgms. of cortisone the night before, and 100 mgms. of cortisone the morning before the operation. He received an additional 50 mgms. of cortisone on the day of the operation and 50 cc. of extract during the operative procedure. The operative procedure itself proceeded extremely smoothly, and the post-operative course was amazingly uncomplicated . . .

The usual treatment of prostatic cancer consists in partial or complete removal of the primary tumor and then a diminution in the male hormone by orchidectomy and in some cases substitution of the female hormone in the form of estrogenic substances. The possibility that male-like hormones of adrenal origin might further stimulate the cancer has been borne in mind by several investigators in the last two years. To date, total adrenalectomy has been carried out on eight patients in the ———— Hospital for reactivated and advanced cancer of the prostate. Six of these patients are living and two have died. One patient showed no improvement whatsoever, and another patient succumbed following marked relief

of pain. The other patients show healing of metastatic disease, regression
of palpable masses in some cases, and marked relief of pain. There has
been a chemical change indicated by a diminution in the serum acid
phosphatase. Results are encouraging. The exact mechanism by which the
result is achieved is still not well understood and studies are under way
to find out if it is due to male-like hormones, or whether it is a non-speci-
fic effect traceable to other principles . . . [18]

The transplantation of an apparently healthy kidney into the body
of an individual dying of renal failure has attracted the hopeful thoughts
of physicians and surgeons for many years. During the past two years,
under the direction of Dr. ———, a collaborative enterprise in medicine
and surgery has been under way. The progress made can best be summarized by saying that in the most recent patient treated, the transplant
survived over three months, during which time it made metabolically
effective urine . . . Although empirical success has greatly been increased,
we are just as much in the dark as ever as to basic mechanisms. It is not
easy to say why this one transplant was so extremely successful nor do we
know why it finally stopped working . . . [19]

Gradually, as such experimental surgery was performed on more
patients, some of the problems of uncertainty that these procedures
originally entailed were mastered. But here again, scientific progress
also inevitably led to the discovery of new problems of uncertainty
that ought to be explored. The case of William Pappas illustrated
this sequence. Mr. Pappas was one of the first patients with advanced
hypertensive disease and coexistent renal disease to undergo a total
adrenalectomy. In a number of ways he improved symptomatically
following the operation:

From his clinical course one can say that adrenalectomy may have prolonged his life three or four years, but gave rise to complications of asthma
and potassium intoxication. From the pathologic findings one can say
that the vascular disease progressed and finally, in addition to potassium
intoxication, resulted in his death from cardiac and renal complications . . .

Throughout most of this postoperative period Mr. Pappas was either
in danger of developing severe edema or actually suffering from it.
At the time, the Metabolic Group could not satisfactorily account for
this aspect of his clinical status. In the few years subsequent to this
patient's death, advances in the knowledge of adrenal cortical physiology have led to the isolation and synthesis of a salt-retaining hormone of the adrenal cortex, aldosterone. A practical method for

aldosterone determination has been developed, and this substance has been found in abnormally high concentration in the urine of patients who, like Mr. Pappas, have congestive failure with edema (as well as patients with nephrotic syndrome and decompensated hepatic cirrhosis). These conditions are now classified as being associated with a syndrome called "secondary hyperaldosteronism." The increased activity of sodium-retaining steroid which these conditions involve is secondary to some metabolic event common to all of them.[20] In the light of this new knowledge it can now be said that:

> There seems little doubt that [Mr. Pappas] presented secondary hyperaldosteronism as an integral part of his clinical picture of refractory edema. Undoubtedly this was intensified by renal changes secondary to congestive heart failure . . . [21]

The advances in knowledge and method which have made it possible to identify the syndrome of secondary hyperaldosteronism eliminate some of the uncertainty originally connected with the edematous conditions of patients like Mr. Pappas. But these advances have also raised new questions, which now call for solution. For example, "the common factor responsible for the high urinary excretions of the sodium-retaining corticoid remains unknown to this date."[22]

Not all of the problems of uncertainty which the Metabolic Group faced were associated with the experiments they conducted. For, as already indicated, medical research comprised only part of their professional activities. The members of the Group also had clinical and teaching duties which were not experimental in nature. They made rounds on various wards and pavilions; served as ward visits, did bedside teaching with third- and fourth-year medical students, acted as consultants for some of the cases handled by other members of the hospital staff; and saw patients in the Out-Patient Department. In these contexts the physicians of the Metabolic Group were confronted with many problems of uncertainty regarding the etiology, diagnosis, treatment, and prognosis of various clinical conditions. As physicians who were also clinical investigators, the Group had a special interest in such problems. Furthermore, they were regarded by their colleagues as experts in dealing with various endocrine and metabolic problems that lay outside the knowledge and control of most physicians. For both these reasons the physicians of the Metabolic Group were likely to see and become involved in working with cases in which it was especially difficult to ascertain what was wrong with a patient, what ought to be done about his condition, and what the outcome of treatment would be.

This patient's problem evoked much interesting discussion. He was seen not only by the house staff, but by Dr. T. and Dr. S. of the Metabolic Group, and Dr. J., in addition to the genito-urinary service and the cardio-vascular service. It was felt most likely that the patient's renal impairment was due to a residual from his renal shutdown due to operative shocks. It was also felt that the patient has some element of pyelonephritis. The other two questions that were raised were whether the patient had a sulfonamide reaction which caused much of his renal damage, or whether the clamp which was placed over part of the inferior vena cava may have caused some thrombosis in the renal vein and [in] this way contributed to his renal difficulty. The main question was whether this patient should be explored. It was decided that the risks of operative procedure at this moment were not warranted, and the patient should be allowed further time for possible improvement of kidney function. If the kidney function does not improve, or if a severe bout of pyelonephritis ensues, it was agreed that the patient should be explored with two possibilities in mind: (1) possibly relieving the venous obstruction by an anastomotic procedure, and (2) to see if there was any sort of obstruction in the outflow tract which might be relieved . . .

The patient was found to be a very difficult problem in regulation. There appeared to be two primary problems. The first was his local re-activity to insulin. This was least marked to beef insulin and most marked to regular crystallin insulin. Intermuscular and intravenous injections of 7½ units of CZI showed only minor changes in blood sugar levels. Later 20 units of insulin was given i.v. again, with only a moderate drop in blood sugar levels. This seemed to establish the fact that he was somewhat resistant to insulin. In addition, a close comparison of his FBS levels as compared with his urine sugars showed that he spilled sugar at a low FBS level. By increasing the amount of PZI taken, his morning sugar values finally were brought under control. However, even though 20 units of CZI were added, the patient still showed 4-plus values throughout the day in pre-meal specimens. It was hoped that the patient would gradually de-sensitize himself . . .

This patient seems to have pure mitral stenosis and symptoms that in any other normal patient would be Grade III and have 3% mortality. With this Addison's disease problem added, we do not know how to take care of the patient's electrolyte problem post-operatively and we are worried about the calcification he might have in the aortic leaflet hinge point . . .

His condition at the time of discharge was excellent, but due to the length and severity of his pre-existing adrenal cortical hyperfunction, it will require many months to ascertain the extent of recovery which he can eventually achieve. Since he has now had both adrenal glands completely removed, he is permanently Addisonian and must therefore receive cortisone, and possibly desoxycorticosterone indefinitely. His prognosis is fairly good, but can be determined with accuracy only after the expiration of from six to nine months. The recovery of his extensive and severe osteoporosis, cutaneous thinning and hypertension must be predicted with some caution in view of the fact that he had severe Cushing's syndrome for a period of over eight years . . .

Problems of Therapeutic Limitation

Like all physicians, the members of the Metabolic Group would have liked to have been able to effect the total recovery of the patients for whom they cared, or at least, to have significantly improved their clinical status. Sometimes they succeeded in doing so:

Eleven years ago, William Barber was diagnosed as having a duodenal ulcer and was treated in the usual conservative regime . . . Due to the intractability of his pain, he was hospitalized again five years ago, at which time a vagotomy was done . . . He experienced complete relief from his ulcer symptoms with the exception of one month's p.o. period in which he had some digestive disturbance consisting mainly of regurgitation. He has been entirely symptom-free. He has not followed any type of regime since: eats, drinks and smokes ad lib now, and to all intents and purposes is completely well . . .

A total recovery like this, of course, was very satisfying to the physicians of the Metabolic Group:

Renewed acquaintance with this old friend. He is a wonderful vagotomy result! I wish they were all this good! Will be interested in the outcome of the studies.

It was partly because they did not often experience this degree of therapeutic success that the physicians of the Metabolic Group were so demonstrably pleased when a patient showed what they termed "such startling improvement." As already indicated, not enough was medically known about the conditions from which many of their patients suffered for the physicians of the Metabolic Group to be able to markedly "benefit" them through the therapeutic measures they applied. In such cases the most these physicians were able to do for patients was to ameliorate or palliate their conditions. There were also many instances in which nothing they did was effective in arresting the course of their patients' diseases, or reversing the damage these diseases had caused.

Looked at from the point of view of how much could be done for them therapeutically, the patients for whom the Metabolic Group were clinically responsible could be classified in the following way:

1. A few patients like William Barber, in whom a total "cure" seemed to have been effected.

2. A sizeable group of patients—predominantly those with Addison's disease—whom (under certain circumstances) it was possible to "almost completely rehabilitate."

Recent advances in understanding of the physiology and chemistry of adrenal secretions had facilitated the development of sound programs for the treatment of patients suffering from this disorder of adrenal function.[23]

However, in spite of these impressive advances in diagnosis and treatment of Addison's disease, if the diagnosis was not promptly established, if there was tuberculosis present, or concomitant anterior pituitary deficiency, the patient's prognosis was negatively affected. Furthermore, the therapeutic management of such patients was still a delicate and intricate matter. Chance infection, the imposition of any type of severe stress, the necessity for undergoing surgery, could suddenly jeopardize the well-being or even the existence of a patient who was previously doing nicely. In this respect, then, the Metabolic Group was faced with complex problems of managing even the particular category of patients to whom they had been able to render the most dramatic therapeutic help.

3. Patients who seemed to be benefited by a form of therapy with which the Group was still experimenting, but in whom improvement was "unpredictable," and could not yet be considered "sustained or permanent" in nature. Patients with hyperadrenalism belonged in this category.

Hyperadrenalism, the clinical and physiologic state associated with over-function of the adrenal glands, was first described by Dr. Cushing . . . Removal of a tumor of the adrenal gland, when such is present, benefits these patients dramatically. Removal of only a part of the hypertrophied adrenal glands may cause moderate to striking improvement in about 80% of the patients so treated. The results, however, are unpredictable and it has seemed worthwhile to investigate total removal of both adrenal glands in this pathological situation where there is "too much" adrenal activity . . . During the last two years nine patients with Cushing's syndrome have been operated on by Dr. ————. Two of them have had total adrenalectomy and in both of these, striking improvement, both subjective and objective, has occurred. The problem deserves further intensive study, not only of the effect of the operation but also of the exact details of replacement therapy.[24]

4. A large group of patients whose response to treatment was symptomatic and temporary, but whose underlying disease process was not modified, and, in fact, often continued to progress. Patients with advanced forms of rheumatoid arthritis and chronic glomerular nephritis were of this type.

This was the fifth admission of this patient who entered the hospital for i.v. ACTH therapy which was received for 10 days and then was tapered. In addition, it was felt that the patient deserved physiotherapy. The rheumatoid arthritis expert was also called. He suggested a high protein diet, liver, laced steel-enforced knee brace, and gold therapy. Received 200 mgms. of gold over 2 week period. Just before discharge had 12 cc. of fluid aspirated in O.R. Thereafter 2 cc., which is 50 mgms., of Compound F was injected into the left knee. Following this there was considerable diminution in the local swelling and pain. Patient was discharged to be followed in the Metabolic Clinic.

Jackie has had 11 observed nephrotic crises in his three years of observation, in addition to a few febrile episodes which were URI's . . . He has accumulated fluid 8 distinct times . . . Score of diureses: Spontaneous: 1; After crisis: 1; After URI recovery: 2; After crisis plus albumen: 3; ACTH alone: 1 . . . His aspects in summary are: Chronic glomerular-nephritis. Evidence: duration of nephrosis, intermittent hematuria and granular casts. Nephrotic crises of presumably GI origin, which as long as chemotherapy is available seem to do him no harm, and may actually initiate diuresis. Frequent URI's which are harmful since on at least 4 occasions they have appeared to activate his disease, in the sense of increased edema . . .

5. Patients with chronic disorders, either progressive or static in

nature, whose conditions did not respond to the various forms of therapy tried.

There is no known treatment that will halt the unrelenting progress of this disease. I believe the only thing we can try to offer this patient is relief of his major symptom. Some drastic measure will have to be instituted to bring this about . . .

This 43-year old male developed progressive muscular weakness of both lower extremities and left upper extremity leading to evaluation and operation by Dr. P. in 1943. Exploration of the cord revealed a reddish grey mass which was thought to be an intra-medullary spinal cord tumor . . . Resection could not be carried out. There has been no progression since that time. Both lower extremities and the left upper extremity are paralyzed . . . Possibilities of rehabilitation are zero. I can see nothing beyond a bed and chair program for him.

6. The group of patients with severe rapidly progressive forms of hypertensive cardiovascular disease, carcinoma of the prostate, and renal disease on whom radical experimental surgery—bilateral adrenalectomy and renal transplant—was being tried.

7. Terminally ill patients to whom it was only possible to give symptomatic subjective relief.

A thin, dyspneic anemic male who appeared chronically ill and in acute distress. With a low white count and a lesion which was known to be radioresistant in addition to his overall clinical state, it was believed that the patient was a terminal case of Hodgkin's disease. It was felt that the greatest comfort might be obtained from ACTH therapy; therefore he was given I.V. ACTH for 5 days. During this time there was a lysis of his fever, but the patient continued to be anxious and due to extreme difficulty in venous punctures, this mode of treatment was discontinued, and cortisone started. The small amount of cortisone had no effect on the patient's overall condition. The patient became increasingly dyspneic and increasingly apprehensive. As a final measure, the patient was treated with TEPA, the new compound, but it seemed to have no effect on the course of his disease. In the final few days the patient had to be kept under sedation. Despite the large amounts used, he remained apprehensive until just before he was discharged to Ward X.

In sum—because the members of the Metabolic Group were qualified to give their patients expert care, and were able to offer them new forms of therapy, they often succeeded in improving the serious and complicated disorders with which many of their patients were afflicted. However, there were also a considerable number of patients whom the members of the Group were "not able to make very much better," and still others whose imminent death they were not able to forestall. It often seemed to the physicians of the Metabolic Group that the patients they failed to help outnumbered those for whom they had done something that made a positive, important, and enduring therapeutic difference.

> ... This business of not being able to make our patients better ... Well, you saw how we all stood around and watched Mickie like a bunch of blooming roses. That's because it seemed so good to see somebody get a break for a change ... Or like, John will say, "Well, I saved a life today!" What he really means is, "God, I wish I had!"

Problems of Reconciling Clinical and Research Responsibilities

> First, have we a right to perform experiments and vivisections on man? Physicians make therapeutic experiments daily on their patients, and surgeons perform vivisections daily on their subjects. Experiments, then, may be performed on man, but within what limits?
> —Claude Bernard[25]

> The problem we face ... presents a true dilemma, being tragic in the classical sense ... A given situation may demand that the attitude of the physician-experimenter and that of the physician-friend be embodied in one person ...
> —Otto E. Guttentag[26]

The fact that these physicians were frequently limited in the extent to which they could improve their patients' clinical status had implications for another constellation of problems with which the Metabolic Group was faced. These were the problems of meeting both their responsibilities as clinicians and their commitments to medical research to the fullest extent possible; ascertaining the limits of each set of obligations; and preventing or reconciling some of the conflicts that existed between them.[27]

In many cases, the clinical and research activities of the Metabolic Group implemented one another. Some of the tests and procedures the Group asked patients to undergo, or the drugs they gave them primarily in order to diagnose or treat their diseases, also provided the Group with basic or general information about such conditions which was relevant to research in which they were engaged. In such instances (providing that things went well), the members of the Group simultaneously fulfilled their obligations as clinicians to further their patients' welfare, and their responsibilities as investigators to advance medical knowledge.

Mr. F. is re-admitted for study. Approximately one year ago he had a bilateral complete adrenalectomy . . . It is our hope on this admission (1) to check with ACTH to make certain that no further functioning adrenal tissue remains. (This has been done and there is no evidence of functioning adrenal cortical tissue); (2) to re-check his renal clearance studies for comparison with his pre-operative values one year ago; and (3) since he was one of the group who had ACTH and was followed by Dr. W. with androgen studies, we would like to repeat this with Compound F for metabolic degradation studies . . . Preliminary observation suggests that (1) renal function has not gotten any worse, and perhaps has actually improved; (2) heart size has not increased; (3) there is no progression in eye ground changes, and, indeed, perhaps there is slight improvement; (4) clinically he is now doing very well . . . EEG should be re-checked.

This interesting 68-year old male is a diabetic Addisonian . . . The coexistence of diabetes and Addison's disease in the same individual is a rare occurrence. Indeed, in a recent review by Stanton only 46 bona fide cases could be found . . . The patient's Addison's disease was supported by the finding of no consistent fall of eosinophiles or rise in 17-ketosteroids with ACTH stimulation. Therefore the patient has been maintained on cortisone. This required re-evaluation of his diabetes which reappeared. It was found that he required 25 units of NPH50. Conclusion of R.Q. studies: (1) Confirms the fact that Mr. P. has Addison's disease and diabetes. (2) In a patient with Addison's disease and diabetes, R.Q.'s fasting and after a test meal do not differ markedly from those in patients with diabetes alone. Insulin and cortisone showed the expected effects on R.Q. . . .

This amiable and cooperative gentleman, having previously been prostatectomized, orchidectomized and adrenalectomized, reenters to be nephrectomized. He has done exceedingly well and offers encouragement to the procedure of adrenalectomy . . . This will be the first major operative procedure carried out in a previously completely adrenalectomized individual. He will be prepared by cortisone in a manner comparable to that used for adrenalectomy. In view of his present good state, he should do well . . .

During first 6 days, i.v. albumin with superb diuresis. Metabolic studies. By 45th hospital day given 100 mgms. of ACTH daily for 7 days in order to study the effect of a high pepid [sic] diet on his respiratory quotient and in order to determine whether in his nephrotic stage he could mobilize fat . . . Upon cessation of ACTH therapy, the patient had a most remarkable diuretic rebound effect. There was 6 kg. weight loss in 2 days so that on the 58th hospital day he had no edema fluid left. Patient discharged on 62nd hospital day, improved.

However, there were also many occasions on which the procedures or drugs which the Group administered to patients did not benefit the persons subjected to them, or proved to have negative consequences for them. Situations of this sort were attributable to a number of factors. To begin with, as we know, the patients under the care of the Metabolic Group were likely to have serious, relatively ill-understood, or complicated diseases. Partly as a consequence, subjecting them to some of the procedures and agents that were used to diagnose or treat their disorders entailed a considerable amount of risk, some of which the Metabolic Group could calculate in advance, and some of which they could not:

This patient was getting i.v. ACTH 20 mgms, in 500 cc. saline in water. Approximately 30 minutes after starting the infusion, patient started complaining of itching in both hands, neck and scalp. The face was showing some congestion, so that ACTH was pulled out in view of what seemed to be an anaphilactic reaction . . .

Insulin tolerance test discontinued at 100 minutes because of probable hypoglycemic reaction . . . All in all, evidence confirms diagnosis of Addison's disease. In view of previous untoward reaction to ACTH, another ACTH test does not seem worth the risk . . .

The adverse effects that certain procedures and substances had on patients sometimes resulted from the fact that the methods or agents employed were relatively new developments. Because the limitations and hazards of such procedures and drugs were not precisely understood, it was frequently not possible to anticipate or prevent untoward effects.

At the time of admission it was the feeling of the staff that the patient had either rheumatoid arthritis or rheumatic fever. It was felt that he might have had a myocardial infarction four weeks before admission. It was thought that his epigastric pain might be due to a hiatus hernia. On the day following admission, the patient started showing daily temperature spikes despite aspirin therapy. Because of his discomfort and the fever, the patient was started on cortisone which was continued for 4 days . . . The patient showed good improvement of his symptoms and the lysis of his temperature with cortisone, but he complained of low chest pain. An ulcer crater was found on the greater curvature of his stomach . . . His cortisone was stopped and at this point his temperature again showed daily rises. Gastroscopy was carried out. The gastroscopist . . . felt that in view of the high uropepsin lesions this might be a benign ulcer of the stomach, probably due to cortisone . . .

Eighteen-year old boy with periarteritis nodosa entered on October 30. After regime of cortisone 100-300 mgms, was started on IV ACTH which was continued 22 days. On 23rd day, December 8, patient became psychotic. He was tapered off ACTH over a 3-day period and transferred to the Psychopathic Hospital, as he became too difficult to manage . . .

For reasons that lay largely outside of their control, in cases of this sort the members of the Group found themselves in a position where they had failed to live up to their aspirations to benefit their patients clinically, or where the methods they employed chiefly for this purpose had contrary effects.

In the words of Hippocrates, "Art is long, but life is short . . . ", and not all experiments performed on men will ever be of value to those particular men. And it is with these breathing men that we are concerned as physicians . . . [28]

The Metabolic Group was also engaged in a considerable amount of research which they undertook primarily to advance general medical knowledge, and only secondarily or incidentally because they thought it might be helpful to patients who consented to act as their subjects. The members of the Group "hoped" that the patients who participated in these experiments might gain some clinical benefit from doing so, and they were pleased when this happened. But to the limited extent that medical ethics allowed them to do so, they subordinated their clinical desire to serve the immediate interests of the particular patients involved in such experiments, and gave priority to the more long-range, impersonal research task of acquiring information that might be of general value to medical science.

The following are the basic principles governing research on human subjects which the physicians of the Metabolic Group were required to observe in order to "conform to the ethics of the medical profession generally . . . and satisfy democratic morality, ethics and law":

1. Voluntary consent of the subject is absolutely essential. Consent

must be based on knowledge and understanding of the elements of the study and awareness of possible consequences. The duty of ascertaining the quality of consent rests on the individual scientist and cannot be delegated.

2. The experiment should seek some benefit to society, unobtainable by any other method.

3. The experiment should be designed and based on prior animal study, the natural history of the disease or problem and other data so that anticipated results may justify the action taken.

4. It should be conducted to avoid unnecessary physical and mental suffering.

5. No experiment should be undertaken where there is reason to believe that death or disability will occur, except perhaps where the experimenter may also serve as his own subject.

6. The degree of risk should never exceed that which the importance of the problem warrants.

7. There should be preparation and adequate facilities to protect the subject against even remote possibility of injury, disability or death.

8. Only scientifically qualified persons, exercising a high degree of skill and care, should conduct experiments on human beings.

9. The subject should be permitted to end the experiment whenever he reaches a mental or physical state in which its continuation seems to him impossible.

10. The investigator must be prepared to end the experiment if he has reason to believe that its continuation is likely to result in injury, disability or death.[29]

The physicians of the Metabolic Group were deeply committed to these principles and conscientiously tried to live up to them in the research they carried out on patients. However, like most norms, the "basic principles of human experimentation" are formulated on such an abstract level that they only provide general guides to actual behavior. Partly as a consequence, the physicians of the Metabolic Group often found it difficult to judge whether or not a particular experiment in which they were engaged "kept within the bounds" delineated by these principles.

This was especially true of the experiments they conducted primarily to advance medical knowledge. The justification for this kind of research did not lie in its potential immediate value for the patients who acted as subjects. Rather, it was premised on the more remote, general, uncertain probability that its "anticipated results . . . their humanitarian importance . . . for the good of society" and the chance of achieving them—would exceed the immediate amount of "suffering" and "risk" the experiment might entail. The criteria on which physicians ought to form such a calculus are not specified by the rules of conduct for clinical research. Thus, without many established or "clean-cut" bases of judgment to guide them, the physicians of the Metabolic Group were constantly faced with the problem of trying to decide whether the particular experiments they were conducting fell within the limits of their rights as investigators, or whether they were overstepping those rights by subjecting the patients involved to more inconvenience and danger than the possible significance of those experiments for the "advancement of health, science, and human welfare"[30] seemed to warrant.

In addition, as we know, the many uncertainties connected with experimentation and the clinical status of the patients who served as subjects made it hard to predict what the actual results of carrying out a procedure or administering a drug would prove to be. For this reason, the physicians of the Metabolic Group sometimes found themselves in situations where their experiments resulted in more inconvenience or suffering for their patient-subjects than they anticipated, intended, or desired.

Accounts of three experiments conducted by the Metabolic Group follow.[31] The primary purpose of these experiments was to obtain scientific information. In this respect, and a number of other ways, they are characteristic of many studies conducted by the Group. Therefore, they suggest or illustrate some of the concrete problems the Metabolic Group faced in trying to determine the boundaries of their responsibilities as physicians to protect and further the welfare of their patients, and their rights as investigators to subject them to a certain amount of discomfort and risk, so as to strike a "proper balance" between these two potentially incompatible aspects of the role of clinical investigator.

This patient [Ray Woodham] with nephrotic syndrome is to be given ACTH 100 mgms. daily for 5 days. The chief purpose of this experiment will be to study the effect of ACTH on "fat metabolism"—namely on serum cholesterol, cholesterol esters, total fat, phospholipids, ketone bodies and on the respiratory quotient. Incidentally the effect on electrolytes, blood sugar and thyroid function will be followed.

The patient was started on a constant diet on February 14th.

The precise, presumptive plan is as follows:

Tuesday, Feb. 14th	Constant diet.
Wednesday, Feb. 15th	Practice on Tissot spirometer.
Thursday, Feb. 16th	R.Q. in the morning.
Friday, Feb. 17th	R.Q. in the morning. Blood as on Feb. 16th (Cholesterol, fat, phospholipids, ketone bodies — Collect).
Saturday, Feb. 18th	Blood as on Friday, Feb. 17th.
Monday, Feb. 20th	R.Q. in the morning. Blood for cholesterol, fat, phospholipids, ketone bodies, Na., K, Eos., PBI to Dr. T.'s Lab.
	Blood for complete blood count.
	Blood for CO_2, BUN, FBS, TP, and A/G to routine lab.
	Radio Active Iodine Uptake.
	ACTH 100 mg q.d. started.
Thursday [sic],Feb. 21st	R.Q. in morning. Blood for fat study.
Wednesday, Feb. 22nd	Blood for fat study.
Thursday, Feb. 23rd	R.Q. in morning. Blood for fat study.
Friday, Feb. 24th	Rest day. Collect 17-ketosteroids. Add acid to urine.
Saturday, Feb. 25	Last day of ACTH. Repeat all studies done on Monday, 2/20, including R.Q.
Monday, Feb. 27th	Blood for fat study. R.Q.
Wednesday, 3/1	Same.
Friday, 3/3	Same. End of Experiment. Off constant diet.

Daily 24 hour urines to Dr. T.'s Lab.
It is calculated that a total of 362 cc. of blood will be required for this experiment.

The purpose of this experiment is to study the turnover rate of plasma phospholipid. We hope to study the effect of cortisone on this by giving the patient another dose of P32 on the day he starts cortisone. We should like to hold off with cortisone until the plasma phospholipid radioactivity following today's injection has reached its peak—which we expect to happen in 4 to 7 days. Besides the above, we will follow blood and urine proteins, respiratory quotient, basal metabolism, cholesterol, protein-bound iodine and urinary sodium and potassium . . .

After initial testing of patient's reaction to ACTH intravenously, the patient [Leo Angelico] was started on a constant diet and 40 units of ACTH-gel intramuscularly daily. These were done to achieve high circulating steroid levels for being able to follow steroid secretion when additional amphenone would be given. Medically, after 25 days of 40 units of ACTH-gel daily and intermittent amphenone administrations, the patient felt definitely very weak, nauseous {sic}, irritable, and hepatic. Physical examination was not relevant, but for the fact that the patient's skin was very dry, and for the fact that he looked sick. Otherwise, examination was negative. At that time there was a loss of weight to 52.8 kilograms coming from 57.8 kilograms. Laboratory data showed potassium of 2.8 mEq/l in serum. At that time further investigation was stopped, and the patient was given plenty of rest with slow tapering of ACTH administration. It was felt at that time that all the patient could have had was adrenal exhaustion or electrolyte disturbance due to concomittant administration of amphenone and ACTH. Two days after stopping of the studies, normal body water and normal extracellular volume were reported. There was a low total exchangeable sodium with a normal plasma sodium. This seems to mean that there was depletion of the sodium source . . .

Like many studies the Group conducted, these experiments had as one of their primary objectives "the striking of a quantitative balance sheet with respect to certain components of intermediary metabolism."[32] Metabolic balance studies of this sort entailed a considerable amount of restriction, control, discomfort, and tedium for the patients who acted as subjects for the Group:

The pattern of [these] studies . . . means a fixed food intake, constant with respect to each dietary constituent, and necessitates the collection of the total excretions. There are, in addition, frequent blood examinations which require venepunctures, as well as other complicated test procedures involving varying degrees of discomfort with the anticipation of equal discomfort on their repetition. The diets are inevitably monotonous since each patient is usually limited to about three daily menus which are repeated in sequence throughout the study. It is a further condition of studies of this character that the patient must take every last morsel of every day's diet regardless of how he may feel or what his mood may be . . . [33]

Another characteristic these experiments had in common is that they all involved the use of a number of procedures which imposed varying degrees of risk upon the patients who underwent them. Most of these procedures were accepted clinical methods for establishing a diagnosis. In this context, risks that accompany these procedures are generally established as "tolerable"—that is, within the confines of ethical medical practice. However, in the research cases we are considering, these methods were not being used to diagnose patients' conditions in order to help them more effectively. Rather, they were being employed for general investigative purposes: specifically, to learn more about the "effect of ACTH on fat metabolism," "the turnover rate of plasma phospholipid," and the pattern of steroid secretion when first ACTH and then amphenone are given. These were inquiries from which the patients acting as subjects could not expect to receive immediate clinical benefit, if any at all. Before they undertook such experiments the Group had to decide whether procedures which had "acquired respectability . . . in a diagnostic setting" could also be justifiably used "in an investigative setting" where the interests of patients were not being directly or immediately served.[34] In these cases, the physicians of the Metabolic Group felt that they were. It was their considered judgment that given the cogency of the research problems they wished to explore, and the fact that the patients who acted as subjects for these experiments were ill with diseases which they could only help symptomatically, the discomforts and risks involved were not excessive.[35]

The problems that the Group sometimes faced in deciding whether it was clinically wise and morally just to subject patients to this kind of investigation are well demonstrated by another experiment they conducted. This is one which had undesirable consequences for the patient, despite the fact that before they initiated the experiment the Group had carefully discussed the risks it might entail, and decided that they were not too great.[36]

Mr. Max Gold, the patient involved, was afflicted with a rarely seen combination of disorders: Addison's disease and mitral stenosis. For the physicians of the Metabolic Group his condition was a "significant experiment of nature." It offered them an extraordinary opportunity to study the metabolic processes underlying a concurrence of disorders which they themselves had neither the moral right nor technical ability to induce.[37] Mr. Gold was also the first patient with both these conditions to have undergone the procedure for surgical correction of mitral stenosis known as mitral valvuloplasty. This enhanced his potential importance as a research subject and the Metabolic Group's interest in studying the patterns of his metabolic processes.

It is a well-established fact that patients with Addison's disease generally have a defect in their ability to excrete administered water. For this reason, one of the phenomena the Group wished to observe was whether this would be equally characteristic of Mr. Gold, or whether because of his heart condition and the surgery he had recently undergone to correct it, his pattern of excretion would be different. For this purpose, the Group considered using what is known as the Robinson-Kepler-Power "water test."[38] This is a simple screening examination: one of the clinical procedures which helps physicians to rule in the possibility that a patient has Addison's disease, or to rule it out. The test lasts for eighteen-and-a-half hours, during which time the patient is not allowed to eat any food or drink any fluids. He is then given a large amount of water to drink over a short period of time. Throughout the test all his urine is collected and its volume and specific gravity are measured. Whereas in normal subjects a prompt diuresis follows ingestion of the water, in patients with Addison's disease the diuresis is greatly delayed. The test is regarded as safe for patients with possible Addison's disease, as well as those who prove not to have it.

Before they finally decided to subject Mr. Gold to the water test, the Group tried to estimate the degree of stress the procedure might impose on him, and discussed the question of whether it was greater than what he ought to be asked to undergo for investigative rather than diagnostic purposes. The major reason for which various members of the Group felt some hesitancy about conducting the test was that it would entail withholding, while the test was in progress, the desoxycorticosterone acetate (DOCA) and cortisone therapy the patient was receiving daily. The possibility was raised that in his postoperative state the patient might "react more radically" than is usually the case to the withdrawal of medication, fasting, and the administration of a large volume of water under these circumstances. However, the members of the Group were somewhat more inclined to believe that because of the therapy he had received Mr. Gold was "well enough stocked" with DOCA and cortisone to sustain the stress of having them withheld for eighteen hours and undergoing the procedure. On the strength of this conviction and because they felt that Mr. Gold "might be the last case of Addison's disease and mitral stenosis that [they] would ever see," the Group decided to proceed with the experiment.

As already indicated, the optimism of the Group regarding the ability of Mr. Gold to withstand the procedure was not upheld. Due to factors they did not anticipate, could not control, and even in retrospect did not understand very well, the patient reacted to the test in a seriously adverse way. Thus, despite the caution with which they proceeded, the effect of the experiment on the patient's clinical status conflicted sharply with what the Group had predicted, and with their desire as his personal physicians to protect him from harm. At the Group's Evening Rounds at the end of the day on which Mr. Gold underwent this test, his untoward reaction to it was described by one physician in the following way:

Well, I guess just about everybody knows that Mickey had a water test today. And out of the blue, he got very hot and dizzy. The room started to spin around, he said. His eyes began to twitch and his vision got blurred . . . His pressure was still 100 over 80 when I took it; but his pulse was feeble and thready. Those symptoms lasted for about a half hour. Right now he's getting saline, desoxy, and Compound F. That should be enough . . . And, of course, it's no longer possible to consider keeping him on a constant diet. We've got no choice but to treat this man. So our experiment ends right here. We might just as well put him on an all-therapeutic program.[39]

The experiments described contain at least two other practices, at once characteristic of the Group's research and essential to it, that produced many of the situations in which they experienced conflict between their obligations to advance knowledge and their responsibility to promote the welfare of their patient-subjects. These were the practices of administering new drugs to patients and of withholding drugs from them, primarily for investigative purposes.

Mr. Leo Angelico, for example, was one of a number of patients to whom the Group gave the steroid amphenone at a time when it had just been synthesized, and had not yet been extensively tried on human beings. Experiments conducted on laboratory animals had indicated that amphenone affected the uterus and thyroid and adrenal glands, and suggested that "this type of compound would be suitable for many clinical studies and therapeutic applications."[40] On the basis of this "promising evidence," the Metabolic Group became interested in giving amphenone to patients in order to learn more about its biological activity and toxicity in man. From experiments such as the one they carried out on Mr. Angelico, the Group gained valuable information about some of the ways in which amphenone affects the functioning of the human adrenal glands, about its potential usefulness as a therapeutic agent, and about some of its undesirable side effects. But in order to acquire this information the Group had to give this compound to a certain number of patients at a time when they did not have enough knowledge about its effects to anticipate the hazards that might be associated with it, or to estimate whether the importance of the problems to be solved by these experiments would outweigh the risks they might involve. The compound produced side-reactions in Mr. Angelico and other patients who received it on this experimental basis that were serious enough for the Group to decide that "amphenone is not a suitable compound for prolonged administration at present."[41] Thus, in this context again, the physicians of the Metabolic Group were faced with a situation in which activities which had positive value for their research also had negative consequences for the welfare of the patients who were their subjects.

In their experiment with Mr. Ray Woodham, on the other hand, what the Group did to implement research interfered with the welfare of a patient in another characteristic way. For the purposes of metabolic study, the Group temporarily deprived the patient of cortisone: a drug which they had good reason to believe would help him excrete the many pounds of excessive water with which his body was swollen as a result of kidney disease. In fact, some of the Group's experiments were conducted primarily for the purpose of determining how long a patient could tolerate not receiving a needed drug, and exactly what the nature of his reaction would be to having it withheld. For example, the Group carried out the following experiment on Mr. Michael Terhune, a patient who had undergone total bilateral adrenalectomy for carcinoma of the prostate, and thus was not capable of producing his own cortisone:

1/7: Mike is at present undergoing DOCA withdrawal for the purpose of demonstrating sodium chloride diuresis. No attempt will be made to prolong this withdrawal; adequate demonstration of the electrolyte defect is all that is desired. Following this, he will resume DOCA therapy, and will then be gradually tapered off cortisone for the purpose of following 17-ketosteroids, FS, and androgenic excretions. In view of the fact that we were never able to withdraw Mr. Carr's cortisone longer than 2½ days without impending crisis, it will be important to determine the length of time Mike can tolerate this procedure . . .

1/26: On 1/14 we began the slow tapering of Mr. Terhune's cortisone dose from 50 mgms. daily p.o. to 0. This is the fourth day off cortisone. The dose of DOCA has been maintained at 5 mgms. I.M. daily
throughout this period. On or about 1/14 he began to complain that the
pain in his back and legs was more severe. This has not been particularly
progressive. There is no doubt that he has been frightened during the
four days off cortisone. On several occasions he has raised the spectre of
death. It has been difficult to reassure him that he is in no danger. This
evening he complained of more marked weakness and excessive perspira-
tion. He has noted some stuffiness in his nose for two days, and since last
night, a dry cough. T 99 degrees (M), BP, 130/80, Pulse 72 min., strong.
He is perspiring excessively about the forehead and neck. No sign of
respiratory infection. We will, however, watch him carefully. If there is
any rise in temperature, we will have to restart his cortisone.
   1/28: 100 mgms. cortisone p.o. at 11:25 a.m.

As this experiment, and also the studies conducted on Ray Woodham and Max Gold demonstrate, the conflict between their responsibilities as clinicians and as investigators which the physicians of the
Metabolic Group faced was a "true dilemma." On the one hand,
their using or withholding a procedure or drug for the purpose of
experimentation often put them in the position where they were not
serving the welfare of the patients who were subjects, or might even
be jeopardizing it. On the other hand, what they did to benefit these
patients or to protect them from harm often curtailed or impaired
their research. Thus, when Mr. Gold reacted adversely to the water
test, for example, in the words of one physician, the Group had "no
choice but to treat this man," which in turn, meant the "end of the
experiment." Similarly, the negative clinical effects of administering
amphenone to Mr. Angelico and of withdrawing cortisone from Mr.
Terhune made it necessary to terminate these experiments despite the
research value that the Group could have derived from prolonging
them. "No matter which way you slice it," a member of the Group
explained,

being a clinical investigator has its problems. A lot of the research you
do is of no benefit to patients, and there's a real possibility that you can
do them harm. So, in order to do research you've got to close your eyes
to some extent, or at least, take calculated risks with the patients on whom
you run the experiments . . . Still, you almost never attain the ideal research . . . You rarely get to the basis of the problem you're investigating,
because it's touch and go all along the way with these patients. Their care

and welfare have to be taken into consideration . . . So, you usually end up by compromising your research goals and standards . . .

Problems of Finding Suitable, Motivated Research Subjects

These conflicts between experimenting on patients and caring for them with which the physicians of the Metabolic Group were confronted were in some ways closely connected with another of their problems as clinical investigators: that of finding patients who would make appropriate subjects for their research, and of motivating them to serve in this capacity.

From the point of view of the Metabolic Group, the ideal research patient would have had the following characteristics. His medical condition would either be directly relevant to the research interests of the Group, or so unusual that it represented an opportunity to study phenomena rarely seen. He would be healthy enough to withstand the inconvenience and stresses of experimentation for long enough periods of time in order to enable the Group to realize high standards of accuracy and evidence in their research, and also to benefit him clinically through the procedures or drugs to which they subjected him. On the other hand, his condition would be sufficiently serious to justify asking him to undergo the degree of discomfort and risk that their experiments entailed, and to accept other than established methods of diagnosis and treatment. Furthermore, such an ideal research patient would not only be willing to submit to the conditions of the experiment, but he would be highly enough motivated to do so for a relatively long time. In short, the ideal research patient would have been one whose physical condition and attitudes allowed the physicians of the Metabolic Group to fulfill both their responsibilities as clinicians and investigators to an optimal degree.

Needless to say, the physicians of the Metabolic Group rarely, if ever, encountered a patient who met all these requirements. For example, the patients whose conditions were severe enough to justify subjecting them to an experimental procedure as radical as a total adrenalectomy, and to motivate them to consent to undergo it, were too ill to endure certain procedures that would have enabled the Metabolic Group to realize high standards of experimental precision, or to derive very much therapeutic value from it. On the other hand, because patients with Addison's disease had received so much clinical benefit from advances in the diagnosis and treatment of their condition which the research of the Group had helped to make possible, they did not present as many "interesting" possibilities for study as they once had, it was no longer justifiable to expose them to the stresses of experimentation on the grounds that there were no effective established means for helping them, and the patients themselves were not as willing as they formerly were to undergo the tedium and rigors of experimentation.

We're witnessing the disintegration of Dr. T.'s Addisonian group. October was always the busiest month for Addisonians. We always had the pot full of them by this time. But so far this fall, we've only had two, and both of those have been new cases . . . We've really *ruined* those people with cortisone! We've made them so well that they simply don't need to come anymore, and so we don't have a chance to do research on them . . . Another trouble with these patients is that there are only a few things left that we can do on them, and not much we can learn from those things . . . [42]

Furthermore, patients who the Metabolic Group were potentially most interested in studying were not always inclined to submit to research; and some of the patients most eager to do so were not necessarily persons on whom the Group wished to conduct experiments:

The patient [Gilbert Mann] is difficult to approach and get a good history or physical examination on.[43] Story good for cholangitis. Path. sections indicate chronic hepatic disease. Patient physically appears to have some type of endocrine deficiency pattern. Suspect hypopituitary state. We would be most interested in studying his hepatic function and its response to cortisone therapy, besides any other endocrine studies indicated. However, he is planning on leaving the hospital once the T-tube is removed, and I would doubt that he would cooperate with us sufficiently to justify studying him . . .

This year I was not asked to come back to the Hospital for metabolic studies [a patient wrote]. I suppose it's good to have a change from research for a while anyway. But I do miss the Hospital very much—so much, that I am forever thinking about it, and the wonderful people I knew, and how wonderful it was to be able to help with research . . . [44]

In sum, the problem for the Group was to find a sufficient number of patients with physical conditions which were suited to their research needs and interests and on whom it seemed morally justifiable to conduct the experiments they had in mind—and, if possible, to motivate those patients to serve as research subjects without violating their ethical responsibility to make known to the prospective subject all inconveniences and hazards the experiment might entail, or imposing any element of force, fraud, deceit, duress, overreaching, or other ulterior form of constraint or coercion upon them in order to obtain their consent to act as subjects.

How the Physicians of the Metabolic Group Felt About These Problems and Stresses

Listening in on what the physicians of the Metabolic Group had to say one evening about the total bilateral adrenalectomy and the patients with hypertensive cardiovascular disease on whom they had carried out this experimental procedure, we hear many of the problems with which they were faced reviewed in this connection, and learn something about the way they were affected by them. The discussion that follows took place during the meeting which the Group customarily held at the end of each day. "Evening Rounds," as these meetings were called, were held in the Group's conference room, which rather appropriately was located half-way between the laboratory and the Metabolic Ward. The Group gathered around the long table in this room to discuss the clinical and research status of various patients for whom they were jointly responsible, and to make any decisions regarding them that were currently necessary. At this particular meeting, the Group were having a difficult time trying to decide what they ought to do for a seventeen-year-old patient with severe hypertension of unknown origin.

DR. D.: There's one thing I want to do before Bob Baum is discharged, if he can tolerate it, and that's a histamine test . . . The thing we ought to consider in following him is doing another retrogram on his left kidney some time in the future. Because if we definitely find bilateral kidney disease that way, then at least we've taken care of one specter . . . He doesn't seem to be a good candidate for an exploratory now. So, what I'd do is send him out, plan to follow him closely, and have him come back in a few months . . . I think our enthusiasm for doing an exploratory on this boy has waned considerably . . .

DR. R.: Actually, I'm not quite sure why we've changed.

DR. D.: I'm not either.

DR. R.: Because we really haven't found out a helluva lot that would make us change our minds . . .

DR. P.: I think there will be a great deal of feeling over exploring this boy, because he's young, and because we can't be sure that he doesn't have a pheo[chromocytoma] . . . Then there'll probably be a great beating of the drums over sympathectomy and adrenalectomy . . .

DR. D.: As I see it, the only reason for discharging him now is for psychological reasons . . .

DR. P.: I agree. The real reason we're sending him out is because he needs more diagnostic tests of a traumatic nature.

DR. G.: It's also a matter, too, of not having any definitive treatment to offer him, isn't it?

DR. D.: We don't want to adrenalectomize him.

DR. G.: Why not?

DR. D.: I'm interested in doing some adrenalectomies, but not on him . . . Do you mean to tell me we're going to start taking every young hypertensive case we find and do an adrenalectomy on them? Let me go on record right here and now, once and for all, about my position on adrenalectomies. I think now—and I've thought from the very first—that the adrenalectomy is a hopeless procedure—not one bit justifiable. There is no evidence whatsoever so far as I'm concerned that it is a bona fide therapeutic procedure. However, once committed to a program, there is the necessity for doing adrenalectomies on a few carefully selected cases for evaluative purposes. If we're going to make a definitive evaluation of the role of the adrenal cortex in hypertension, we've got to select a group of patients who don't have such serious complications as the patients we've done adrenalectomy on up till now . . . But I don't want to do it on this patient.

DR. G.: It's just about time you went back to clinical medicine, Jim.

DR. D.: You're perfectly right . . . Because this group has been puttering around with adrenalectomy for two years now. It seems to me that once and for all the technique deserves some sort of real trial. This is the one place where that can and should be done. So, I'm willing to try it on ten carefully selected cases.

DR. G.: Quite apart from therapeutic considerations, then.

DR. D.: Right.

DR. R.: I think the patients who have survived adrenalectomy are doing very well. (*Group laughter*) No, I mean it. I'm serious. Howard Beech, for instance, was just about as bad as this patient is . . .

DR. D.: Oh, was he? Well, the fact of the matter is, he was much, much better than he is. He was far and away the earliest case of hypertension we did . . . You can list Will as a good result—I'll take that. You can list Mr. Hemming, but he falls in a different category entirely . . . Mr. Ardsley's pressure is 230 over 160 . . . So, it's been a tremendous triumph!

DR. C.: Well, I'm not enthusiastic about the procedure at all. But in Abe Samuelson's case, I really think it's done something for him.

DR. D.: Sure, it's done something for him. But he's become a real invalid as a result.

DR. H.: A vegetable . . .

DR. D.: He's been sitting in the house for 400 consecutive days now, not moving a muscle, having his family wait on him hand and foot, and doing nothing but listening to the radio and watching TV all day. Even without the operation, on *that* regime his pressure would have come down!

DR. R.: So it's been a therapeutic success, but not a psychological one. (*Laughter*)

DR. D.: What you're doing, Bob, is evaluating these people as good merely on the basis of their not being dead, because so many of the others have died . . .

DR. C.: Bill Pappas is a good result . . .

DR. R.: And Walter Cousins was . . .

DR. D.: Except he's now dead.

DR. R.: Well, you can't live forever! (*Group laughter*)

DR. P.: Well, we took a gamble, and maybe we lost.

DR. D.: I don't know . . .

DR. C.: Now that we've gotten off *that* depressing subject, let's talk about the Cushing's disease cases . . .

Problems of uncertainty and therapeutic limitation, problems concerning the ethics of human experimentation, the selection of patients for research subjects, the conflicts between standards of rigorous investigation and those of good medical practice, are all discussed with considerable feeling in this exchange of comments. Total bilateral adrenalectomy, of course, was one of the most audacious experimental undertakings of the Metabolic Group, and this debate took place during what one member of the Group referred to as the "black period" in the development of this procedure. It was a time when the members of the Group were particularly discouraged about the high mortality rate connected with the operation, the ambiguous and limited nature of what this procedure had done to improve the clinical status of the patients who had survived it, and about the relative paucity of what they had been able to learn from it about the possible role of the adrenal cortex in patients with severe hypertensive vascular disease.

In other research contexts, the Group encountered in less serious and disturbing form the kinds of problems discussed here. However, there is quite a bit of evidence to indicate that by and large these problems imposed a considerable amount of stress on the physicians of the Metabolic Group. The discussion previously quoted is a magnified version of the kinds of interchanges that frequently took place between members of the Group. For example, as we shall see, the expression of doubt and discouragement, the banter about taking leave of the life of the clinical investigator in order to return to medical practice, the macabre jokes, were characteristic of the meetings that the Group held at the end of each day.

Some of the entries that the members of the Group made in patients' charts also reflected the fact that they often felt subject to strain:

A truly pathetic thirteen-year old boy who developed nephrosis several months ago and has had marked edema since . . .

This unfortunate man has terminal uremia . . . He needs to be handled with kid gloves . . .

There is no known treatment that will alter the unrelenting progress of this disease. I believe the only thing that we can try to offer this patient is relief of his major symptom. Some drastic measure will have to be instituted to bring this about . . .

Occasionally, feelings of elation over signs that a patient had improved or that an experiment had "turned out as it ought" found their way into the charts. Such entries point up both the relative infrequency of these occurrences, and how much the physicians of the Metabolic Group "wished that more of [their] cases were that way":

On the 18th hospital day, the patient was subjected to bilateral adrenalectomy . . . The operative procedure proceeded extremely smoothly, and the post-operative course was amazingly uncomplicated . . . Most exciting finding was that there has been improvement in bone metastases by x-ray! {sic}

In some of the letters that the members of the Group wrote to colleagues, patients, and the families of patients there is evidence that they were personally affected by their inability to help some of these patients, or by the discomfort and risk to which they had to subject them for the sake of an experiment:

We discharged Mr. Engles on Friday. He is an extremely pleasant fellow and I am sorry that we were unable to do more for him or to give him a better prognosis . . . He has the nephrotic stage of chronic nephritis, and I am afraid with beginning nitrogen retention and hypertension. I am afraid that his prognosis is poor. I should expect that perhaps he may have a period when he loses his edema before he goes into frank renal failure. He was discharged on a 2 gm. salt diet with added potassium acetate. I am afraid that the prolonged use of resins in his case would only result in acidosis. I should be happy to send you some of the Dirnate if his edema recurs, although I am afraid that our therapeutic weapons are inadequate . . .

We have now got back the results of our studies done when you were in the ward. I know that you did not enjoy these strenuous tests very much, but the results are very valuable to us. Thank you for suffering so stoically . . .

We were all shocked by Walter's sudden death. We are grateful for his pioneering spirit and his great cooperation with all of us, which enabled significant progress to be made in the field of high blood pressure. We can only regret that he did not live longer to enjoy the fruits of this progress . . .

Finally, in moments of special intimacy or when they were under particular stress, the members of the Group sometimes made outright statements to the sociologist about how "disturbing" the life of the clinical investigator could be:

Being a clinical investigator takes a lot off your gastric mucosa . . .

It takes spiritual fortitude to spend any time at all with the Metabolic Group . . .

Every morning and every night I have to go past a Mr. Engles, a Mr. Markham, and a Mr. Hale in rapid succession, knowing there is absolutely nothing I can do to help them . . .

There are times when this business makes me feel like a Dr. Jekyll and a Mr. Hyde . . . I'm a different person when I make rounds to see patients and find out how they are; I sit down and shoot the breeze with them like a good doctor should. But I'm another person when I'm doing research on them. Then it's just, "hello," and not so much "How are you?" as "How are your eo[sinophil]s today?" You give them the needle, and then, a quick goodbye . . .

We're caught in an eternal conflict between being physicians and medical researchers . . .

On the bulletin board, in the Metabolic Group's Laboratory, the following sign was posted:

"Where life is, there are tensions and antitheses. Harmony and lack of tension mean death."
Is this significant?
Yes—0.01.

Ostensibly, this sign referred to the fact that one of the major research interests of the Group lay in studying the effects of physical and psychological stress on man (particularly the role that the pituitary-adrenal system plays in reactions to stress). However, knowing what we do about the Metabolic Group, there are several additional things that we can "read" in this sign.

We can assume that the "tensions and antitheses" to which this quotation referred were not simply the stresses that the Group was studying, but also some of those with which they themselves were confronted as clinical investigators. Furthermore, we note that the quotation expressed a positive acceptance of the fact that these tensions and antitheses exist. It suggests that they considered accommodation to such stresses necessary and desirable.

The efficiency and enthusiasm with which the members of the Group carried out their professional duties, and the fact that they have all continued to engage in clinical investigation, indicate that they achieved a satisfactory degree of accommodation to the problems and strains that these various medical activities entailed. The question that arises, then, is: What enabled the physicians of the Metabolic Group to meet these problems so well? Specifically, what kinds of mechanisms helped them to come to terms with some of the aspects of the "laboratory life" that were inherently stressful? The sign on their laboratory bulletin board also suggests a partial answer to this question.

The fact that the members of the Group all seemed to find the motto relevant, amusing, and wise indicates that they felt they *shared* certain tensions and antitheses. The comments that were penciled at the bottom of the sign ("Is this significant? Yes,—0.01.") were also meaningful in this connection. The symbol for a high level of statistical significance obviously referred to the collaborative research in which the Group was engaged, and to the laboratory studies on which their studies depended. It will be noted that they were humorous remarks: a joking exchange about one of the kinds of problems with which the Group as a whole was faced, the problem of uncertainty. This sort of humor, the research activities of the Group and their sense of unity, along with some of their attitudes toward chance, and their special relationship to patients who acted as their research subjects—all contributed to their ability to meet the stresses of clinical investigation with relative equanimity, and to find gratification in their work. This is what we shall consider in detail in the next chapter: how the physicians of the Metabolic Group came to terms with their problems and stresses.

NOTES FOR CHAPTER II

1. These comments were taken from the questionnaire which the physicians of the Metabolic Group were asked to fill out.

2. For what was perhaps the first systematic sociological discussion of "the uncertainty factor" in medical practice and its significance for the physician, patient, and patient's family, see Talcott Parsons, "Social Structure and Dynamic Process: The Case of Modern Medical Practice," Chapter X of *The Social System* (Glencoe, Illinois: The Free Press, 1952), especially pp. 447-454. See also Renée C. Fox, "Training for Uncertainty," in *The Student-Physician*, pp. 207-241. In this essay, an attempt is made to distinguish various kinds of uncertainty the doctor faces, as well as to identify some of the experiences, agencies, and mechanisms in medical school that teach students to recognize these uncertainties and to cope with them.

3. A phrase used by Raymond B. Fosdick in discussing the nature of medical research. *The Story of the Rockefeller Foundation* (New York: Harper & Bros., 1952), p. 305.

4. As we have said, physicians in practice are continually faced with problems of uncertainty. But because they work within the confines of what is medically known to a greater extent than clinical investigators do, their encounters with uncertainty are probably more evenly distributed among the three types we have designated: uncertainty attributable to the stage of development of the field, uncertainty that results from personal limitations, and uncertainty in distinguishing between these two.

5. An arbitrary listing of the titles of some of the articles published by members of the Metabolic Group is indicative of the role their work played in this regard:

> "Pathophysiology of Edema"
> "Determination of Total 17-Hyroxycorticoids in Plasma"
> "The Use of Intravenous ACTH: A Study in Quantitative Adrenocortical Stimulation"

"The Administration of Oral Cortisone"
"Effect of Cortisone on the Abnormal Distribution of Intravascular Water in Adrenal Cortical Insufficiency in Man"
"The Clinical Usefulness of ACTH and Cortisone"
"Advances in the Diagnosis of Altered States of Adreno-cortical Insufficiency"
"The Treatment of Adrenal Dysfunction"

6. On the whole, we shall be concerned with the ways in which the uncertain and chance elements connected with their work as clinical investigators imposed a considerable amount of stress on the physicians of the Metabolic Group. However, chance also plays an important positive role in scientific discovery. Happy or lucky chance, or what Robert K. Merton has called the "serendipity pattern," has led many scientific investigators down unforeseen paths toward an unanticipated discovery.

For a discussion of serendipity, see Walter B. Cannon, *The Way of An Investigator* (New York: W.W. Norton, 1945), Chapter VI, "Gains from Serendipity," pp. 68-78; Robert K. Merton, *Social Theory and Social Structure,* rev. ed. (Glencoe, Illinois: The Free Press, 1957), pp. 103-108. Merton and Elinor G. Barber are now engaged in investigating and clarifying the variety of meanings of chance that are lumped together under the notion of serendipity by different users of the term. See also Bernard Barber and Renée C. Fox, "The Case of the Floppy-Eared Rabbits: An Instance of Serendipity Gained and Serendipity Lost," *The American Journal of Sociology,* Vol. LXIV, No. 2 (September, 1958), pp. 128-136. This is a case study of two distinguished medical scientists who independently observed the same phenomenon in the course of their research: reversible collapse of rabbits' ears after injection of the enzyme, papain. One went on to make a discovery based on this serendipitous or chance occurrence; the other did not. Intensive interviews were conducted with each of these scientists and analyzed for the light they shed on the process of scientific discovery in general, and on the serendipity pattern in particular.

7. "Report of the Physician-in-Chief" in *Forty-Third Annual Report of the* ———— *Hospital* (For the fiscal year ended September 30, 1956), p. 54.

8. *Ibid.*

9. James B. Conant, *Modern Science and Modern Man* (New York: Columbia University Press, 1952), p. 29.

10. *Ibid.*, pp. 28-29.

11. The experiments conducted by the Metabolic Group were not always this speculative, of course. A considerable amount of their research was based on working hypotheses derived from existing medical concepts and facts which they tried to rule out systematically or rule in by means of planned experimentation. However, in the words of one of the members of the Group, a good deal of their research was of the "you can't tell ahead of time what you're going to do, so you feel your way along" variety, illustrated above. As already indicated, this was attributable to current gaps in medical scientific theory and knowledge, to the bold nature of some of the research undertaken by the Group, and to certain characteristics of doing research on human subjects who are patients. We shall have occasion to demonstrate this more fully as we go along.

12. Fosdick, *The Story of the Rockefeller Foundation*, p. 110.

13. Such advances in therapy sometimes lead to the discovery of a new clinical syndrome. For example, agammaglobulinemia was first delineated as a disorder in

1951. The development of antibiotics was partly responsible for this. Before the era of antibiotics, most victims of agammaglobulinemia died very early in life, due to the severe infections they contracted. Antibiotics made it possible for persons with this disorder to survive such infections, and this in turn led to the recognition that their susceptibility to infection was due to an underlying defect in their ability to produce antibodies. See David Gitlin and Charles A. Janeway, "Agammaglobulinemia," *Scientific American*, Vol. 197 (July, 1957), pp. 93-106.

14. See George W. Thorn, F.A.C.P., J. Hartwell Harrison, John P. Merrill, Modestino G. Criscitiello, Thomas F. Frawley, and John T. Finkenstaedt, "Clinical Studies on Bilateral Complete Adrenalectomy in Patients with Severe Hypertensive Vascular Disease," *Annals of Internal Medicine*, Vol. 37, No. 5 (November, 1952), pp. 972-1005.

15. "Report of the Surgeon-in-Chief" in the *Thirty-Eighth Annual Report of the ——— Hospital*, for the year 1951, p. 85.

16. "Report of the Surgeon-in-Chief" in the *Thirty-Ninth Annual Report of the ——— Hospital*, for the first nine months of the calendar year 1952, p. 57.

17. Thorn *et al.*, "Bilateral Complete Adrenalectomy," p. 974.

18. "Report of the Surgeon-in-Chief" (*Thirty-Ninth Annual Report*), pp. 57-58.

19. "Report of the Surgeon-in-Chief" in the *Fortieth Annual Report of the ——— Hospital*, for the fiscal year ended September 30, 1953, p. 75.

20. See Jerome W. Conn, M.D., "Primary Aldosteronism, A New Clinical Syndrome" (Part II of Presidential Address presented at the Twenty-Seventh Annual Meeting of the Central Society for Clinical Research, Chicago, Illinois, October 29, 1954), *Journal of Laboratory and Clinical Medicine*, Vol. 45, No. 1 (January, 1955), pp. 6-16.

21. G. W. Thorn, A. E. Renold, E. R. Roesch, and J. Crabbé, "Pathophysiology of Edema," *Helvetia Medica Acta*, Vol. 23 (1956), p. 22.

22. Conn, "Primary Aldosteronism," p. 7.

23. George W. Thorn, M.D., "The Fifteenth Charles Value Chapin Oration . . . Advances in the Diagnosis and Treatment of Adrenal Disorders," *Rhode Island Medical Journal*, Vol. XXIX (August, 1956), p. 1.

24. "Report of the Surgeon-in-Chief" (*Thirty-Ninth Annual Report*), p. 57.

25. Claude Bernard, *An Introduction to the Study of Experimental Medicine*, trans. by Henry Copley Green, A.M. (New York: Dover Publications, Inc., 1957), p. 101.

26. Otto E. Guttentag, "The Physician's Point of View" ("The Problem of Experimentation on Human Beings"), *Science*, Vol. 117 (February 27, 1953), p. 210.

27. The following works, concerned with the ethical and legal aspects of experimentation on human beings, contributed to the author's understanding of these problems and conflicts which the Metabolic Group faced:

Leo Alexander, M.D., "Medical Science and Dictatorship," *New England Journal of Medicine*, Vol. 24 (July 14, 1949), pp. 39-47.

W. B. Bean, M.D., "Testament of Duty: Some Strictures on Moral Responsibility in Clinical Research," *Journal of Laboratory and Clinical Medicine*, Vol. 39 No. 3 (1952), pp. 3-9.

Otto E. Guttentag, "The Physician's Point of View" ("The Problem of Experimentation on Human Beings"), *Science*, Vol. 117 (February 27, 1953), pp. 207-210.

Alexander M. Kidd, "Limits of the Right of a Person to Consent to Experimentation on Himself" ("The Problem of Experimentation on Human Beings"), *Science,* Vol. 117 (February 27, 1953), pp. 211-212.

Irving Ladimer, J.D., "Human Experimentation: Medicolegal Aspects," *New England Journal of Medicine,* Vol. 257, No. 1 (July 4, 1957), pp. 18-24.

Walsh McDermott, M.D., "A Consideration of the Present Ethics of Clinical Investigation." Presented before the Practitioners Society at the Century Association, December 10, 1954 (Unpublished paper).

Alexander Mitscherlisch, M.D., and Fred Mielke, *Doctors of Infamy: The Story of the Nazi Medical Crimes.* (New York: Henry Schuman, 1949.)

Michael B. Shimkin, "The Research Worker's Point of View" ("The Problem of Experimentation on Human Beings"), *Science,* Vol. 117 (February 27, 1953), pp. 205-207.

Willard L. Sperry, *The Ethical Basis of Medical Practice.* (New York: Paul B. Hoeber, Inc., 1950.)

28. Otto E. Guttentag, "The Physician's Point of View," p. 208.

29. United States Adjutant General's Department, *Trials of War Criminals before Nuremberg Military Tribunals, under Control Council Law No. 10: Nuremberg, October 1946—April 1949.* Vol. 2, *United States vs. Milch (Medical Case).* (Washington, D.C.: Government Printing Office, 1949), p. 181.

30. *Ibid.*

31. The accounts of these experiments which are quoted in the text were recorded by members of the Metabolic Group in the hospital charts of the patients who acted as subjects.

32. Ephraim Shorr, M.D., "The Emergence of Psychological Problems in Patients Requiring Prolonged Hospitalization," in *Medical and Psychological Teamwork in the Care of the Chronically Ill,* ed. by Molly Harrower, Ph.D. (Springfield, Illinois: Charles C. Thomas, 1955), p. 33.

33. *Ibid.*

34. McDermott, "A Consideration of the Present Ethics of Clinical Investigation."

35. Partly because they had conditions for which not very much could be done therapeutically, many patients were not merely willing to act as subjects, but quite eager to do so. In turn, this made the physicians of the Metabolic Group feel that they could be somewhat less conservative and more bold about the experiments they conducted on such patients. Some of the factors which motivated patients to be so interested in serving as research subjects will be discussed in later sections of the book.

36. With regard to the conduct of research on human beings, at least one writer expresses the opinion that this kind of experimentation is "too hazardous and implies too many responsibilities to be undertaken by lone investigators. It should be a group effort supported by a proper consultative body." See Shimkin, "The Research Worker's Point of View," p. 206.

37. Perhaps the most renowned, intensively studied experiment of nature in medical history is the case of Alexis St. Martin. In 1882, St. Martin, a French-Canadian *voyageur,* accidentally received a shotgun charge in the stomach. He was attended by Dr. William Beaumont, a surgeon in the U.S. Army, who was stationed in the Michigan territory, where the accident took place. Under the care of Dr. Beaumont, St. Martin regained his health. However, an opening remained below his left nipple which communicated with an opening in his stomach. This enabled

Beaumont to look directly into the cavity and observe the stomach at work. As a result of eight years of intermittent observations on St. Martin, Beaumont was able to correct many erroneous ideas about digestion which had previously been accepted, to describe gastric juice, and to show that one of its most important constituents is hydrochloric acid. See William Beaumont, M.D., *The Physiology of Digestion with Experiments On The Gastric Juice.* 2nd ed.: Corrected by Samuel Beaumont, M.D. (Burlington: Chauncey Goodrich, 1847.)

In the Preface to the First Edition of this book (which is reprinted in the Second Edition), Dr. Beaumont describes the experiment of nature which he encountered, and his grounds for feeling he was justified in studying it, in the following way:

> I had opportunities for the examination of the interior of the stomach, and its secretions, which have never before been so fully offered to any one. This most important organ, its secretions, and its operations, have been submitted to my observation in a very extraordinary manner, in a state of perfect health, and for years in succession. I have availed myself of the opportunity afforded by a concurrence of circumstances which probably can never again occur, with a zeal and perseverance proceeding from motives which my conscience approves; and I now submit the results of my experiments to an enlightened public, who I doubt not will duly appreciate the truths discovered, and the confirmation of opinions which before rested on conjecture. (p. 10)

38. For a description of this procedure see Thomas Hale Ham, M.D., ed., *A Syllabus of Laboratory Examination in Clinical Diagnosis* (Cambridge, Massachusetts: Harvard University Press, 1950), p. 410. For a brief discussion of the relationship between this procedure and the ability of patients with Addison's disease to excrete administered water, see Joseph F. Dingman, M.D., David H. P. Streeten, M.D., D. Phil., and George W. Thorn, M.D., "Effect of Cortisone on the Abnormal Distribution of Intravascular Water in Adrenal Cortical Insufficiency in Man," *Journal of Laboratory and Clinical Medicine,* Vol. 49, No. 1 (January, 1957), p. 7.

39. The nature and significance of the Group's Evening Rounds will be discussed in the next chapter ("How the Physicians of the Metabolic Group Came to Terms with Their Problems and Stresses").

40. "Report of the Physician-in-Chief" in the *Forty-Third Annual Report of the* ——— *Hospital,* for the fiscal year ended September 30, 1956, p. 53.

41. *Ibid.,* p. 54.

42. The conflict between their interests and responsibilities as clinicians and as investigators which the members of the Metabolic Group often faced is reflected in two adjectives they sometimes used to describe cases which confronted them with this dilemma. An "interesting" case was typically one that was experimentally stimulating partly because it was clinically nonoptimal. (E.g., "George is an interesting case. He has more of an adrenal response than we would like him to have.") A "ruined" case, on the other hand, was usually one in which clinical developments, either beneficent or noxious, had undermined its research value for the Group.

43. We will meet this patient again later.

44. This is an excerpt from a letter written to the author by Leo Angelico. Other passages from this letter will be quoted in Chapter VII, where it will be considered from the point of view of what it indicated about the relationship of the author to the patients on Ward F-Second.

CHAPTER III — How the Physicians of the Metabolic Group Came to Terms With Their Problems and Stresses

Research As a Way of Coming to Terms

THE RESEARCH in which the physicians of the Metabolic Group were engaged constituted one of their primary means for coming to terms with some of the problems they faced. Through the studies they undertook, the members of the Group hoped to learn more about the metabolism of the human body and the nature of various metabolic and endocrine diseases, and also to develop better methods for conducting their investigations and dealing with the disorders which were their special concern. To the extent that these studies actually enabled the Group to realize these goals, their research provided them with a logical-rational way of resolving medical uncertainties and of increasing their ability to help patients. In turn, this made some of the experiments they conducted seem more fully justified, both to themselves and to the patients who participated in them as subjects.

For the members of the Metabolic Group, the most persuasive evidence that research could advance knowledge and skill in all these respects lay in their experience with Addison's disease. As already indicated, the advent of ACTH and cortisone, an event which had very recently taken place, had made an important contribution to the diagnosis and treatment of this condition.[1] It had definitively transformed Addison's disease from the "obscure and deadly" condition it had been in the past, to a state that could be "frequently anticipated, easily recognized and successfully treated."[2] The Metabolic Group had made important contributions in helping to bring this about—through their studies on the role of the adrenal cortex in the metabolism of water, salt, and carbohydrates; their development of laboratory methods for the assessment of adrenal function; and their testing of ACTH and cortisone on patients when these steroids had first become available.

Most of the members of the Group had not been affiliated with the research unit in what one patient referred to as "the days B.C. (Before Cortisone)" when, as he put it, "we people with Addison's disease were very poor examples of this human race." However, from such patients, and the Professor of Medicine who was their Chief, the members of the Group had nonetheless gained a vivid impression of what it had been like in the "B.C." era.

Have you heard the Chief describe what the Metabolic Ward was like in the old days? It was practically all Addisonians at that time, and practically all of them were dying, or pretty close to it. The mortality rate was well over 50%. First, they were only getting salt and some questionable steroids. Later, they got salt and desoxycorticosterone. But the atmosphere on the ward when anyone got the slightest cold, for instance, was really something! They'd seen it turn into pneumonia and end in death too many times . . .

I want you to know that I am forever grateful for this medicine [a patient with Addison's disease wrote to the Metabolic Group]. I only wish you, the scientists, and the companies producing these miracle drugs could know the peace of mind a patient has when after all these years he is able to get help and relief. And your group and your hospital have made this available to me . . .

Such firsthand descriptions of the earlier "black period" in the history of Addison's disease, and knowledge of the role that the research of their predecessors had played in making the "new period of light" possible, helped the members of the Group to cope with some of the discouragement they felt about their current research. This was especially true because many of their studies were closely related to work with Addison's disease. For example, the experimental adrenalectomy operations that the Group was performing were based on their demonstrated ability to "maintain in excellent general health a relatively large group of patients with Addison's disease":

Up to the present, complete surgical removal of the adrenals has not been justified because of the severity of symptoms known to be associated with Addison's disease. However, the recent synthesis of cortisone, together with its relatively low cost and its efficacy when administered orally, has made it possible to maintain in excellent general health a relatively large group of patients with Addison's disease. Many of these patients have now been followed for several years on cortisone therapy supplemented by small doses of desoxycorticosterone. It would appear, therefore, that bilateral complete adrenalectomy is justified as an experimental approach in man in an effort to determine the possible role of the adrenal cortex in patients with severe hypertensive vascular disease . . .[3]

The research-borne advances in knowledge and management of Addison's disease not only made some of the studies in which the Group was engaged more feasible, and ethically tenable. It also helped to reassure the Group that the day might come, as it had with Addison's disease, when their present studies would help to dispel some of the uncertainties, therapeutic limitations, and moral ambiguities with which they were grappling.

Belonging to the Metabolic Group, then, provided a heritage of significant research that was both intellectually and symbolically important to its members. It also supplied a number of other resources which helped them to deal effectively with their mutual problems.

Membership in the Group as a Way of Coming to Terms

To begin with, the physicians of the Metabolic Group found deep personal and professional gratification simply in being associated with one another:

I made some of the finest and firmest friendships of my life [in the Metabolic Group]. It also provided a wonderful atmosphere for learning. My associates were all of high calibre, and I was tremendously stimulated by them . . .

The enthusiastic, sound group spirit was outstanding. It was really a terrific amount of fun working with, arguing with and laughing with the members of the Group . . .

The "fun" and "stimulation" that the members of the Group derived from working together helped to counterbalance some of the strains to which they were subject. Their unity made it possible to exchange opinions and feelings about common problems, and to share responsibility for them in ways that made them somewhat easier to handle.

The particular situation which gave the members of the Group the best opportunity to consult with one another about their mutual problems and to express how they felt about them were the Evening Rounds. We have already had occasion to quote some of the conversations that took place at these meetings: specifically, the Group's discussion about whether or not to subject a young patient with severe hypertension to adrenalectomy, and their consideration of Mr. Gold's untoward reaction to the water test. Some other discussions and interchanges which occurred at Evening Rounds follow.[4]

Dr. P.: Poor Mr. Sparrow looks as though he's just about at the crossroads.

Dr. D.: The only thing we can do now, I guess, is to just sit tight and wait and see what happens to him . . . Did Mike develop cardiac arrhythmia, too, before he died?

Dr. C.: I don't think so. The terrific thing about Mike was how much sweating he did that last week there before the end. Do you remember?

Dr. M.: Leo got one unit of ACTH today.

Dr. D.: His eos fell 42% this time, 70% last time. Of course, the actual per cent fall of the eos doesn't make a damn bit of difference. All we want to know is what kind of a dose, when given, say, to ten or twelve normal subjects, will result in a drop of about 50% in the eos with no rise in hydroxycorticoids.

Dr. D.: Here's Barton's protocol from the last time he was here. You can see how much ACTH he got just by glancing at it. One, two, three—ten days of I.V. ACTH. After the first few days his eos behaved all right. But his keto[steroid]s never did anything. He'll stay this time until his adrenal responds, even if it takes six months. We won't let him out until it does. (Group laughter)

Dr. C.: Mr. Green had a lot done today. Practically the works. EKG, EEG, X-Ray, skull plate, radio iodine . . .

Dr. D.: Does anyone want to test him to see if he really has Addison's disease?

Dr. S.: That would be a mighty good idea. (Group laughter)

Dr. C.: I'll give you 10 to 1 that he has it.

Dr. D.: I won't take it. But we need to document the fact that he has it. Lou Atkinson, for instance, was a lovely case. The only thing is we never proved he had Addison's disease.

Dr. D.: Now, Frank, here you are, dear boy: a case of Addison's disease with diabetes. What's your pleasure, Doctor?

Let's all be thinking as hard as we can in the next few days about what we can do to Mr. Powers to get the most information, because this is a priceless situation. In 1950, I think, there were only 23 or 24 reported cases of Addison's disease and diabetes, and out of those, only 3 had gotten Addison's disease before they had diabetes . . .

Before cortisone, it was very hard to take care of these people. They were always in a hypoglycemic state. Look at the chart of Howard, for instance. He had 50 hospital admissions. Every time he came in it was for hypoglycemia of the severest sort. Cortisone has changed the outlook completely . . .

So, we have *two* cases like this on the ward at once, which is fantastic. This is a fascinating combination of diseases, so let's move carefully with Mr. Powers . . .

Dr. E.: We have another new patient with a very interesting gland, well worth feeling. It's described in the chart as being the size of a grape. But it must be a very large California grape!

Dr. D.: Well, let's stop by tomorrow, hear, see, and feel. Sounds like a good problem, David.

Dr. D.: Here comes Alex now. Alex, we've got a program all set up for you.

Dr. P.: I bet you have! Oh man, you're not going to do that to me!

Dr. D.: You're our stress subject for the week, boy!

Dr. P.: Not during my ruddy Board exams!

Dr. D.: Phil, you can get eos on him every morning before he jumps out of bed.

Dr. P.: Not Phil in the morning.

Dr. C.: Besides, he doesn't jump out of bed.

Dr. P.: I'll have to carry a bottle around with me, because I'm sure to have polyuria next week.

Dr. D.: We've just *got* to get steroids on Alex. It's a priceless opportunity.

Dr. P.: Actually, Jim, there's no point in doing it. Because I'm not under any stress at all!

Dr. P.: Mr. Starr . . . Well, the poor guy is likely to go out in the next 24 hours.

Dr. E.: Really!

Dr. P.: He's a wonderful candidate, of course, to die in adrenal crisis. The question is whether we should treat him as an Addisonian.

Dr. E.: What's killing him?

Dr. P.: This infection, and dehydration, plus a big Factor X . . . Suppose he goes into crisis tonight, which is a great possibility. Suppose he starts yorking his head off, and his pressure goes down to say, 90 over 60 . . . How far should we go with him?

Dr. D.: I'd treat him for crisis.

Dr. E.: He should be covered by hormone therapy, I think.

Dr. D.: By all means. We certainly don't want to be guilty of common neglect! (*Group laughter*)

Dr. G.: Anybody interested in Mr. Bard's ketos?

Dr. E.: What's your guess about them?

Dr. C.: I bet the ketos went down.

Dr. G.: You can leave now. The ketos went up from 3.7 to 11, and the eos went down. Way down, in fact. They dropped 86%.

Dr. E.: Here's a lead pencil, Jim. You can cross him off the list.

Dr. M.: Allen seems to get quite a charge from one unit of ACTH. When I was there today, his bed was vibrating and everything.

Dr. P.: Pretty soon, now, everybody on the street will be wanting to come in for an ACTH assay, if that's the case.

Dr. M.: It's a nice feeling. Like coffee.

Dr. D.: And an assay is not expensive.

Dr. M.: It may not be the ACTH at all that's having that effect on him. It may just be your magnetic personality, Frank.

Dr. E.: Mr. Forde?

Dr. C.: He's just dandy! (*Group laughter*) Well, he is!

Dr. E.: He's a nice fellow, too.

Dr. D.: How's his diarrhea?

Dr. C.: The diarrhea's just about gone now.

Dr. D.: If Bruce were here now he'd say, "See, cortisone is a constipating drug!"

Dr. E.: Mr. Forde will have to be watched very closely tonight, I should think. Because we really don't know how fast F runs out, do we?

Dr. D.: No, we don't. Dr. T.'s theory was that it would last as long as the oral stuff, but we don't really know. And agents that go in fast usually go out fast. So, we still have to watch him. This would be a heckuva time to lose him . . .

Dr. M.: You know, 25% of our present patients on the ward are diabetic Addisonians! (*Laughter*)

Dr. D.: The disease is getting more and more common.

Dr. C.: Now if we discharge a few patients, the per cent will go up even higher.

Dr. E.: We have two adrenals and four pancreases on the ward.

Dr. P.: Remember the time last year when we had seven patients with one adrenal between them? (*Group laughter*)

Dr. P.: Bob's withdrawn, depressed, headachy, nauseous [*sic*].

Dr. D.: Well, Doctor, he's your patient. What do you want to do with him?

Dr. P.: Well, we can't let him go out of the hospital the way he is now. So, what I'd like to do, I think, is try some hypotensive drug on him while he's here.

Dr. D.: What drug would you want to give him?

Dr. P.: I'd say hexamethonium.

Dr. D.: Phil?

Dr. C.: Apresaline.

Dr. D.: Joel?

Dr. E.: Apresaline, too.

Dr. D.: Ed?

Dr. M.: I don't know enough to say.

Dr. D.: Neither do the rest of us. (*Laughter*) Dan?

Dr. H.: Hexamethonium. But by mouth.

Dr. D.: How much would you give him, Dan?

Dr. H.: God, I don't know! I'd have to look it up. (*Laughter*)

Dr. E.: Tomorrow's the day of the operation? I think I would like to give Mr. Graham a couple of milligrams of desoxy today. I just have a queer feeling that with a little desoxy, these people might do better from a vascular point of view. I don't know why. It's probably emotional on my part, but I think I'd feel better if he got some desoxy.

Dr. D.: You would? Of course, he's going to be getting 100 mgms. of cortisone today and 100 tomorrow. Two milligrams of desoxy won't make much difference. But philosophically, it seems to me that it contradicts our program of the past month. Well, we'll compromise. I'll settle for giving him cortisone three times before the operation instead of twice. I think he should have some cortisone earlier today, before the party. Let's say a half unit p.o. at lunch.

Dr. G.: Actually, he would be a wonderful subject for a continuous I.V.

Dr. D.: Delightful! But I wouldn't dare try it on him.

Dr. E.: Well, I guess we're all happy about him now. There's no real scientific basis for our decision, of course. But we feel better . . . (*Laughter*)

As we develop our analysis of the Group's ways of coming to terms, some of the details of these complex interchanges between the physicians of the Group will become more intelligible. For the moment, our primary intention is to convey something of the atmosphere which characterized their intimate discussions, and illustrate some of the more general ways in which these discussions helped the members of the Group to cope with problems of clinical investigation.

As these excerpts from their meetings indicate, the members of the Group (in the words of one physician) did a great deal of "sounding off" to one another about the strains they experienced in the face of the elements of uncertainty and unpredictability in their professional situation, their limited ability to help many of their patients, and the conflicts between "good medical practice" and "good research" to which they were subject. At Evening Rounds, and in other more informal contexts, the members of the Group expressed a good deal of tension, frustration, and disquietude over these problems. The combined effect of sharing these feelings with colleagues who were also friends, who faced the same problems, and who often reacted to them in the same way, as one physician put it, was that it gave the members of the Metabolic Group "a lift" which they needed and welcomed.

In addition to listening sympathetically to one another, the members of the Group also gave one another active encouragement and support. For example, when Dr. P., who was scheduled to be "on call" for the night, asked his colleagues what he should do if Mr. Starr, one of the patients on the Metabolic Ward, went into crisis, they assured him that they would be unequivocally in favor of his treating the patient, even though this would undermine the experiment they were conducting on him.

As other of their interchanges at Evening Rounds demonstrate, the members of the Metabolic Group were not always so thoroughly in accord with one another. In fact, often they quite openly disagreed. However, on the whole, the members of the Group considered such differences of opinion and the discussions they provoked "stimulating" and "valuable." From their point of view, "arguing with one another" in this way usually led to decisions that were scientifically and ethically more sound because of the active critical process out of which they had emerged. It is not within my layman's capacity to judge the objective quality or merit of such decisions. What can be said, however, is that the debates which preceded them enhanced the ability of the Group to cope with their problems by strengthening their felt conviction about the validity and justification of the decisions that they made in this way.

Laughter from the Conference Room and the Laboratory

As these excerpts from their Evening Rounds also suggest, a salient characteristic of the relationship between the members of the Metabolic Group was the frequency with which they "joked and laughed with one another." A highly patterned and intricate form of humor was one of the most important ways that the Group had evolved for coming to terms with their problems and stresses. "Our humor is a kind of protective device," one of the members of the Group explained. "If we were to talk seriously all the time and act like a bunch of Sir Galahads or something, we just couldn't take all this."

A close inspection of the humor of the physicians of the Metabolic Group reveals that many of their jokes focused around the major problems they faced as a unit. For example, they joked about the problems of uncertainty with which they were confronted in their clinical and research-oriented activities, and about the rather whimsical, trial-and-error nature of their so-called scientifically-based efforts to cope with these uncertainties.

Dr. T.: There's been something brewing with this man from the very first that we haven't succeeded in putting our finger on . . . Oh, I can always *explain* it. But I don't know if it's *right!*

Dr. P.: Mr. Thayer's a State of Maine-er. So you can expect his keto-steroids to do just about anything!

Dr. D.: Does anyone know what's wrong with this patient? Evidently, there's no difference between his oral and rectal temperatures, for one thing. What *that* means, I don't know.
Dr. G.: Maybe it's just that he has a hot mouth and a cold rectum!

Dr. D.: Barton?
Dr. G.: Well, when I went down to see him, he was sitting on the bed wrapped in a huge blanket. "Are you cold?" I asked him. "Yes," he said. Thyrotoxicosis, indeed!

Dr. D.: Let's go around the table quickly on what this boy had at 15.
Dr. P.: Pyelonephritis.
Dr. C.: I reserve judgment. (*Laughter*) Hypertension.
Dr. M.: Essential hypertension.
Dr. H.: Pyelonephritis.
Dr. G.: Pyelo.
Dr. E.: Pyelonephritis.
Dr. S.: I think probably hypertension.
Dr. D.: I thought you were arguing for the other point of view before. (*Laughter*)
Dr. T.: Pyelo.
Dr. W.: Pyelo.
Dr. D.: That makes 6 pyelos and 4 hypertensions. There's no answer, of course. It's just a matter of opinion. (*Laughter*)

Dr. W.: Mr. Flanders? Well, Flander's unchanged. I've checked him for several nights now, and he always has a little pitting edema. I would say about point seven's worth. (*Laughter*)
Dr. P.: Point 0 seven plus-or-minus-five? (*More laughter*)

Dr. D.: Moore came in this summer with an infarct and we thought he was a goner. But he pulled through all right. And so far as I know, he's been doing pretty well since. His pressure's better.

Dr. P.: Infarct: the new treatment for hypertension! (*Laughter*)

Dr. G.: Are you *sure* Mr. Stark's adrenals are out?
Dr. H.: They *must* be. His carcinoma got better.

Dr. E.: There's no real scientific basis for our decision, of course, but we *feel* better . . . (*Laughter*)

The members of the Group also made numerous jokes about their inability to "cure" patients, or even to help them symptomatically. In this connection, they joked frequently about the impending death of some of their patients, and especially about their failure to "rescue" or "save" patients from death.

Dr. W.: Mr. Benjamin [a patient with carcinoma of the prostate] has an ingrown toenail. He complains about it every day. Couldn't we have the chiropodist come up to see him? It's a very painful thing to have. I know.

Dr. P.: I love that fellow feeling! (*Laughter*)

Dr. D.: Mr. Goss is still alive.
Dr. S.: Is he putting out urine?
Dr. D.: No.
Dr. E.: Is he having hemodialysis?
Dr. D.: No.
Dr. C.: Then how is he alive? (*Laughter*)

Dr. H.: One more thing, *doctors*. We finally figured out what caused the death of that goldfish that Nellie kept in the lab. The flame photometer was throwing off fumes . . .

Dr. T.: What was the cause of most of the deaths? Hypertension itself?

Dr. C.: Four or five died of adrenal insufficiency, we think. Some of the others, as you say, died of hypertensive disease. One man died just being turned over on the operating table.

Dr. M.: He wasn't a very good case anyway! (*Laughter*)

Dr. H.: I don't like this discouragement about Mr. Simmons. All he's suffering from at the moment is a mild psychoneurosis.

Dr. P.: The only trouble is, he's dying of it!

Dr. W.: Why not give him some "F," then? That's our newest cure-all.

Still other jokes characteristic of the Metabolic Group centered around the moral ambiguities and conflicts that conducting research on patients entailed. There were jokes about the non-relevance of many studies to the clinical welfare of patients; the deprivations and risks that experimentation imposed on patients; the particularly radical nature of some of the Group's research; the disappointing and untoward consequences of various experiments. The members of the Group also joked about the fact that in spite of the discomforts and hazards that participating in their studies entailed, they nonetheless continued to ask patients to be subjects.

Dr. G.: Mr. Powers' test will be over on Wednesday. What are the plans for his management after that?
Dr. S.: Why, I suppose we'll finally get around to *treating* him.

Dr. P.: Flanders looks and feels much better, doesn't he? Good. We must do some nice experiments on him before he goes home . . .

Dr. M.: We've really hit pay dirt this time. Mr. Lane's a wonderful research case! Now if we can only see him in crisis at some point along the way . . . But we can always *arrange* that . . .

Dr. G.: Mr. Messing doesn't like studies very much. And he doesn't like too many doctors. He says the more doctors there are, the more pokes he gets.
Dr. C.: He's only going to get eleven pokes from eleven of us in eleven days . . .

Dr. P.: What's Mr. Thayer getting? Let's see—F, Estinyl, Cortisone, Digitoxin, Elkisin, Percorten, Potassium, Citrate . . . Is that *all?*

Dr. T.: We have another new patient, sixty-six years old, who's had hypertension of five weeks' duration. His pressure is 240 over 90, and it's been accompanied by anxiety, sweating and weakness . . .
Dr. D.: Wonderful! Sounds like epinephrine! The perfect candidate for an adrenalectomy!
Dr. P.: We don't have to do tests on him. Just operate, eh?
Dr. C.: Sounds *too* good . . .

Dr. D.: Let's assign a good doctor to Mr. Kaye. Are there any good doctors around? Ah, there's one.
Dr. C.: Put that knife down when you say that!
Dr. D.: The trouble with you is that you worry about all sorts of inconsequential things, like your patients' welfare.
Dr. C.: The trouble with me is that when a patient has hypertension

and it obviously has something to do with his home, I like to try to get to work on that home.

Dr. D.: It's much easier to take out his adrenals than to burn down his house!

Dr. M.: "Adrenals are the tonsils of our time" ought to be our Group slogan.

Dr. T.: What we need is a patient with cancer of the prostate, leukemia *and* hypertension!

Dr. E.: We have two adrenals and four pancreases on the ward.

Dr. P.: Remember the time last year when we had seven patients with one adrenal between them?

Dr. E.: I've got a pearl!

Dr. C.: We've got the basket out!

Dr. E.: Well, so far the only people we *haven't* done adrenalectomies on are those with bad kidneys. So, it seems to me that the thing to do in cases like those is to *transplant a kidney.* Then, if you need another kidney, you just transplant another. When the kidneys start to work, you go in and do an adrenalectomy. So, when you're all finished, you're left with no adrenals, and an indeterminate number of kidneys! I think it's a brilliant idea!

Dr. D.: You'll be interested to hear, I'm sure, that according to the latest issue of *The Reader's Digest,* no one has to worry about cancer of the prostate any more. All you have to do, you see, is have your adrenals removed! Incidentally, Mr. Thayer was sitting up in bed this morning reading that article. I'll tell you one thing. He's much better off reading *that* version of the operation than the beauty of a report *we'll* have to write!

In the ironic words of the physician quoted earlier, the members of the Metabolic Group were not a "bunch of Sir Galahads" splendidly fitted out with all the knowledge and equipment necessary to conduct rigorous, meaningful research, protect patients from discomfort and harm, "rescue" them from death, and "cure" them. Their humor reflects the fact that in their role as clinical investigators they were subject to uncertainty, limitation, and conflict, and as a result, to considerable strain.

In part, the humor of the Metabolic Group was cathartic. It enabled the Group to express some of the tension they felt over the problems they faced. Their humor was also counterphobic and somewhat impious. The members of the Group were especially inclined to make jokes about events that disturbed them a good deal, or about which they had other very strong, and serious feelings—for example, the death of a patient, or the failure of a major experiment. To some extent, this kind of humor was defiant. By laughing at such events the members of the Group expressed their refusal to accept them as inevitable, and asserted that from their conference room and laboratory something more effective than laughter for coping with such situations would eventually come. At the same time, joking about things they regarded as particularly important helped the members of the Group to "make light" of their feelings, and in that way, achieve a more detached attitude toward their problems.

It is relevant to note that in its admixture of bravado and "blasphemy," the humor of the Metabolic Group resembled a type of humor known as "grim humor" or "gallows humor." (*"Galgenhumor"*). This sort of joking typically occurs in situations where a group of individuals (more generally men than women) are faced with a considerable amount of stress—above all, firsthand contact with death. For example, gallows humor is characteristic of prisoners who have been sentenced to death, individuals interned in a concentration camp, and soldiers on the front lines of a battlefield.[5] The fact that the humor of the Metabolic Group was reminiscent of the kind of joking that takes place in such precarious and dangerous situations supplies evidence to support our assertion that the problems they faced as clinical investigators imposed a considerable amount of stress on the physicians of the Metabolic Group, and that their humor was a way of coming to terms with this stress.

It is equally important to note that the humor of the Metabolic Group was also compatible with a type of joking so generally characteristic of physicians that it is sometimes referred to as "medical humor." In the earliest years of their medical training, physicians learn that an effective and appropriate way to handle their reactions to death and other stressful or emotionally provocative professional situations is to joke with their colleagues about them in much the same look-it-in-the-face-and-laugh manner as the members of the Metabolic Group did.[6]

In sum—by freeing them from some of the tension to which they were subject, enabling them to achieve greater detachment and equipoise, and strengthening their resolve to do something about the problems with which they were faced, the grim medical humor of the Metabolic Group helped them to come to terms with their situation in a useful and professionally acceptable way.

The "Game of Chance" Behavior of the Metabolic Group[7]

The humor of the Metabolic Group was closely related to another of their characteristic ways of coming to terms: the guessing and wagering behavior in which they engaged.

As the excerpts from Evening Rounds suggest, in their discussions with one another the members of the Metabolic Group not only expressed themselves through humor, but also in what might be termed the language of the game of chance:

> Dr. C.: I'll give you 10 to 1 that Mr. Green has Addison's disease.
> Dr. D.: I won't take it . . .

> Dr. P.: 8 to 1 he won't react to glucose . . .

> Dr. E.: We're waiting for Mr. Flanders to go into negative balance, if he will.
> Dr. H.: Actually, we may be studying the exact reverse of what we set out to study. We may be studying the period of recovery in this man . . . Well, we'll just have to sit tight until we see his chemistries.
> Dr. T.: It's quite a gamble, but I think it's worth it . . . It would be a real ten-strike to get his 17-ketos and 17-hydroxy[corticosteroid]s . . .

> Dr. G.: Anybody interested in Mr. Bard's ketos?
> Dr. E.: What's your guess about them?
> Dr. C.: I bet the ketos went down.
> Dr. G.: You can leave now. The ketos went up from 3.7 to 11 and the eos went down. Way down, in fact. They dropped 86%.

In part, the gambling lingo that the physicians of the Metabolic Group used to describe some of the phenomena they encountered on the Metabolic Ward or studied in their laboratory was simply descriptive of the high degree of uncertainty, unpredictability, and risk-taking that characterized a considerable proportion of their work. However, this lingo was also intended to be humorous. In part, when the Metabolic Group talked about an experiment as a "gamble" or findings it might be possible to get as a "ten-strike," they were joking about the many unknowns with which they were faced, and laughing at their attempts to be "scientific."

10 to 1 he has Addison's disease . . .

8 to 1 he won't react to glucose . . .

Not only did the Metabolic Group use gambling jargon. It was also their custom to take bets[8] on the possible outcome of various laboratory tests they conducted:

Let's all take a guess at what Bob's eos will do. Here's mine. With ACTH and epinephrine, a 50 to 60% fall; with ACTH alone, a 20 to 30% fall; and with epinephrine alone, a 30% fall . . . Your turn next, Jim . . .

This group wagering had several functions. First, it was a stimulating intellectual exercise, which gave the members of the Group an organized opportunity to think out loud about clinical and research problems, and try to formulate predictions that were based on sound medical reasoning. Second, as one of the members of the Group explained, their betting was also a form of "friendly competition":

We knew each other well, and liked each other a lot. We were all good friends, and we were also interested in competition. The betting was a form of gamesmanship in the spirit of fun, that livened things up. Part of the fun lay in tricking the other person into making a bet in which the odds were against him so that he stood a poor chance of winning . . . In other words, you tried to get the other guy to walk into a loaded bet . . .

The betting game that the Metabolic Group played also had more latent, noncognitive functions. In this connection, certain details about the game of chance are revealing. The Group was most likely to take bets about the outcome of tests that were especially important to them from a clinical or research point of view, but which they had "no good scientific basis" for predicting. They often formalized the betting they did under these circumstances by writing down the guess of each member, sometimes on the same kind of paper they used to record laboratory findings. The giving and taking of bets was usually carried out in a rather ceremonious fashion, and was always accompanied by a great deal of banter and joking. On several occasions when they were registering such bets, the members of the Group laughingly referred to the following incident. It seems that

a year ago they had invited the dietician to join them in making a
bet about how a certain experiment would turn out. "And she came
closer to guessing the results than we did!" the members of the
Group recalled with amusement. This was "because she had no idea
how the experiment was *supposed* to turn out," they contended.[9]

The kind of joking that accompanied the Group's wagering suggests that to some extent it overlapped with their characteristic humor. In part, their betting was an ironic game in which they laughingly acted out some of their feelings about the uncertainties and
limitations with which they were faced. Our ignorance is so great,
they said through their wagering, and there are so many things we
do not have enough knowledge to predict, control, or explain, that
some of our so-called scientific endeavors are like organized lotteries.
What we do is try to make reasonable guesses about some of the
problems with which we work. If we are lucky, things turn out as
we anticipated or planned; if we are unlucky, they do not. For the
relative accuracy of many of our predictions and the success or failure
of some of our undertakings seem to depend as much on chance as
on knowledge and skill. For example, witness the fact that the dietician came closer to predicting the outcome of an experiment than any
of us did.

In this way, the physicians of the Metabolic Group wryly acknowledged that their scientific efforts were often confounded and
sometimes defeated by unpredictable chance elements. However, the
attitude toward uncertainty and chance which they expressed through
their betting was not simply a resigned one. Their game of chance,
like their humor, was also a form of assertion. In a sense, betting
about how an experiment or a clinical undertaking would turn out
was the Metabolic Group's way of making predictions *in spite of* the
fact that they did not have sufficient knowledge to do so "on scientific grounds." When they recorded their bets on the kind of paper
they used for laboratory data, it was as if they were saying: Ideally,
our judgments and decisions *should* be scientific and laboratory-pre-
cise. In this case, we don't have enough knowledge for that. But we
won't let that deter us. We'll use the relevant information and techniques available to us, take our chances, and proceed on that basis.

Dr. E.: We're waiting for Mr. Flanders to go into negative balance,
if he will.

Dr. H.: Actually, we may be studying the exact reverse of what we set out to study. We may be studying the period of recovery in this man . . . Well, we'll just have to sit tight until we see his chemistries.

Dr. T.: It's quite a gamble, but I think it's worth it . . . It would be a real ten-strike to get his 17-ketos and 17-hydroxys . . .

The fact that the physicians of the Metabolic Group were more prone to make bets when the project they undertook was very important to them suggests that their wagers were also petitions for success. Some of the Group's betting seems to have been a way of collectively expressing the hope that the results of their endeavors either would confirm their predictions or yield new knowledge that would increase their certainty and ability to control.[10]

The Physicians of the Metabolic Group and Their Patients

Sometimes patients become the common interest of everyone in a department, even at times seeming as close as one's immediate family. It is of particular sorrow, therefore, to record the death of two of our special patients, each exceptional in his own way. Don Mahoney, whom we had cherished for fourteen years, whom many generations of residents had known, and for whom we never gave up hope, finally succumbed to his disease, xanthomatosis, in January. Don always cooperated as soon as his inevitable question of "Why" was answered. We shall miss him. The other special patient was Robert Holmsby, the last survivor of Dr. ————'s group of 83 patients with cerebellar medulloblastoma. Robert died in December, 14 years after his tumor was identified at operation . . .

(From the Report of the Roentgenologist in an Annual Report of the Hospital.)

We soon learned that it was not enough to assure these patients that we are aiming at their physical rehabilitation, and that in order to obtain their cooperation in these tedious studies, it was necessary to instill in them an appropriate motivation. To some we could promise relief of varying degrees, to others, a correction of their difficulties; but in almost no cases would these effects be so dramatic and rapid as to serve per se as an adequate motivation. Here then was a microcosm which incorporated all the various problems which challenge any group concerned with the chronically ill. It was an enriching experience to see how the difficulties inherent in this research program were overcome and to come to understand the many factors that went into their resolution . . . Our medical staff which had been accustomed to brief hospital admissions, now had to learn to assume a broader relationship to their patients and soon began to recognize the desirability of serving as substitute for important outside relationships—for the employer, the father or mother . . .

> —Ephraim Shorr, M.D., "The Emergence of Psychological Problems in Patients Requiring Prolonged Hospitalization."

He had settled down as one of the physicians who are companions in suffering to the patients in their care; who do not stand above disease, fighting her in the armor of personal security, but who themselves bear her mark . . .

> —Thomas Mann, *The Magic Mountain.*

Finally, some of the distinctive characteristics of the Metabolic Group's relationship to their patients also contributed to their ability to cope with their shared problems and stresses.

Like other social roles, the role of the physician is defined and governed by a system of normative ideas and values. The physician is expected to orient his professional behavior to certain standards—to try to live up to them in the various situations and relationships with which he deals as a physician. Among the values and norms that structure the relation of the physician to the patient are the following.[11]

—The primary obligation of the physician is to do what he can to protect and further the welfare of the patient.

—In the "emotional aspects" of his relationship with the patient, the physician is expected to maintain a dynamic balance between attitudes of "detachment" and "concern."[12] He is expected to be sufficiently detached or objective toward the patient to exercise sound medical judgment and maintain his equanimity. He is also expected to be sufficiently concerned about the welfare of the patient to give him compassionate care.

—The physician is required to strike a comparable balance with respect to the *scope* of his relationship and involvement with the patient. The physician is expected to confine his relations with the patient to matters which pertain to the handling of medical problems. However, he is also expected to establish a relationship with the patient which is comprehensive enough to enable him to "know the patient as a person and give substantial attention to [his] psychological and social circumstances."[13]

—Closely related to the last two pairs of norms are those which have to do with the degree and kind of authority that the physician is expected to apply to his relations with the patient. By virtue of his special, institutionally-validated scientific knowledge and skill, the physician is invested with the right to exercise a considerable amount of authority over the patient. He is permitted and expected to manipulate, manage and control many aspects of the patient's behavior and activities. However, the physician is expected to restrict his authoritative influence over the patient to things which bear upon the patient's medical problems, and to use this authority primarily to facilitate his competent handling of those problems.

Some of the materials already presented suggest that in certain ways the relations of the physicians of the Metabolic Group to their patients diverged from these normative standards. The scope of their relationship to patients and the degree of their emotional involvement with them exceeded what is usually expected of physicians. As we shall demonstrate, to some extent these characteristics of the Metabolic Group's relationship to their patients were connected with the fact that in their capacity as clinical investigators they were required to give as much emphasis to conducting research on patients as to caring for them, and that for the purpose of advancing knowledge they had to subject their patients to greater risks and more stringent controls than physicians ordinarily do.

First, we will more fully describe and illustrate some of the rather special characteristics of the Metabolic Group's relations with patients.

"Friends of the Family"

In certain respects, the relations of the Metabolic Group with patients were more "personal" than "professional" in nature. To some extent, as one physician put it, the Group treated their patients "like one of the family," or, at least, "like friends." For example, they allowed certain of their patients to address them by their first names, rather than as "Doctor"; they joked a good deal with some of their patients; they told them a considerable amount about their extraprofessional activities; and in certain instances they were interested or involved in the events of their patients' lives on other than a "strictly professional" basis.[14]

These personally-toned elements in the Metabolic Group's relations with patients are illustrated by the following passages from letters which they wrote to patients:[15]

On December 1st I shall find myself out in California in a permanent appointment as associate professor of medicine at the ——— Hospital . . . So, Mrs. G., our nine-year old and our one-year old baby, Beth, will move across the country in a wagon (1951 Chevrolet) to our new home in the late fall. I shall be a bit closer to Texas, and once we are settled out there I shall make a real attempt to see you on one of my speaking tours . . .

. . . With regard to the vaccination, I would go ahead and have it done, but would take 50 mg. of cortisone on the day of vaccination and a couple of days thereafter. With regard to the name of a doctor in Mexico City, Dr. R. is your man . . . He was with Dr. T.'s group for two years, and just returned to Mexico City last summer. Finally, with regard to any "names of any likely prospects among the Señoritas down south of the border," I suggest that you contact Dr. R. immediately on arrival in Mexico City. He is a caballero of long-standing, and although married at the present time, he is, I am sure, in close contact with Mexican females of incomparable attractiveness . . . I do hope this will help you out. Have a wonderful time! I'm sure you will . . .

Many thanks for your letter of September 28th. We will book you for Ward F-Second on November 1st, if this is convenient for you. I do not anticipate that you will need to stay in any longer than two weeks. If you can manage it, would you bring down some of your Kodachrome pictures. I know that we would all like to see them, especially of the Maine coast line. Looking forward to seeing you . . .

My conscience bothers me when I think that I never came to your cocktail party—first, to eat the figs from your garden, and when they were gone, the apples. Life is difficult for me right now, and has been for the past few months, with my wife having had a miscarriage and being in the hospital, and I with two little children to take care of. I regret sincerely that I did not come to your home . . .

"Red-Carpet Treatment"

"We'll have the 'red carpet' put out on March 17th," one of the physicians of the Metabolic Group wrote to a patient who was scheduled to be admitted to the Metabolic Ward on that day. Though intended half-humorously, this remark aptly describes another characteristic of the relationship between the Metabolic Group and their patients. In certain ways, the physicians of the Metabolic Group gave their patients "red-carpet treatment"—that is, they granted them special privileges and considerations not accorded to the "usual" hospital patient.

The Group planned and supervised the construction and decoration of the Metabolic Ward on which most of their patients were hospitalized, so that the unit would be as attractive as possible. They provided the patients on this ward with a television set, books, and games. They did everything they could to staff the ward with a high ratio of nurses to patients, and tried to "hand-pick" nurses for this unit. They encouraged the nurses they chose to give personal attention to patients, to be "especially considerate of any complaints they might have," and to "try to keep them busy and happy." Through the dieticians who worked with them, the Metabolic Group saw to it that top-quality food was purchased for patients, and that the food was well-prepared and attractively served. If they felt that a patient was well enough, and if he was not undergoing an experiment which required that he stay in bed, the physicians of the Metabolic Group permitted him to move freely about the ward, to visit patients in other parts of the hospital, and, sometimes, to go out of the hospital on a temporary pass. The Group also allowed patients to stay up later at night than patients on other wards generally did. Except for those instances in which they temporarily deprived patients of certain drugs or procedures in order to conduct an experiment, the Metabolic Group made a special effort to give their patients the best medical care that the hospital could offer, and especially the benefits of any promising new medical developments to which they had access. They also followed their patients closely after they were discharged from the ward, and encouraged them to return to the hospital for periodic check-ups. The Metabolic Group charged many of their patients less than the prevailing hospital rates, and gave some of them free hospitalization and medical care.

"Patient-Colleagues"

In addition to the personal and privileged forms of treatment they accorded patients, there were certain respects in which the Group dealt with patients as if they were professional equals.

They provided patients with a considerable amount of information about their disorders: the state of knowledge concerning them; their characteristic signs and symptoms; the technical intricacies of treating them; and their prognoses. The Metabolic Group also told patients a good deal about the experiments in which they participated as subjects:

... As far as the dibenzylene is concerned, I would suggest that you try one tablet twice a day and increase it to one tablet three times a day if necessary. I would not at present go any higher unless you have some bothersome symptoms. There is no rule as to maximum dosage, since this is variable from individual to individual. The warning symptoms of overdosage are excessive flushing, headache and nausea, as well as lightheadedness when getting up from a chair ...

... The best indicators of the need for extra salt are your weight and salt-craving, especially the former. It would be wise for you to weigh yourself regularly, every other day or so. Any significant decline is an indication for an increased salt intake ... The book by Dr. T. to which you refer is the second edition of the book which you undoubtedly already have. The new material included in it is chiefly that related to cortisone. The title of the book is: *The Diagnosis and Treatment of Adrenal Insufficiency,* published by —————— ...

Now on this chart, I've plotted the results of all your tests ... Each day when we were doing your test, you see, your blood sugar started way up here. On various days we gave you insulin, or hydrocortisone, or both together. This day here you got insulin alone, in a very small amount, and as you can see, your blood sugar came sailing down to a normal range ... The next day, indicated by the blue line, we gave you insulin and then started Compound F right away. Your blood sugar came down, you see, but not quite as much as before ...

Sometimes the physicians of the Metabolic Group gave patients quite a bit of information about the medical status of fellow-patients hospitalized on the ward:

Our mutual friend, Martin Kane, spent the summer on the North Shore without losing any weight, and when he came back, we removed his second adrenal. He had a most uneventful recovery from the operation, and feels wonderful now ... Mr. Henderson isn't doing too well, having had a severe psychological disturbance which has little to do with the disease. We just re-admitted him with a question of further surgery. We don't know yet ...

The members of the Group also allowed patients to visit their laboratories and offices, and sometimes asked them to help with minor tasks.

. . . Shortly before the patient was discharged, he took a considerable interest in aiding the members of the Metabolic Group in making up charts of laboratory data . . .

Through behavior of this sort, the physicians of the Metabolic Group implied that they regarded their patients as "colleagues" or "collaborators" whose qualified services they welcomed or needed. They were especially inclined to treat the patients who acted as subjects for their experiments in this way, and sometimes actually told such patients that they thought of them as working members of the Group.

Dr. T. and I are currently engaged in completing some studies of great importance. Our deadline is September fifth. Because of your wonderful help during last winter and your precision in such matters, we thought perhaps you might be interested in the following: We must administer to an Addisonian some intravenous infusions of adrenal cortical hormones. Although the action exerted by these potent agents would, I am sure, give you a considerable boost, we feel that we should provide compensation for any person taking part in the study since the work is, at this stage, purely in the interest of research . . . We should be happy to pay all transportation, plus $10 a day while in the hospital . . . Certainly no one deserves a stipend more than you do . . . I shall await your reply with interest . . .

I regret the necessity of having to write this letter without having had the pleasure of seeing you again this summer. It is, however, necessary to inform you that I shall be leaving the Hospital on July 1st, in order to assume my new duties at the University of ——— Medical School. You should therefore address your future communications to Dr. C., who is taking my place in the laboratory. I am certain that you remember him, and know that he is both capable and cooperative . . . I sincerely hope that both you and your wife continue to enjoy many years of comfort and happiness. Also, please accept my thanks for your wonderful cooperation during the past two years with the various studies which you were so successful in carrying out. It has been a pleasure to have such an intelligent and cooperative patient working with the Group. We are grateful for your help, and the studies in which you took part have meant a great deal to the progress we have been able to make during this time . . .

The "Celebration" of Patients

As these excerpts from their letters demonstrate, the physicians of the Metabolic Group did more than politely acknowledge the services of some of the patients who acted as their research subjects. They praised and congratulated them for their willingness to serve in this capacity, for the proficiency with which they did so, and even for any evidence of their having derived clinical benefit from the experimental drug or procedure to which they had submitted:

I am glad to hear that you are getting along so well. You are a real advertisement for the Addisonian group. It sure is amazing what a few pills of cortisone will do . . .

Above all, the physicians of the Metabolic Group told patients when the experiments in which they had participated had made an important contribution to the advancement of medical scientific knowledge and to its application in the practice of medicine:

. . . You will be interested in knowing that the results from the big experiment in which you were involved are of the greatest interest not only to us, but also to many scientists who work on the new steroids in Switzerland and elsewhere . . .

The trip you made to the hospital will benefit humanity greatly through the data we obtained . . .

You are now quite a famous person . . . The article you appeared in was a teaching paper and has proved to be of considerable value to a large number of practicing physicians . . .

"We celebrate our patients," was the way a member of the Metabolic Group once described these aspects of the Group's relationship to some of their patients. He also was referring to the many conferences and "rounds" at which the Group presented their patients to other physicians and medical personnel. In this context, too, the Group sometimes expressed their indebtedness and gratitude to patients for the role they had played in facilitating research:

This is Leo Angelico . . . Leo has been assaying ACTH for us for three years now. And we've gotten some wonderful baseline studies with his help. He's been written up in many of our papers. Wherever you see the initials L.A. . . .

The Group also gave personal citations to patients in some of their professional publications:

We are indebted to the patient, without whose enthusiastic cooperation this study would not have been possible . . .

We are most indebted to Mr. Leo Angelico, whose unfailing cooperation allowed us to work out the fundamentals of intravenous administration of ACTH . . .

Dedicated to a loyal friend and patient, L.H.F. . . .

For reasons which we will explore in greater detail in later sections of this book, many of the Metabolic Group's patients were potentially "newsworthy." Popular magazines and newspapers were eager to publish what they considered their "exciting medical stories." This provided the physicians of the Metabolic Group with another way of publicly celebrating their patients. In the prepared stories about their research activities which they released to the press and in the interviews they granted science reporters, the Metabolic Group often singled out individual patients for special mention:

Before the days of miracle drugs a man could not have lived more than a few weeks after surgical removal of his adrenals (the endocrine glands which lie astride the kidneys). Last week the amphitheatre at ——— Hospital was crowded with standees as Dr. John T. described cases in which patients have lived as long as nine months after the removal of the adrenals and are still going strong . . .

Dr. T. described twelve cases in which the operation had been performed. Four cases had died; eight others had been kept alive by the administration of desoxycorticosterone and cortisone, given in place of adrenal hormones.

One patient went ice fishing in New Hampshire a few weeks after the operation; his only complaint was that he got uncomfortably cold, which was to be expected because the body's conversion of food into heat depends, in part, on the activity of the adrenal glands.

Another, Walter Cousins, 32, had been given six months to live. He had a roaring in the head which made it impossible for him to work. He had the operation nine months ago, responded so well that he got a job as a night orderly at the hospital. Cousins takes a cortisone tablet twice a day and gets a daily injection of desoxycorticosterone.

It is too early to say what success the technique may have in treating extreme high blood pressure, and Dr. T. was bending over backward to be conservative in his report. But four of the patients surviving without adrenals had shown a marked drop in blood pressure. In all eight cases, the enlarged, overburdened hearts had been reduced in size. And the maintenance of life by artificial hormones after removal of the vital adrenal glands was exciting medical news.

Arthritis sufferers holding out pleading arms the country over for healing grains of the newest "miracle" drugs, Compound E and ACTH are finding that there isn't enough money to buy them. Yet in some 17 or 18 of the best clinics in the country, the victims of this crippling and deforming disease are receiving in their veins the solutions which give them strength to start life over again. These are human "guinea pigs" on whom doctors are working to test the good and bad effects of ACTH, and with whom they already have proved that mild arthritis can be cured, that disseminated lupus, a more virulent form of arthritis, is through as a killer, and that rheumatic fever, crippler of children, has met its match . . .

The "lucky few" getting the experimental doses of ACTH are showing the doctors that although in cases of severe rheumatoid arthritis it is no "cure" once the drug is suspended, the permanent improvement is about 50 per cent . . .

One patient, Louis Bontadini, who contracted severe gout and arthritis, is able to walk for the first time in seven years. Now on his second course of injections, he says: "I just felt better almost over night, and now I'm a new man. This medicine is something from God. I'm going to get off the shelf and go back to work . . ."

There was a story in the Tribune of November 9 about William J. Barber, and the ordeal he was submitting to in the name of science. The word "ordeal" is loaded, we'll admit, but we like it for the purposes of this narrative because getting needles stuck into you, as a result of which you acquire assorted symptoms of a disturbing nature, is not fun. By any man's definition. The ordeal is over now, so we can take inventory of what it meant for Mr. Barber.

By way of backfill, let us point out that Mr. Barber was selected for the experiment in the first place because he is one of the few persons in the country who has had his vagus nerve severed to cure an ulcer. In round and very unscientific terms, Dr. R. and other researchers wanted to see what effect the relatively new glandular extract ACTH has on a system which, because of the vagotomy, produces little or no stomach acid. That's approximately the story as we understand it.

Anyway, since the experiment started about a month ago, Mr. Barber has had more milligrams of ACTH injected into his body than anybody now living. Three thousand milligrams, at least—well over $1,000 worth, we are told. The first couple of weeks, he spent in a hospital; during that interval he could lie back and enjoy the dubious luxury of having someone else administer the ACTH. But, as of Nov. 5, he was on his own; he had to handle the hypodermic syringe himself. Since that time he has punctured his thighs and arms 93 times for the greater good of humanity, which, in the opinion of anyone who is at all queasy about "shots," so-called, is ample justification for the use of the word "ordeal."

As we have indicated, he picked up a few symptoms en route. His face has puffed out and has, along with the rest of his body, taken on a peculiar tannish coloration. As the experiment progressed, he noted alternate phases of marked euphoria and lassitude. At times, his pulse slowed down from 78-80 to a lethargic 45. Toward the end, he experienced severe pain in his knees; they were of such severity that they would not permit him to sleep. He has been assured, of course, that the effects of the ACTH will be only temporary, that the puffiness of his face, the discoloration of his skin, and the pains will disappear.

However, there aren't too many people who would care to endure what Mr. Barber has endured even for all that ACTH. And be it known that he did what he did strictly for science; the only thing he can expect to get out of it is conspicuous mention in some medical journal. This, plus the satisfaction that comes from having helped a good doctor and a good cause . . .

Survives After Rare Operation: Wayne William is congratulated by Dr. Herbert N. on his ability to walk again after having been bedridden five years. Nurse Elizabeth M. is helping Wayne to pack in anticipation of leaving ———— Hospital. Dr. N. said that Wayne's case was the first time in medical history that a faulty heart valve had been restored through surgery . . .

Thus, in the lay press and professional publications, at conferences and rounds in the hospital, in letters, and in face-to-face relations with them, the physicians of the Metabolic Group gave special recognition to some of their patients. The patients they most frequently acknowledged in this way were those who had continuously served as research subjects without receiving any personal clinical benefit, and those whose apparent clinical improvement from an experimental procedure or drug made them "walking testimonials" to the fact that it might have positive therapeutic value.

These, then, were some of the characteristic features of the relationship of the physicians of the Metabolic Group to many of their patients. The question we now want to consider is: What was the connection between the professional situation of the Metabolic Group—particularly, the problems and stresses they faced as clinical investigators—and the special intimacy, favor, respect, and acclaim with which they treated some of their patients?

In part, certain aspects of the Metabolic Group's relationship with their patients were by-products of their continuing association with them, and of the teaching-hospital environment in which the Group carried on their professional activities.

We already know that many of the patients for whom the Group cared were ill with chronic diseases which were often serious in nature, and that a considerable number of these patients served as research subjects for the Group. As a consequence of their clinical and research status, patients were repeatedly hospitalized on the Metabolic Ward, in some cases, for long periods of time. Whenever it was possible, the Metabolic Group continued to supervise the care of these patients after they were discharged from the hospital, or simply to follow their clinical progress. By scheduling periodic clinic or office visits with patients, or writing letters to them, the physicians of the Metabolic Group "kept in touch" with them. The Group maintained this sort of contact with some patients over a period of many years. It was partly because they had "known them for a very long time" and had seen them or heard from them regularly that the physicians of the Metabolic Group became deeply, and in some ways rather personally, involved with their patients.

To some extent, the superior medical care that the Metabolic Group gave their patients was also connected with their continuous relationship to them. At least, their opportunity and ability to give patients good care was enhanced by frequent and enduring contact with them. It also followed naturally from the fact that they were physicians of demonstrated special abilities who were affiliated with an outstanding research unit, in an excellent teaching hospital. Thus, the Metabolic Group had all the resources necessary to give patients the best care which modern medicine can offer.

Certain of the privileges the Group made available to their patients were also connected with the unusual resources of their hospital. The specially-constructed ward on which the Group hospitalized its patients, the excellent nursing care, choice food, and other accommodations with which they provided them, the reduced hospital rates and "Free For Science" arrangements they made for some of their patients—these were all contingent on the high quality of staff and the sorts of endowments, grants, and special funds that their renowned, medical-school-affiliated hospital could command.

Some of the ways in which the Metabolic Group "celebrated"

their patients were also related to the organized facilities and reputation of their hospital and of their own unit.

As we already know, the hospital of which the Metabolic Group was a part was not only organized to care for patients and conduct research; it was also an important teaching institution, contributing to the training and education of medical students, physicians, nurses, and many other types of medical personnel. At formal conferences and lectures in the amphitheatre of the hospital, at informal meetings and seminars in various conference rooms, at "rounds" on the wards and private pavilions, at sessions held in out-patient clinics, members of the hospital staff described their clinical and research activities, presented medical facts and tentative findings, expressed opinions, exchanged ideas, and discussed their problems. In this way they furthered their own medical knowledge and understanding and that of the students and mature medical professionals who had come to learn from them and with them. Generally, these conferences, teaching sessions, and rounds involved the presentation of actual hospital cases; and it was common procedure for the patients who were discussed to be introduced to the assembled medical group, who questioned and examined them. Because they were renowned for their special competence in caring for endocrine and metabolic diseases, and were engaged in important clinical research, the physicians of the Metabolic Group were frequently required to conduct these various types of sessions at which physicians, medical students, and hospital staff "went to school on patients," as one F-Seconder put it. Thus, simply by meeting their obligation to do so, the Group focused special attention on many of their patients. In addition, as we know, they often celebrated their patients in a more deliberative sense on such occasions by describing their cases, in their presence, as especially "interesting and important," and expressing their gratitude to patients for having allowed certain studies to be made.

Other characteristics of the Metabolic Group's relationship with patients were not so directly connected with the organization and function of the hospital. They were more closely related to some of the conditions imposed on these physicians by the serious, chronic nature of their patients' diseases, and by their status as research subjects. A certain amount of the teaching and informing of patients in which the Metabolic Group engaged fell in this category.

Because they were chronically ill, many of the patients for whom the Group cared needed enough information about the nature of their conditions, treatments, and prognoses, to rationally organize their daily activities and plan for the future. In many cases, the knowledge required for this purpose was complex and vast, for, as we know, a considerable number of the Metabolic Group's patients had diseases which were not only chronic, but also serious and rather intricate to manage. In addition, some of the Group's patients had undergone radical experimental surgery, and many were receiving new drugs whose properties were still not thoroughly understood. This made their conditions more unusual: harder to interpret and manage. It also meant that there were not many physicians as qualified to handle their problems as the Metabolic Group was.

Thus, in order to equip their patients to lead as normal and independent lives as possible outside the hospital without taxing or jeopardizing themselves too greatly, the Metabolic Group had to teach them a good deal. Patients had to be trained to take responsibility for their prescribed medication and other aspects of their regimen, to make small adjustments in it, to handle minor upsets, to distinguish these from more serious developments, to recognize such major difficulties quickly enough to contact the Group if necessary, and to make sure whenever they were seen by a local physician that the way he handled their problems was in keeping with what the Metabolic Group would have advocated. Before they discharged their patients from the hospital, the Metabolic Group gave them detailed oral and written instructions pertinent to all of these things:

If you take your insulin and your cortisone every day, Mr. Powers, you ought to be well protected. Unless something unforeseen happens that puts an extra stress or strain on your system—like a sore throat, or an upset stomach, or a temperature. When any of those things happen, the first thing to do is to increase your cortisone.

Now, so far as your medication is concerned, you'll be taking cortisone—a half tablet, twelve-and-a-half milligrams—two times a day. During any illness, you'll step that up to twenty-five milligrams, every six to eight hours.

The cortisone is the thing that takes care of your stresses and strains, which your adrenal glands aren't doing for you, because they're lying down on the job. The other thing that the adrenal glands do is take care of salt. The trouble, you see, is that your automatic regulation is gone. The best way we've found to help that is to give percorten. So, before you leave, we hope to switch you to desoxycorticosterone acetate. We call it by its chemical name: DCCA.

It's a good idea to weigh yourself often at home. We want you to have a steady weight gain; but if you should start gaining too fast, that weight is likely to be fluid rather than flesh. There are several things you can do about that. You can put away the salt shaker and start to eat salt-free bread. Or, before you resort to that you can take sodium chloride pills. We've found, you see, that those tend to neutralize salt. Of course, if the picture is reversed at any time, and you start to *lose* weight fast, then you may need to take extra salt.

Now for the diabetes. You'll be taking N.P.H. insulin. Unfortunately, no one has yet found insulin that will last for a month, so this you'll have to take every day. Now, ordinarily, we tell our diabetic patients to think of food acting to bring their blood sugar up and insulin to bring it down, and the problem is to balance the two off. Well, the same applies to you as to other diabetics, except that you are also taking cortisone which works to bring the blood sugar down.

We'll want you to test your urine three times a day. And I think we're going to try to keep your blood sugar up a little; we don't want your urine blue too often, that is. If it is, then you can either eat more or take less insulin.

Your general rule of thumb, then, is to keep on taking all your medicines, sometimes cut down on the insulin, sometimes step up the cortisone a little. I hope that when you get adjusted to all these things you'll be able to live a normal life . . .

INSTRUCTIONS FOR PATIENTS WITH INSUFFICIENT ADRENAL FUNCTION
(For Mr. Tony Costello)

On discharge from hospital, you will take ½ tablet (12.5 mg) cortisone twice daily and ½ cc DCTMA monthly. You will need approximately this much hormone each day. Under no circumstances should it be omitted unless instructed to do so by a physician.

You will need additional hormone if:

(1) You have a cold, any other sickness or injury.
(2) You have a stomach upset with vomiting and diarrhea.

If you have any of (1). take one tablet (25 mg.) cortisone by mouth twice a day (morning and evening). If the illness is worse than mild, call your physician or phone one of the doctors of the Metabolic Group (local 474 or 481).

If you have (2)., you should have intramuscular injections as follows:

cortisone —— 2 cc.
percorten — 1 cc.

and you should be seen by a doctor as soon as possible. He may consider it advisable to give you intravenous fluid containing hydrocortisone. It is your responsibility to carry adrenal hormone preparations suitable for injection if you travel far away from your supply at home.

Additional Medications: Unicaps — one capsule daily.

Instructions for Mr. Todd

Your daily medication will consist of 37.5 mg of cortisone. Instead of a daily administration of DOCA, you have been given an intramuscular injection of 30 mg. of a long-acting DOCA preparation. The effect of the cortisone will be to make you feel more alert, more energetic, and to keep your appetite at a normal level. DOCA, on the other hand, is effective in regulating your salt balance. You can be practically certain that 37.5 mg. a day of cortisone will easily meet your requirements under all but unusual circumstances. In cases of illness of any sort, such as a cold, grippe, gastrointestinal upset or any condition associated with fever, you should increase your cortisone dosage to 74-100 mg. a day and get in touch with us. During the next month, any problems in regulation you might have will be related to regulating your salt balance. Should the dose of DOCA already administered be excessive, you will know of this by a tendency to gain weight and develop swelling of your hands and feet. In this event you should cut back on your salt intake (i.e. use no salt shaker, for approximately one week). You will be able to recognize evidence of insufficient DOCA by weight loss and by generally feeling poorly. In this event you might help yourself by taking added salt approximately 3-6 gm. extra a day.

If there is any question in your mind as to the adequacy of your control, you should not hesitate to bring this to our attention. Our telephone number is LE 4-4373.

The following exchange of letters between Howard Oates, a patient, and Dr. D., of the Metabolic Group, illustrates several of the ways in which the information and instructions with which the Group provided patients helped to protect and foster their welfare:

Dear Dr. D.:

. . . I'll wait until I hear from you before I take my injection, because I feel somewhat concerned about the soreness in the muscle where I have gotten the injection. Mind you, there is no soreness there now, but there was for at least one week and perhaps ten days after the injection . . .

Howard Oates

HOWARD: WIRE IMMEDIATELY LOT NUMBER UPPER RIGHT HAND CORNER OF LABEL. HOLD INJECTION UNTIL INSTRUCTED.

Dr. D.

Dear Howard:

We have had five reactions of the type you describe to Lot No. 2179, but we must admit that we are not certain why this particular lot has caused these reactions. It is essentially no different from previous lots in any way we have so far been able to determine, except for the obvious important fact that no reactions have ever occurred with the other batches . . .

Dear Dr. D.,

I have enough long-acting DOCA for one more injection, which I will take before I leave on my vacation. Will you, if possible, send me enough for at least three more doses, which will last me until September?

Can you give me the name of a doctor whom I might consult if the occasion arises in Honolulu?

Shall I, if I get an infection, continue to do as I have been doing: take 4-250 mg. tablets of Terramycin and up to 4.25 ms. tablets of cortisone per day?

Incidentally, the last two injections of long-acting DOCA have not bothered me. I would say, in general, that I prefer this method of taking desoxy to the pellets.

I hope you have a pleasant summer. My regards to Dr. T. and the others.

Howard Oates

Dear Howard:

The trip sounds wonderful and I am most envious. We are mailing the following to you: five bottles of the long-acting desoxycorticosterone, and one bottle of cortisone suspension for injection. The desoxycorticosterone should be sufficient to carry you adequately and represents material to which you have had, I believe, no unfortunate reactions. The cortisone suspension is merely insurance for possible situations which might preclude cortisone by mouth.

Your program for possible episodes of infection is positively professional. Only one word: the continuous use of one antibiotic, in this case, terramycin, might on occasion leave in its wake a group of organisms which may eventually become quite resistant. In such a case, therefore, it becomes necessary to switch antibiotics, and I am sure that either chloromycetin or aureomycin in the same dosage would do admirably.

In case of difficulties in Honolulu, we would suggest Dr. ———.

Best wishes for a successful and happy summer. Do not hesitate to call either Dr. E. or myself in case of difficulty—depending on your location at the moment. We shall see you next fall, I trust.

Best wishes,
James D———, M.D.

Because Howard Oates had acquired enough medical knowledge

from the Metabolic Group to regulate his therapy and evaluate his symptoms with skill and acumen, he was able to take long trips in spite of his illness, to handle effectively and sometimes forestall the potentially dangerous infections with which he was continuously threatened, and protect himself and other patients from what might have proved to be very serious side-effects of a newly-synthesized drug.

Another reason the physicians of the Metabolic Group deliberately educated their patients to the extent that they did, was in order to train them to write the kinds of reports about their conditions and reactions that would have research value. Mr. Todd had undergone adrenalectomy, the major surgical procedure with which the Group was experimenting. Both Mr. Costello and Mr. Oates had Addison's disease, the endocrine disorder on which a considerable amount of the Group's research was premised. Mr. Powers was afflicted with a rare combination of diseases: Addison's disease and diabetes. And all of these patients were receiving new steroid compounds. For these reasons, it was important to the Group from a research point of view to obtain detailed, accurate, competent reports from such patients about their status after they were discharged from the hospital. For example, the following letter from a patient was regarded by the Metabolic Group as an "interesting and valuable report": one that contained the sort of data which contributed to their research. It could not have been written if the Group had not taught the patient to make the observations on which it was based:

Dear Al [Dr. S.]:
This perhaps will not be the scientific report you hope it to be. The reason: I've been more or less on the move ever since I left the hospital on October 23rd, and as a result, have not had access to the same set of scales each morning to compare my weights. Nevertheless, here are my observations for what they are worth:
50 mg. of fluoro-hydro-cortisone made me feel well enough, but after a few days, brought on some edema in the face (but not in the ankles or any other observable place). Since then I have cut down to 25 mg. each day, and have maintained my weight (a nice round 185) quite nicely.
As far as how I "feel," the answer is not as well. I do not have much zip, and cannot keep up sustained physical exercise the way I could on the old combination of trimethyl and cortisone. I tend to get hypoglycemic much faster . . .

There were at least two other factors connected with their research which impelled the Group to promote the "knowledge and comprehension" of their patients. First, as we know, they were required by the ethical and legal tenets which govern medical research to "obtain the voluntary consent" of the patients who participated in their experiments. For this purpose, it was essential that they give the patients who acted as their subjects "sufficient knowledge and comprehension of the elements of the subject-matter involved as to enable [them] to make an understanding and enlightened decision":

> . . . Before the acceptance of an affirmative decision by the experimental subject, there should be made known to him the nature, duration, and purpose of the experiment; the methods and means by which it is to be conducted; all inconveniences and hazards to be expected; and the effects upon his health and person which may possibly come from his participation in the experiment . . .[16]

Thus, in order to obtain the sort of knowing agreement from their patient subjects which was ethically and legally required, the Group had to explain the "details of the contemplated procedure to them."

Reinforcing the moral reasons for which the Group conscientiously gave patients a detailed explanation of the experiments in which they participated, was another more pragmatic one. It was the doctors' impression that telling patients a good deal about experiments increased their motivation to act as research subjects, and made them more "cooperative" about the demands and restrictions the studies imposed on them. Thus, to some extent the Group provided patients with information about experiments in order to secure their compliance as research subjects. This was done in conjunction with some of the other ways in which they treated patients as valued colleagues and privileged friends.

For example, this process was particularly apparent on one occasion when the Metabolic Group deliberately tried to "convert" a "recalcitrant and difficult" patient into a "cooperative" research subject. The patient involved was mentioned earlier. Mr. Mann was hospitalized on the general medical ward with a serious liver disease, and on examination also appeared to have an endocrine deficiency suggestive of a hypopituitary state. At the request of the house staff, he was seen on a consultation basis by the Metabolic Group, who entered a note in his chart saying that although they would be "most interested" in studying the patient, they "doubted if he would co-operate sufficiently to justify" their doing so. Nevertheless, the Group later decided to transfer the patient to the Metabolic Ward for "indicated liver and endocrine studies." Once he was admitted to their ward, the Group made an organized effort to transform Mr. Mann into a willing and suitable candidate for research. The studies he was to undergo were elaborately explained to him. The potential value they might have for his own welfare and for the progress of medical science was emphasized. Reduced hospital rates were arranged for him. The staff of nurses and dieticians were instructed to "get behind the doctors . . . and try to make it pleasant" for Mr. Mann on the ward. In spite of the Group's strategy, the patient continued to "balk" all studies. He refused to take part in them, and ten days after he was transferred to the Metabolic Ward, he "signed out against advice."

Mr. Mann's refusal to cooperate was unusual. In fact, his resistance seems to have been associated with rather special psychological difficulties, for his chart indicates that on three subsequent admissions to the hospital in a nonresearch capacity, he signed out against advice. Eventually, a decision was made to follow him in the out-patient department, but not to readmit him to the in-patient service.

In more usual cases, the special ways in which the Metabolic Group treated their patients did seem to enhance their desire and ability to be "good research patients":

> One of the reasons they're more liberal with us on this ward is because so many of us are research patients, and they want to solicit our cooperation . . . Like when you're on a constant diet, for instance. You could drink a little more than they want you to; eat in between meals— things like that. But when they explain things to you and they're so nice to you as they are here, you don't have the desire to cheat. You don't even feel much resistance inside![17]

To summarize: In part, some of the special features of the relationship of the physicians of the Metabolic Group with their patients resulted from their continuous association with them; the requirements of effectively caring for their chronic, serious, intricate conditions; certain characteristics and facilities of the teaching hospital in which the Group was based; and various physical, socio-psychological, and moral conditions they had to meet in order to conduct research on patients. As we have seen, to some extent the type of relationship the Group established with patients was a by-product of these conditions and requirements. To some extent, the Group deliberately fostered it in order to realize their clinical and research goals. In either case, the various ways in which the Metabolic Group dealt with their patients enabled them to carry out effectively their duties and activities as clinical investigators in a manner that was in keeping with certain standards of technical and moral excellence.

Treating their patients as personal associates and professional colleagues, according them special recognition and privilege, also seemed to make the members of the Group "feel better" about "how little" they could do to improve the clinical status of many of their patients, and about the restrictions, discomforts, and hazards they asked them to undergo in the context of their experiments. This was particularly true of the things the Group told their patients and did for them which did not seem to be a direct or necessary consequence either of the characteristics of the hospital or of the practical and moral dictates of their roles as clinical investigators:

. . . Mr. Henderson isn't doing too well, having had a severe psychological disturbance which has little to do with the disease. We just readmitted him with a question of further surgery. We don't know yet . . .

Looks like I'm the toughest case of my kind Dr. I. has had to do this operation on. He told me they had to cut in terribly deep. He said you can only cut in just so far and then you have to start pulling. Well, they had to do a lot of pulling on me. In fact, Dr. I. said he wore out two assistants in the process . . . And you know what else happened in the operating room? Dr. I. was sitting down to do some cutting or sewing, he said. I guess he was kind of tired, because it was toward the end of the operation. Well, anyway, he got up, caught his foot in something— a piece of bandage, I think—and he fell right down on the floor!

The Group also told some patients exactly where professional articles in which their cases were included had been published. For example, they told one patient they had used his photograph in a specific textbook to which they had contributed. Another patient was informed that the studies in which he was involved would be "reported in part in the ——— Medical Journal." We also have seen that some of the physicians of the Group told patients about intimate details and events in their personal lives.

There are also things the Metabolic Group did for their patients which did not appear to be strictly or even primarily determined by the practical and ethical demands of their situation as clinical investigators in a teaching hospital. For example, we have already noted that the Group arranged a "first birthday party" for a patient who had survived the adrenalectomy operation one year. They gave another patient reprints of an article in which they had expressed their "indebtedness" to him for his "unfailing cooperation" in serving as a subject for the experiments on which it was premised. At Christmas time the Group presented one of their younger patients with a stethoscope and a laboratory coat. Several members of the Group made it known to one of the patients that they carried a picture of him in their billfolds. In this picture the patient was puffing away on a big cigar after having been successfully dialyzed on the artificial kidney machine to which he was still "hooked up."

"Thank you for suffering so stoically," the Group wrote to one of their patients after he had been discharged from the Metabolic Ward. This seems to have been one of the primary things they were implicitly trying to convey to patients through the behavior described. The intimate and extra things they shared with patients enabled the members of the Group to show their personal and professional concern over the "suffering" to which illness and research subjected patients. It also seemed to have given the physicians of the Group some feeling that they were compensating patients for their suffering, or at least, that they were doing something to help counterbalance it. Thus, one of the latent functions the special ways they treated patients seems to have served for the physicians of the Metabolic Group is that it helped to relieve them of some of the anxiety and guilt they felt about "not being able to make patients better" and about subjecting them to the strictures and hazards of experimentation.

In addition, the members of the Group derived a considerable amount of pleasure, support, and even "inspiration" from "knowing some of [their] patients so well." This also helped to offset some of the strain to which they were subject, and reinforced their motivation to "go on living the laboratory life" they had chosen. "When the Group came by on rounds," a patient observed,

they'd often stop for maybe fifteen minutes or so in Tony's or Barney's cubicle just to talk to them. Because Tony and Barney could make jokes out of anything. So you'd hear all this laughter coming from their cubicles . . .

The letters that the Group received from patients also gave them "pleasure" and helped to "raise their morale":

Dear Dr. E.:
    According to my informants, you recently became a proud poppa. May I offer you my belated but nonetheless sincere congratulations . . . I have continued to get along nicely on the dosage you prescribed . . . My very best, as always, to Dr. T., and all of his metabolic and diabolic friends, including you . . . And a happy April shower to you, too . . .

Dear Dave:
    Thank you very much for your letter, always refreshing and filled with clever witticisms. Thank you also for your congratulations on my fatherhood which I am proudly enjoying . . .

Finally, the Group was "very impressed" by the "courage . . . energy . . . and understanding" shown by many of their less fortunate patients. To some extent, their close relationship to such patients "strengthened [their] determination" to learn more about the diseases with which they had been afflicted:

We need not tell you how damaging high blood pressure of your husband's type was . . . We are grateful for his outstanding cooperation with all of us in the studies we conducted . . . By further research we hope we can gain more insight into this disease, so that in the future we can help others, as we know Martin would want us to do . . .

We have discussed certain patterned characteristics of the Metabolic Group's behavior primarily from the standpoint of their bearing upon the problems which confronted this team of clinical investigators. On the whole, the type of relationship the members of the Group established with patients and with one another, their humor and their games of chance, in conjunction with some of their research activities, seem to have helped them to meet the uncertainties, limitations, and conflicts they faced in a proficient and equipoised manner. However, it should also be stated that on several occasions that we observed, the same patterns of behavior which ordinarily served as ways of coming to terms made it harder for the physicians of the Group to carry out their clinical and research activities with detachment and efficiency. The instances of this sort we can cite seem to have resulted from the close relationship that existed between the Group and their patients. For example, when a patient died, the members of the Group were inclined to feel "upset" or "depressed" in a "rather personal sort of way":

> You get to know patients so well that when something happens to one of them, it's almost as though he were a personal friend of yours . . . That's the way we felt about Walter . . .

In another context, when one of their patients began to experience some nausea and vomiting from an experiment he was undergoing, the Group was in favor of discontinuing it. Although these side-effects were "moderate," concern for this patient who had been under the care of the Group for almost ten years was greater than commitment to the experimental procedure. It was only because the patient himself "insisted" on having the experiment go on that the Group carried it through. This incident is described in the patient's chart in the following way:

> This patient has had severe gout for a period of at least 10 years, and was suffering from continued and increasing articular deformities of all the extremities. Hemodialysis was planned as an experiment to determine the influence of ACTH on renal excretion of uric acid. The patient was fully informed of the experimental nature of the procedure, and consented to having the experiment carried out . . . The cutdown was effected in the usual manner without incident. 120 mgms. of heparin were administered and dialysis begun . . . The patient after the first hour began to experience moderate nausea and occasional bouts of vomiting. In spite of this he requested that the experiment be continued to the end . . . Run lasted 5½ hours . . . The same evening the patient felt perfectly well, no longer complained of joint pain, and was quite thrilled with the idea of having participated in an experiment.

It is a cardinal principle of social life that persons who are brought into continuous and meaningful contact with one another in a common situation will mutually influence one another. The foregoing incident suggests that this was particularly true of the relationship between the physicians of the Metabolic Group and their patients. Here we have a case where, partly as a consequence of their long-term and intimate association with a patient, the physicians of the Metabolic Group were reluctant to subject him to the discomforts and risks of an important experimental procedure. On the other hand, partly as a result of his contact with this group over the years, the patient was persuaded that medical research was "very important" and was "quite thrilled with the idea" of contributing to it. Thus, it was largely because of him and the pressure he exerted on the Group that the procedure was carried to its ultimately successful end.[18]

As this incident demonstrates, the physicians of the Metabolic Group and their patients were so intricately and closely entwined, that neither can be well understood without considerable knowledge of the other. Physicians and patients were unified by the situation they shared, and they greatly influenced one another.

We turn now to a consideration of the problems and stresses of the men who were the Metabolic Group's patients, and their characteristic ways of coming to terms. In so doing, we move to the Metabolic Ward—Ward F-Second—to listen to the words spoken by these patients in their cubicles, around the card-table, and on the porch. Occasionally, what we shall hear will sound remarkably like some of the discussions that took place in the conference room and laboratory of the physicians of the Metabolic Group. For the problems, stresses, and ways of coming to terms of the physicians of the Metabolic Group and the patients of the Metabolic Ward were mutual ones.

Notes for Chapter III

1. George W. Thorn, M.D., Peter H. Forsham, M.D., Thomas F. Frawley, M.D., D. Lawrence Wilson, M. D., Albert E. Renold, M.D., Donald S. Fredrickson, M.D., and Dalton Jenkins, M.D., "Advances in the Diagnosis and Treatment of Adrenal Insufficiency," *The American Journal of Medicine*, Vol. X, No. 5 (May, 1951), p. 609.

2. *Ibid.*, p. 610.

3. Thorn *et al.*, "Clinical Studies on Bilateral Complete Adrenalectomy in Patients with Severe Hypertensive Vascular Disease," pp. 972-973.

4. In the discussions of the Metabolic Group quoted in the text it will be noted that Dr. D. acted as chairman at these Evening Rounds. Dr. D. was appointed by the Professor of Medicine, Dr. T., who was the Chief of the Group, to be in charge of its members and of the Metabolic Laboratory. A great deal of

sociological interest and pertinence could be written about the social organization of the Group and its relationship to the Hospital and Medical School as social systems. However, we have defined such considerations as falling outside the orbit of this particular study.

5. For example, many of Bill Mauldin's "Willie and Joe" cartoons from World War II typify this kind of humor. See *Bill Mauldin's Army* (New York: William Sloane Associates, Inc., 1951). In his account of his internment in four different Nazi concentration camps, David Rousset writes that "the discovery of [this kind of] humor enabled many of us to survive." See David Rousset, *The Other Kingdom*, trans. by Ramon Guthrie (New York: Reynal and Hitchcock, 1947), especially pp. 18-19, 76-77, and 172. Arthur Koestler has termed such humor "blasphemous hilarity," and described it as characteristic of the R.A.F. in wartime. See Arthur Koestler, "In Memory of Richard Hillary," *The Yogi and the Commissar* (New York: The Macmillan Company, 1946), pp. 53-56.

Probably the most brilliant analysis of "grim humor" or "gallows humor" is set forth in Sigmund Freud's essay entitled "Humor" (*Collected Papers*, V, London: The Hogarth Press, 1950, pp. 215-221). A frequently cited sociological analysis of this sort of humor is Antonin J. Obrdlik's "'Gallows Humor'—A Sociological Phenomenon," *The American Journal of Sociology*, Vol. XLVII (March, 1942), pp. 709-716.

We will have occasion to consider this kind of humor in detail again when we discuss the patients of Ward F-Second, since, as we shall see, this was also one of their important ways of coming to terms with their situation. In this connection, it is interesting to note that in the only other extensive sociological study of physically ill patients in a hospital setting of which we know, the author reports that humor of this type was also characteristic of the ward communities she observed. See Rose Laub Coser, "The Role of the Patient in a Hospital Ward" (Unpublished Ph.D. dissertation, Columbia University, 1957), pp. 236-254.

6. This kind of joking begins in the first year of medical school in the Anatomy laboratory where students dissect a human cadaver. It continues to be characteristic of medical students in later stages of their training, particularly whenever they are confronted with situations that are stressful or involve contact with death. See Renée C. Fox, "Training for Detached Concern in the Anatomy Laboratory," and "The Autopsy: Its Place in the Attitude-Learning of Second-Year Medical Students" (Unpublished papers). Both these papers are part of what can be described as "a sociological calendar of the medical school," which I am engaged in writing. This is a detailed chronological account of important stages of learning through which medical students pass in the course of becoming physicians. It is primarily based on firsthand observations of students in various medical-school situations, focused interviews with them, and journals which several of them kept. Since humor is a very important means of tension-release, social control, socialization, and adjustment for students, many sections of the "Calendar" will contain examples of it, as well as discussions of its meaning and functions in various medical-school contexts.

7. I acknowledge my indebtedness to the unpublished Ph.D. dissertation of Edward C. Devereux, Jr. ("Gambling and the Social Structure," Harvard University, 1949), which helped me to perceive some of the more latent functions of the Metabolic Group's "game of chance."

8. Sometimes the bet involved stakes, usually the price of a beer. The members of the Group who lost the wager treated the others to a beer.

9. On one occasion I was invited to guess the outcome of an experiment. When I asked the members of the Group to explain the rationale for the experiment so I would be able to make a reasonable guess, they denied me this information on the grounds that I would have a better chance of winning if I did not make a "scientific guess." This was consistent with the Group's interpretation of why the dietician won the lottery in which she participated, and, as we shall see, indicative of one of the functions the betting served for the Group.

10. In this respect, the wagering of the Metabolic Group served the kind of function that is usually attributed to magic. As Bronislaw Malinowski indicates in his classic essay, "Magic, Science, and Religion," (in *Magic, Science and Religion and Other Essays*, Glencoe, Illinois: The Free Press, 1948, pp. 1-71), magic typically occurs when men are engaged in pursuit of what they consider an important empirical end and when there is great uncertainty regarding the successful outcome of that activity. In situations of this sort, magical practices help man to cope with "unaccountable influences" by providing them with a "mental and practical technique . . . to bridge over the gaps . . . and ritualize [their] optimism." From a certain point of view, then, the game of chance of the Metabolic Group could be considered the functional equivalent of magic.

Occasionally, when they were engaged in an important experiment or faced with a critical situation, and were very uncertain about its outcome, the members of the Group behaved in a way that was unambiguously magical. For example, in the course of a discussion about a patient the evening before he was scheduled to undergo an adrenalectomy, several members of the Group laughingly knocked on wood and crossed their fingers. Another example of magical behavior on the part of the Group occurred in connection with a "first birthday" party they decided to give a patient with malignant hypertension who was still alive one year after his adrenalectomy operation. The Group devoted several minutes of earnest discussion to the question of whether or not they ought to light the candle on the cake they had ordered for this party, before they reached the bedside of the patient they were celebrating. In the opinion of several physicians, this was not advisable because the candle might be blown out by a draft or by the physical motion involved in carrying the cake. They implied that this would be a bad omen, signifying imminent death for the patient. Their opinion prevailed, and the Group lit the candle on the cake *after* they presented it to the patient.

One further note of relevance. Since magic and religion are often found in close association with one another, and some of the problems with which the Group was faced were of the type which might have been conducive to a religious response, the reader may wonder about the role that religion played in the Group's shared modes of adjustment. We know from the responses they gave to several items of our questionnaire that three members of the Group felt that religion was "very important" to them, two felt it was "fairly important," and six, that it was "not too important." No member of the Group checked the response "not important at all." Thus, religion may have played a significant part in enabling members of the Group to come to terms with some of the problems and stresses of their professional situation. However, we did not observe any behavior which provided evidence in support of this fact. If religion did help members of the Group to cope with some of the problems and stresses we have delineated, it seems to have operated on a more private, individualistic level than the other ways of coming to terms we have described.

11. The norms and values governing the role of the physician cited here are

based on an examination of medical codes of ethics, descriptions of the physician's role as incisively identified by Talcott Parsons (*The Social System*, Glencoe, Illinois: The Free Press, 1951, Chapter X, pp. 428-479), and the continuing study of the processes through which medical students learn to be physicians, conducted by the Bureau of Applied Social Research of Columbia University, with which I am affiliated.

12. For a more detailed discussion of this important requirement of the physician's role, see Renée C. Fox, "Training for Detached Concern in the Anatomy Laboratory."

13. Robert K. Merton, "Some Preliminaries to a Sociology of Medical Education," in *The Student-Physician*, p. 74.

14. This type of intimacy was not equally characteristic of all the physicians of the Group, nor of the relations of any particular physician with all his patients. However, as we shall see, because certain characteristics of the professional situation they shared were conducive to it, in varying degrees all the physicians of the Metabolic Group tended to structure their relations with many of their patients along these intimate, personal lines.

15. In this section, for illustrative purposes, we will draw upon that part of the correspondence between the Metabolic Group and their patients which the Group had kept in their files. A great deal of this correspondence was carried on by the young physician designated by the Chief to be head of the Group and its laboratory. The correspondence we examined spans a good many years, and thus includes letters written by five physicians who served at different times in this capacity, as well as by numerous other members of the Metabolic Group. For this reason, we feel justified in assuming that the patterned consistencies we found in the content and tone of these letters were not simply a function of the personality attributes of particular physicians, or merely a matter of letter-writing "style."

16. This is one of the "ten basic principles which must be observed in order to satisfy moral, ethical and legal concepts . . . in medical experiments on human beings."

Sometimes the Metabolic Group obtained the informal, spoken consent of the patients who participated in their experiments. However, for those which involved a considerable amount of hazard and risk, they usually had the patients involved (or their closest of kin) fill out the following form:

> I, _____, hereby certify that I have had explained to me the details of the contemplated procedure and assume full responsibility for any results of such a procedure.
>
> Signed_____
> Date _____
>
> Witnessed
>
> _____

Putting the patient in possession of technical information not only protects his welfare; it also fulfills the moral prescriptions of science, and, in so doing, helps to perpetuate and give momentum to scientific investigation as an institution. There is evidence to indicate that when these moral precepts are violated, scientific creativity is impaired. The case of the Nazi medical crimes provides documentary evidence in support of this hypothesis. According to Dr. Leo Alexander, one of the chief prosecutors of the Nuremberg Trials, in the Nazis' search for vaccines and drugs against typhus (for which purpose they used concentration-camp prisoners as subjects—needless to say, without their consent), they completely overlooked an important experimental lead. For, in the midst of their experiments, one of the strains of the typhus rickettsia proved to be avirulent for man.

"Instead of seizing upon this as a possibility for developing live vaccine," Dr. Alexander writes, "the experimenters, merely annoyed at the fact that the controls did not die, discarded the strain, and continued testing relatively ineffective dead vaccine against a new, virulent strain." Leo Alexander, M.D., "Medical Science and Dictatorship," *New England Journal of Medicine*, Vol. 24 (July 14, 1949), pp. 39-47.

17. As we shall see, one of the reasons for which patients tended to be receptive to the effort the Group made to inform and educate them is that acquiring medical expertise was one of the preferred ways their ward community had evolved for coming to terms with their situation. In fact, to some extent patients exerted pressure on the physicians of the Group to explain things to them.

18. How such a reversal of roles could come about will be easier to understand once we have learned more about the patients and their characteristic ways of coming to terms.

CHAPTER IV — The Patients of Ward F-Second: Some of Their Problems and Stresses

> Our townsfolk were like everybody else . . . They disbelieved in pestilences. A pestilence isn't a thing made to man's measure; therefore, we tell ourselves that pestilence is a mere bogy of the mind, a bad dream that will pass away. But it doesn't pass away and, from one bad dream to another, it is men who pass away . . . Our townsfolk went on doing business, arranged for journeys, and formed views. How should they have given a thought to anything like the plague, which rubs out any future, cancels journeys, silences the exchange of views. They fancied themselves free . . .
> —Albert Camus, *The Plague*

I HAVEN'T BEEN a very good patient compared to the others on the ward," Mr. Engles remarked during his first admission to Ward F-Second:

I've probably been the worst patient on this ward over these last few weeks. And I'm probably less ill than anybody else on the ward. Almost everybody else is sicker than I am.

But I'm not like the other fellows. I can't act the way they do: happy and making the best of everything. I just haven't been able to take all this the way they do. I came in so cheerful, and I've been down most of the time I've been here. I've been thrown all out of balance somehow.

My stomach has been upset, of course. But there's more to it than that . . . Everyone around me is so sick . . . Everyone is so sick . . .

I've never been in a hospital before. Never been sick. Never saw any of this. Never believed it existed. I never knew there were so many people so sick.

114

The suffering I've seen here . . . the things I've seen . . . would turn anyone's stomach! Three or four died right before my eyes!

"Mr. Engles's having a rough time of it," one of the "veteran" patients on the ward agreed:

It's particularly hard on him to be sick: harder than for most of us. Because he doesn't exactly comprehend things the way some of us do. Everything's a mystery to him. With you and me, it's different. We've been through this thing before, and we know what it's all about. It's not that way with Mr. Engles. So far as sickness and hospitals are concerned, he's completely green . . .

As the comments of these patients demonstrate, illness is not just a biological "upset." ("There's more to it than that . . . ") Illness is also a disturbance in the psychological and social functioning of an individual. Particularly when his illness is a serious one, "being sick" greatly modifies the ordinary patterns of a man's existence. It removes him from the sphere of his normal social activities and sets him down in a "new world" of "sickness and hospitals, doctors and patients." Until he begins to "comprehend" these aspects of illness and what they require of him, a man who is sick is likely to "have a hard time." Even after he has come to "know what it's all about," and how to "make the best of [it]," being sick "still isn't easy," the patients of Ward F-Second testified.

To put this in sociological terms: Illness is more than a biological condition; it is also a *social role* with certain patterned characteristics and requirements.[1] In our society, a sick person is considered to have some degree of impairment or disturbance in his ability to carry out his normal tasks and responsibilities. For this reason, he is "exempted" from some of his activities and obligations. He is not simply "allowed" to withdraw if he wishes. To some extent he is encouraged —and even required—to do so. The sick person is also exonerated from certain kinds of responsibility for his illness. He is not held morally accountable for having gotten sick; nor is he expected to make himself better. Again, this is more than an option. It is considered undesirable for the person who is sick to blame himself for his illness, and unwise for him to care for himself, unless his illness is a minor one. Rather, the sick person is expected to seek competent advice and help—in our society, preferably that of a qualified physician. In so doing, he becomes a patient. As a patient, the sick person is expected to submit to the techniques and facilities of medical science which the physician brings to bear upon the diagnosis and treatment of his condition. If his physician deems it advisable, the sick patient may be confined to bed, either at home or in a hospital.[2] In any case, once he puts himself under the surveillance, supervision, and care of a physician, the sick person is expected to cooperate with his physician, and in this way do everything he can to facilitate his recovery.

To be ill, then, is to be cast in a role which is "partially and conditionally legitimated."[3] But the legitimacy of the sick person's exemption from responsibility for his condition and for his normal social obligations is based upon his "recognition . . . that to be ill is inherently undesirable, and that he therefore has an obligation to try to get well by cooperating with others to achieve this end."[4]

It was from these general characteristics and specific attributes of the sick role that many of the problems and stresses of the patients of Ward F-Second derived. Although they were "different sorts of people, from different walks of life and different parts of the country," as one patient put it, "F-Seconders all shared the common problems of illness." By listening to what patients who had "never been sick before" said about the "hard time" they were having, and to what the "experienced patients" of the ward said when they "swapped memories . . . of the first time they went to the hospital," or when they felt discouraged, we learn in detail about the nature of those "common problems."

Problems of Incapacity and Inactivity

From one point of view, the exemptions from normal duties and activities granted to a person who is ill constitute privileges. They free him in a certified way from some of the responsibilities that a well person is required to assume. However, to many patients on Ward F-Second, these exemptions of illness felt more like penalties than reprieves.

Particularly when they were first hospitalized, patients missed their families and worried about them a good deal:

When I first came here, I wasn't only worried about myself. I was worried about my family, too. Kind of thought of them most of the time, and wondered how they were getting along. I've noticed that in other patients, too . . .

The men of Ward F-Second were also concerned about the jobs and businesses they had left behind, and about the financial consequences their inability to work might have for themselves and their families:

> Listen, if they keep me in here much longer, by the time I go home there'll be a sign on the door reading, "Cottage for Sale" . . .

When two ex-patients who were well enough to return to their jobs came back to visit the ward, patients who were still hospitalized on F-Second looked with envy and longing at signs that they had resumed normal activity:

> I'd rather be like Pat, working hard on the railroad than doing this any time. Or like Joe . . . He's laying bricks and he's happy. Did you see his hands? All rough and cut up. It's better than having lily-white hands like mine . . .

Young and old patients alike yearned for the activity, the fast tempo, and the variety of their healthy, nonhospitalized days:

> You see, before I was sick, I was so active. I went to school and to work. I had dates, went dancing and to parties. I just never had a minute to spare, my life was so full . . . So to have my life so empty and unbusy was a hard thing for me to get used to . . .

> Take Mr. Frank, there. He's not very young, but he's been an active man all his life. He's like a caged lion. He can hardly wait to get out . . .

It was difficult, then, for many patients on Ward F-Second to accept the state of incapacity and inactivity that illness and the sick role imposed on them. Of course, there were certain advantages to being exempted from the duties and problems of the "world outside," an occasional patient sometimes half-jokingly admitted:

> I like it so well here, with a good bed, three squares a day, and the company, that—like I was telling Dr. O.—I think I'll stay until May. I never had it so good on the outside . . .

We shall also see that as they learned to adjust to illness and the hospital, most of the patients of Ward F-Second found other more active satisfactions in their association with one another and with the physicians of the Metabolic Group,

but no matter how you are, how long you've been here and how well you've learned to tolerate it, you never completely adjust to being cooped up and tied down this way . . . Take me. There are lots of times when I wish I could be on the outside, on the move and the go, doing what other strong, healthy, vigorous men are doing. That's normal . . .[5]

Problems of Isolation

The allusions that F-Seconders made to being "cooped up" and "caged in" are partly related to another of the problems they shared: their isolation from "the world outside the Hospital."

The patients of F-Second were affected by the extent to which their confinement to the hospital shut them off from "the sights and sounds . . . comings and goings" of the "world outside":

Have you noticed the snow flurries today? When I was looking out the window after lunch, I noticed them. They were sort of nice to see, because you can't see very much out of the windows in a hospital— especially not up here . . .

When I first came to the hospital, I was over on Ward A where I could watch the people come and go in the front door. I rather enjoyed that . . . But now there's not much to look at . . . except the rest of the building . . . the laboratory . . . the clouds . . . sometimes a sunset . . . and the yard down there, that is rather fading . . .

The patients of F-Second not only felt that they were physically separated from the people and events of the "well world"; they also felt a "kind of apartness" that was social and psychological in nature. For example, many old F-Seconders reported that they had been "very homesick" during the early days of their first admission to the hospital, and that they had felt "so individual." ("At first, you think about yourself, how sick you are, how bad off, and how alone . . .") A new patient described the difficulty he had trying to speak to his wife on the telephone:

I got so choked up, I couldn't say a word to her. She kept saying, "What's wrong? What's wrong?" And I just couldn't say a thing . . .

"What *can* you say, anyway?" the patients of Ward F-Second asked.

Part of the problem, they explained, lay in the fact that "people who have never been sick just don't know how the other half lives. They have no idea . . . and in a way, they don't want to":

> When you're outside on the sidewalk there, you don't know what the hell's going on in here, and furthermore, you don't really care. It never enters your mind. You know there's sick people in there in the hospital, and that they're cared for the best that they can, but that—that's just breezed right through your mind. Because you're out. You're walking on the street . . .

Old patients and new patients agreed, "There's no way we can tell those people out walking on the street . . . what it's really like" to be sick on a ward such as F-Second. "Not being able to tell well people" what they were experiencing also gave F-Seconders the feeling that "the world outside this room is very far away."

Problems of "Submission to Medical Science . . . the Doctors, and the Hospital"

Ward F-Second, as we know, was a "world of medical science," committed both to caring for patients and to conducting research on them. It was supervised by a team of physicians who were clinical investigators; and it was an integral part of the teaching hospital in which it was located.

Like all patients, the men of Ward F-Second were expected to entrust themselves to the physicians responsible for their care; to undergo the procedures that these physicians felt were necessary for the diagnosis and treatment of their conditions; to take the medications which had been prescribed for them; and, in general, to "follow the doctors' orders." As patients in a teaching hospital, they were expected to permit medical students and physicians other than their own to interview and examine them and sometimes to participate in their care. As patients on a research ward, they were under a certain amount of psychological and moral pressure to allow their physicians to try new procedures and drugs on them.[6] Agreeing to do so meant accepting the hazards, discomforts, and rigorous controls that conducting experiments on human subjects entails.

These various ways in which the patients hospitalized on Ward F-Second were asked to submit to the apparatus and conditions of

medical science, and to "whole groups of doctors," posed many difficulties for them.

The Tests, the Machinery, and the Drugs

It has been remarked that as a result of "the scientific advances of
recent years . . . diagnostic and therapeutic procedures have tended to
become so complicated [that] the medical ward sometimes resembles
a laboratory rather than a sickroom."[7] Ward F-Second, of course, was
just such a laboratory-sickroom: equipped with all of the latest apparatus and medicaments that were relevant to investigating and
treating the particular cross-section of diseases with which its patients
were afflicted. "Tubes and needles . . . boxes and bags and hanging
bottles . . . electrical hook-ups . . . artificial kidneys . . . wonder
drugs and magic pills"—to many new patients on Ward F-Second,
this complex equipment was a "mystery" and "frightening." ("You
lie there, you see all this, and hear about it . . . and you wonder . . . ")

Before very long, such a patient was called upon to undergo
some of the procedures for which the apparatus was designed. For
example, there were "all those tests for proper diagnosis in the situation," a patient explained "I was willing to undergo them, because
I figured they were necessary to get the right diagnosis. But I didn't
like them . . . The cardiograph . . . the brain test . . . and the test
of your adrenals." The procedures to which this patient referred were
an electrocardiogram (EKG), electroencephalogram (EEG), and an
ACTH test which he had undergone to evaluate the action of his
heart muscle, the pattern of electrical currents in the cortex of his
brain, and the functioning of his adrenal glands, respectively. These
were the objective, rational purposes of the tests he was asked to undergo, but the patient reacted to them in other more subjective, nonrational ways. As he experienced it, an EKG was an "ordeal" which
made him "shake all over":

> This other fellow came in with the cardiograph machine and a couple
> of them boxes. He had me lay down on the bed trying to get the cardio-
> graphs . . . But I really couldn't relax. I was shaking all over . . .

An EEG was a "brain test," capable of passing judgment on his
relative maturity:

It's the brain test—a test to figure out what kind of brain I've got . . .
If I had a four-year-old brain, or a twenty-year-old brain, or if I was
almost normal . . . It could prove that I didn't have the brain of a thirty-
two-year-old man . . .

And an ACTH test was a camouflaged "operation":

He pulled in this cart loaded with tubes, and needles, and lots of bags
. . . That starts me to thinkin' . . . I'm wonderin' what the heck's under-
neath all those covers. 'Cause I'm gettin' all that . . . I figured almost I
was gonna have the operation right there . . .

The symbolic meaning of tests for this patient, the intensity of
his reaction to them, and the fervor with which he reported his responses were partly associated with deep-rooted characteristics of his
personality.[8] Thus, in substantive detail the way he responded to procedures was not necessarily indicative of how other patients felt about
them. However, there is a general sense in which the reactions of
this patient were representative of those of many F-Seconders. For
him and for numerous of his fellow-patients, the stress of some of
the procedures they underwent seemed to be as much connected with
"feelings" of being helpless, passive, and constrained that such procedures aroused in them, as with the physical discomfort they entailed.

Dr. B.: How do you feel about all the tests?
Mr. F.: Well, they are necessary for getting over the operation properly, getting nourishment and fortifying the system against infection . . .
But I don't think anyone likes intravenous. They tolerate it. They know
they have to do it, but—Well, I'll quote what I said to a doctor up there
on the ward. I said, "I don't like these because I feel I'm tied up like a
dog!"
Dr. B.: What did you mean?
Mr. F.: Well, hour after hour of intravenous makes you feel like you
are tied up . . . You can't get away from that bottle. You've got to keep
your eye on it, be quiet, just lie in bed.
Dr. B.: You said "tied up like a dog"?
Mr. F.: Well, that's just a comparison. It reminds me of a dog on a
leash. Can just go so far and then you can't go any farther . . . You have—
you have the symbol, if you will, right there—being tied up to that bottle
there. You've got to stay there . . .
Dr. B.: You would not become angry at something that was doing
you good?
Mr. F.: I tried not to . . . I might be a little irked, not exactly angry.

Oh, you complain. I've heard many other people on the ward say, "I wish I didn't have this darn thing stuck in my arm all day," or something like that. But in a way, that's just an expression. They do. They have to tolerate it, and I do too . . .[9]

Since most of the patients on F-Second received infusions of adrenal compounds for diagnostic, therapeutic, or investigative purposes, the experience of "being tied up" by "hour after hour of intravenous" which this patient described is one that he shared with "many other people on the ward." As a consequence, "the intravenous" (I.V.) became an important symbol for the ward. Patients sometimes jokingly referred to F-Second as the "Hall of I.V." (after a popular television program), and to the infusions they received as "Battles of the Bottle." We shall gradually come to see that the "I.V." was a complex social symbol which stood for a number of different things in the patient community. As both the "I.V. jokes" and the comments of the patient quoted above suggest, one of the things intravenous infusions signified to patients was the restriction and dependence which their illness and its scientific management required. Having to "tolerate" this seems to have entailed some degree of stress for most F-Seconders.

Many patients reacted in a similar way to the strict regulation of intake and output of food and fluid to which they were subject. As we know, most of the patients on Ward F-Second were placed on calculated diets, and also required to save all their excretions. The extraordinary degree of control this imposed on them is indicated by the instructions that nurses were expected to give new patients "in regard to food and fluid intake and collecting specimens for study":

Patient can eat only what is given on his tray. Absolutely nothing else. He must eat every crumb of food on his diet, every grain of measured salt, if any, every bit of butter, sugar, bread, etc.
Patient is to drink only the distilled water which is given him in his carafe. He is not to drink water from the faucet or fountain.
Repeat. Repeat. Repeat. Patients may have no candy, cake, fruit, soda or chewing gum which visitors might bring in. Only foods on the diet may be eaten.
Patients may not use regular toothpaste because it contains calcium.
Each patient has his own urinal and bedpan in the utility room marked with his name . . . Remind patients to empty bladder when voiding. Urinal should be left on shelf in utility room with tag noting patient's name and time of voiding.

Special Time for Voiding
  a. Between 6-7 A.M. to complete 24-hour collection.
  b. Between 9:30-10:30 (before going to bed).
  c. Before defecating.
  d. Before going to bath.
  e. Before going off the ward for any reason.
Procedure for Defecating:
  a. Ambulatory patients void, then place a white enamel stool can inside the commode. Can and lid are left on shelf in utility room and tagged with patient's name and time of defecation.
  b. Bed patients void in urinal, then defecate in separate bedpan which has been lined with 2 layers of wax paper.[10]

The jokes and comments that patients made about their diets and collection of specimens indicate that along with the hunger and thirst and inconvenience they experienced as a result of these regulations, patients suffered from a sense of having lost the right to be active, independent, and self-determining as they were in their days of health.

Around here, they run you on and off like a faucet. And there's a shortage of everything you can think of. Food, water, salt—even a shortage of urinals!

One thing for sure—I'm going to have a Thanksgiving dinner at home this year, like the ones I used to have in the old days . . . I'm not going to be in here for Thanksgiving like I have for the past two years. I'm gonna have my Pop get the biggest turkey he can buy. And I'm gonna bust my diet that day and eat all the things I used to—because it's gonna be my day. About five plates of turkey, lots of olives and stuffed celery, and all different kinds of vegetables: potatoes, boiled onions, squash, turnips . . . Then I'll sample every kind of pie they can give me: mincemeat, punkin [sic], squash . . . Then, after dinner, I'm gonna dig into a big bowl of fruit and nuts . . . I'll probably gain ten pounds a day after that, but it'll be worth it . . .[11] Why do you know what I used to eat for breakfast when I was well and workin' on the farm? I'd think nothin' of having about four slabs of bacon a quarter inch thick, three or four eggs, a whole batch of hash brown potatoes, and about three or four glasses of milk to wash that down. At every meal my plate would be heaped this high, and practically spilling off the sides . . .

When I was well, I used to go to the delicatessen and eat two, maybe three, hot dogs. You know, the great big fat ones . . . And with those hot dogs I'd have some nice sour pickles, maybe, and a coupla glasses of beer or gingerale . . . It didn't matter which . . . Now I can't eat those things no more . . . For more than fifty years I was a healthy man. I ate and slept and worked like a horse. But those days are over for me now. I'm sick . . .[12]

> "It's a topsy-turvy world, all right, more
> doctors than patients . . ."
> —*The Plague*

Supervising and administering the many procedures and the strict regimen to which patients were asked to submit were the eleven physicians who comprised the Metabolic Group. The patients of Ward F-Second, then, were subject to the control, scrutiny, and care of a "whole team of doctors" rather than to the ministrations of "only one." "Being taken care of by a host of doctors" had certain advantages, patients felt:

I was figuring to myself that if there was only one doctor there, and he didn't come to the right conclusion, he probably wouldn't know it. But when there are six there, and they all get their heads together, why they come up with something that picks you right up . . .

But the kinds of observation and control that being under the jurisdiction of "all those doctors" entailed could also be disturbing to patients. Particularly when the "doctors all put their stethoscopes on you" or "two or three of them tried to get a needle into your vein," patients sometimes felt "like a special curiosity . . . trapped . . . at the mercy of the doctors."

When there were six guys on me, and they had their stethoscopes on . . . I was just like a caged lion . . . I was all ready to get up and push the whole six of them aside and say, "Let me the Jesus out of this place!"

Dr. ——— jabbed me four times, and then he got the needle half in the vein and half out of it. Finally, he said, "That's all," gave up, and asked Dr. ——— to try. Then *he* took three shots at it before he got into the vein . . . Those jabs hurt! And there was blood all over the sheet by the time they got through! I had to lie there and let them make a human pincushion out of me![13]

As we know, the patients of Ward F-Second were not only examined and cared for by the physicians of the Metabolic Group. Their cases were "of interest to many other groups of doctors," as well:

Wheeling that cart around with the files in it, these different groups of doctors come into the room. All day long, they come and they go. First one group, and then another. They all look at you and talk about you . . . It can get to be exhausting!

Some of the doctors who come, patients explained, are "those new young doctors just over from the Medical School—medical students, you know":

One time there, Dr. L. came around with a group of them. First he listened to my heart, and he said, "Yes, definitely a seagull murmur." Then, the students listened. Finally, they all went away. But after that, the whole day long, bunches of students came to see me. "Did you hear?" they'd ask one another. "What's a seagull murmur?" "I think what it is, is that the heart goes along, skips a beat, and then there's a high-pitched squeak." Let me tell you, at the end of that day I was pretty worn out!

This morning I was having some kind of test where they put a needle in your arm and have a bottle hung up. I think it was an ACTH test. This young doctor or student was in the midst of changing the bottle. The seal on the bottle wasn't right, and it started to leak. So he had to change the cap and when he went to do that, he noticed the stuff was cloudy. So he handed it over to find out about it. Well, anyhow, he found out and got another solution. Then, when he come back with that, evidently there was a clot. I don't know—whatever stopped it from goin' in anyhow. It wasn't goin' through the veins, so he had to try to punch again . . . My veins evidently roll when they get the needle. I mean, I could even see them roll myself . . . Then the dietician come to the door, and she saw him and said, "How much longer are you gonna be here?" He says, "I'm all done right now," he says. "I'm leavin'." The test was out, of course, so I had to have it again . . .

Thus, as one patient put it, because "medical students and doctors would learn quite a bit on [them]," F-Seconders had to "tolerate" the stress of having neophyte and graduate physicians "go to school on [them]."

Their status as research patients increased the amount of supervision and observation to which many F-Seconders were subject. Accuracy was essential to the kinds of studies in which they participated. Thus, as we noted, the food and fluid intake of research patients and the collection of specimens from them were especially tightly regulated and constantly checked. Furthermore, as we have seen, acting as a research subject entailed undergoing many additional tests and procedures. The following outline of an experiment conducted on a patient is typical of the sort in which many F-Seconders participated. It involved a planned diet, collection of urine, frequent blood examinations which required venipunctures, and infusions of adrenal steroids administered intermuscularly and intravenously.

Leo will again serve as an assay subject for corticoids and ACTH preparations. The present plan:
1) Calculated diet
2) Discontinuous 24 hour urine collection
3) Collect in cold with preservative, 8AM-12:00 and 4PM-8PM, 12-4PM.

He will receive at 12 noon, immediately *before* lunch on successive days:
a) 25 mg. ACTH, I.M.
b) 0.2 mg. Epinephrine in 200 cc, NS, IV, during a 30 minute infusion.
c) 50 mg ACTH IM
Skip 8/17
d) Oil unit Crystalline insulin Kg, IV with BS at 0', 15', 30', 60', 90'. Test to be given at 12 noon. Do not withhold breakfast. For all studies Eos will be drawn at 0 and 4 [12 and 4 P.M.].

Patients who were the subjects for more radical experiments—archetypically, studies connected with bilateral complete adrenalectomy—were subject to an even greater number of exacting procedures. For example, the following series of tests "designed to establish baseline values of cardiovascular, renal and adrenal function" were performed on patients with hypertensive vascular disease who underwent an adrenalectomy:

Cardiovascular Studies: Values for blood pressure designated as "basal" were measured in the early morning before the patient arose. A sedation test, using amytal, was performed to determine blood pressure levels during sleep. A benzodioxane test was performed routinely to investigate the possibility of pheochromocytoma. The cardiac status was evaluated with standard 7-foot heart films, electrocardiogram and measurement of vital capacity, venous pressure, and arm-to-tongue circulation time. Plasma volume was measured with T 1824. Cardiac catheterization studies were performed in four patients prior to adrenalectomy . . .
Renal Studies: In addition to periodic urinalyses, serial modified Addis counts, blood urea nitrogen levels, phenolsulfonphthalein excretions and urea clearances were determined. Urine concentration and dilution tests

were likewise obtained. Glomerular filtration was estimated with inulin or with sodium thiosulfate. Renal plasma flow was measured with the para-amino-hippuric acid clearance.

Endocrinological Studies: The state of adrenal cortical function was ascertained by measuring the fall in circulating eosinophils in response to ACTH. Urinary 17-ketosteroid and 11-oxysteroid excretions were determined before and during administration of ACTH as a 48-hour test. Following operation an intravenous ACTH test was performed . . .[14]

Patients who acted as subjects for the Metabolic Group's experiments, of course, were of "special interest" to the Group itself, and to "lots of other doctors, too." Thus, they were all the more likely to have "different groups of doctors crowd into the cubicle and stand around and look at" them, in the words of a patient, "as if [they] were Exhibit A."

Problems of Uncertainty

Their hospitalization on a research ward not only subjected patients to the rigors of being under strict medical control and surveillance. It also meant that they were faced with a converse set of problems. These were problems of uncertainty which derived from the many uncontrollable, unpredictable elements in their situation as research patients:

I think that perhaps in the long run an operation like the adrenalectomy has a certain effect on a person's nervous system . . . I think to most people it's a traumatic experience, mainly because of the unfamiliarity of the patient regarding the operation . . . Anything that's new, like this operation which apparently only happens in this hospital, or maybe a very few in the United States is, I believe, from the patient's viewpoint— is looked upon with apprehension. You think, well, this is—this is pretty new, and I wonder if it's the thing that's meant for me, or is it still too experimental . . .Although some of the doctors have told me all about it, I just wonder if it will be successful . . . There is uncertainty as to the outcome of the operation, and just what benefit it will actually be, and what type of benefit that will be, too . . .

I think that the human body as it is made is supposed to—that everything is in it to take care of all your needs . . . So, sometimes I wonder, if parts like the adrenals are placed there, why don't they function correctly? Why is it necessary to take them out? . . . And when they are taken out, I wonder whether it will change my way of life radically. In other words, will I be able to go on as I have planned—or will this stand

in the way of almost any of these activities? Will it slow my reaction up?
Will it make me less alert? Will I have to be a burden for the rest of my
life? For the rest of my life will I always be wondering just how this is
gonna be and that's gonna be, and whether I'll have to fly back to the
Hospital if I get feeling bad? . . .

What if sometime I couldn't get ahold of cortisone? What would
happen then—say if we had a war and the source of supply were cut
off? My life would depend on getting it. There are a number of contingencies like that . . .

I just don't like the idea of the uncertainty of the whole thing attached
to the operation . . . I mentioned there is fear that—that perhaps all will
not go well . . . and even that you might die. It's been known to happen . . . But those fears aren't even so great as the uncertainty . . . It's the
uncertainty you fear most of all . . .[15]

The degree of uncertainty which faced this patient and others
like him who consented to undergo adrenalectomy was, of course,
extreme. Such patients were literally "taking a life-or-death gamble"
when they agreed to submit to this highly experimental radical procedure. As we know, their diseases (severe hypertension, carcinoma
of the prostate, or hyperadrenalism) had "failed to respond to practically all forms of medical therapy." "On the chance that it might
benefit" them, they underwent this operation which was "so new"
that the physicians of the Metabolic Group were just beginning to
work out some of the intricate technical problems associated with it,
and had reached only the most tentative conclusions regarding its
feasability and potential clinical value.

The uncertainties which confronted other F-Seconders were generally less serious. A more common form of uncertainty experienced
by patients was connected with the fact that many of them were receiving newly-synthesized adrenal steroids. As we have seen, not
enough was yet known about the properties of these hormones to
predict accurately how individual patients would react to them.

These uncertainties were complicated by the ambiguities associated
with the patients' characteristically ill-understood diseases:

This is a very peculiar disease I've got. It's got all kinds of phases,
and God only knows what phase you're in at what point. The doctors
can't tell you exactly . . . After you've had this for a while, you either go
in one direction or another. You reach a point where you either get better, or you get worse. And there's no foolproof way of telling in advance
which way you're going to go . . .

This patient was referring to the clinical difficulties involved in determining whether he had that form of glomerular nephritis (kidney disease) which unaccountably seems to "heal itself" or "burn itself out," or whether by insensible degrees he was moving from a latent phase of the disease toward a degenerative stage and, ultimately, death.

When a relatively new hormone extract was tried on a patient whose disease represented so many unsolved problems, the question of how he would react and what the drug might do for him were all the more difficult to determine in advance. The strain that "living with this uncertainty" could impose on patients (and their physicians, as well) is dramatically suggested by the circumstances under which one F-Seconder experienced a "psychotic-like" reaction to ACTH.[16] (The account of this episode was recorded in the patient's chart by the psychiatrist who was called in as consultant):

The patient [Charles Macoby] is a man in his 40's with severe nephrotic syndrome, who was given a 15-day course of ACTH, terminated 5 days ago. He showed some euphoria while taking the drug and the usual depression after it was stopped . . . Yesterday and today he has been overactive and confused from time to time . . . When I saw the patient, he was quite restless, and nurses had difficulty persuading him to stay in bed. He had a bright, fixed smile and talked to everyone in the most amiable, childlike, good-natured way, chirping merrily, "I think I'm dead. I don't know whether I'm in Heaven or Hell. I've been taking a ride through Heaven, and I don't know where I am now. I think I'm dead." He grinned, and sat feeling his thighs and legs which were swollen with edema. The Resident said he has been asking whether these were his own legs, whether they were really there, etc. . . .

Impression: Similar episodes of confusion with massive depersonalization and disturbances of body image, position, space and time have been observed in other patients receiving ACTH. No psychotic episodes of precisely this character have occurred after ACTH was stopped, at least as far as I know . . . Dr. O. also points out that this patient has just undergone some purely emotional experiences which have been thoroughly disturbing. Treatment was begun with considerable justified optimism, and he expected to have a diuresis during the 15 days. When this did not occur, it was expected in the days following the termination of the drug, and when this, too, failed to appear, the patient must have sensed the disappointment in the entire ward personnel. It is likely that both the drug and emotional factors had something to do with this clinical picture.[17]

As the psychiatrist's note indicated, Mr. Macoby's psychotic episode was not only connected with some of the problems of uncertainty which confronted F-Seconders. It also seemed to "have something to do with disappointment" over the fact that the ACTH had
failed to benefit him. In this respect, Mr. Macoby's psychotic reaction
stemmed from what was perhaps the most basic of the problems
F-Seconders shared: the problem of "not being able to get better."

Problems of Not Being Able to Get Better

I dreamt that I got all well, and had gone back home from the hospital. Only I came back to the ward to visit. And when I got here, I found
that everybody had changed. Everyone was well . . . Leo was standing in
the corridor playing catch with George. Bobby's kidney had grown back.
And everybody was well, running around and everything . . .

The "real" Ward F-Second was quite different from the "dream
ward" of this twelve-year-old patient. Leo's arms and legs were paralyzed by an inoperable spinal tumor. George was incapacitated by a
severe, progressive form of rheumatoid arthritis. Bobby's kidney had
been surgically removed and would never "grow back." And the boy
who dreamed this dream was entering the degenerative phase of a
kidney disease from which he subsequently died.

Some of the patients on Ward F-Second did "get all well," of
course, and others made significant progress. But as we already know,
many patients were ill with chronic diseases which failed to improve,
or got worse in spite of all that was done medically to treat them:

Many of us have diseases you can't fight against, or help with, or
cure. We're up against a stone wall . . .

He may have looked wonderful *this* time. But the next time he comes
in he'll look worse. And the next time, a little worse than that . . . When
you've been in and out of the hospital as much as we have, you know it's
only temporary, and that you'll be back in again with the same trouble
in worse form . . .

It was hard for patients to accept the fact that nothing curative could
be done for them:

Dr. E.: I talked to Mr. Kaye for almost an hour last night, but I don't
think it did very much good. He just doesn't seem to realize there's almost

nothing we can do for him. The problem is to make him understand that there just isn't one medicine, or *any* medicine, that will cure him . . .

If you have excellent medical care administered by physicians as highly qualified as those here, patients reasoned, and if you do everything you can to cooperate with them, then you can expect to "get better":

Well, the operation is over and done, and I'm rather optimistic about what the results will be. I hope the blood pressure will gradually come down, or at least be held in check by the operation . . . I've done what I was advised to do. I was recommended by my own doctor whom I trust very much to come here. And I have a great deal of trust in the doctors here, too. And I've done the best I could not to stand in the way of any good they might be trying to do. So, the way I feel at this point is that it would be rather stupid not to look forward with some degree of eagerness to what's going to take place . . .

When such a patient began to realize that he probably would not make much progress, he felt "frustrated . . . disappointed . . . discouraged":

I've kinda been thinking things over a little . . . I—I thought to myself, well, you mean to tell me I've gone through all this and not—maybe—maybe the desired effect hasn't been achieved, or even achieved in part. That makes a person feel pretty frustrated . . . I was pretty well given to understand that by going through this operation that would benefit the blood pressure and lower it, and that lowering the blood pressure would bring about naturally more helpful effects on my entire system . . . Well, so far I haven't seen any direct result. I don't think it's lowered my blood pressure any . . . I—I sort of figured at the time of the operation that I would—well, I'd have this and then things would be much better. And the way I look at it now is—I've lost the adrenals, still have the blood pressure, and I've got something else added on top of the whole thing. See—see what I mean. It doesn't look like there's any gain at all. It's very disappointing . . . and discouraging . . .

Even F-Seconders who had less serious problems and could realistically expect to get better, had to learn to cope with the realization that "many patients don't get well." They had to watch other patients who were "not as lucky" as they go through the difficulties of being inexorably or terminally ill:

That sickness of Leo's is a terrible thing. There's not much hope for him getting better, is there? Believe me, he's got it tough! His back's up against the wall . . .

We all have our concern with one of the patients, a young fellow who's having a tough time of it. He's—he was on the ward for about 3 or 4 months, I guess, since June anyway, and we're all wondering just how he's going to turn out. That is the thought in everybody's mind that knows him . . . His name is Paul O'Brian. I think he has Hodgkin's disease. And he's just having a hell of a time, lying in bed, quite discouraged about it. It seems to a—something that we're hoping he'll be able to come out of positively and quite soon because it is tough on him. You can just see him draining all his personal resources . . . I have wondered what more could be done for him . . . It's just a question—my little old question mark . . . But I wonder what—what—I wonder why . . .

Problems of Meaning

The question "why" was one that the patients of Ward F-Second frequently asked themselves and each other:

Why do some people get sick and others stay perfectly healthy? . . . Why are the people in here sick and those outside well? . . . Why am *I* sick? . . . You lie there and think, "Why? Why Leo? Why me?" I've tried to be a good man. I've gone to Temple, given money, never cheated, tried to help my fellow man . . . I don't understand . . . I don't know . . .

Through the process of asking these crucial whys, F-Seconders tried to account for their illness—to find "meaning" in the untoward thing which had happened to them.

Perhaps their illness was due to some "purely physical cause," they ventured:

Mr. A.: I don't know. Have you ever read those statements in the papers that people write about how they lived to be as old as they are? Well, some of them say they ate, and smoked, and drank all their lives. And others of them say they didn't eat very much, and never smoked or drank. What are you going to make of that?
Mr. F.: Yeah, there's this guy I know. He did everything wrong. And he used to drink a quart of raw alcohol. He lived to be 95 anyway.
Mr. G.: And what about those stumblebums? They never work. Or they work just to make enough to drink. And they don't eat good food. And they sleep just about anyplace. *They* never seem to get sick . . . Right behind the place where I used to work, there was an alley, and all the rummies used to sleep on the ground out there. In the middle of the winter they'd spread some paper on the ground, put their heads in a cor-

rugated box to keep the wind off, and go to sleep. Nothing ever happened to them . . .

If those who "can't eat good food," who smoke and "drink raw alcohol" and "sleep on the ground in the middle of winter" stay well, then how could you explain the difference between the healthy and sick "solely in physical terms"?

Although in our society persons who become ill are not held responsible for having incurred this state, many patients on Ward F-Second turned to the realm of personal morality for answers to the why's of their illness:

It boils down to this. I brought this on myself, either through improper living or improper thinking . . . That's all . . .

I will admit that I probably haven't lived as good as I could've. I mean I could've been a helluva lot cleaner in my living . . . and I probably wouldn't be in the hospital today if I had . . .

"Who of us really believes that his own bodily infirmities . . . are natural occurrences? To the most rational of civilized men health, disease, the threat of death, float in a hazy emotional mist . . . "[18] Because physicians could not provide adequate scientific explanations for their illness, the patients of Ward F-Second were all the more inclined to attribute their "infirmities" to nonrational, nonphysical causes:

Maybe I shouldn't say this, because I have heart trouble myself. But the way I look at it, the kind of life you lead and the thoughts you think affect your heart. For instance, jealousy, envy, greediness . . . Being envious of the other fellow because he has more than you do . . . All those things are bad for your heart . . .

Sometimes I thought there might be some physical cause for my high blood pressure, like I've had my kidney stones removed, and so forth . . . Or, it might be due to my mental outlook on things. Perhaps I'm more keenly aware of things and let things bother me more than I should . . . I think a person can worry . . . Probably I have worried and not been aware of it, and by doing that, maybe boosted the blood pressure. Or maybe way back somewhere there's something hidden that—that pains me, and I don't realize what it is . . . There may be something about my life or my particular makeup that—that bothers me and I am not aware of the fact that it's bothering me. I don't think—I'm not entirely content with my life. I know that . . . I don't think I'm leading a full life . . .

"Still, it's hard to believe that you get sick just because of your thoughts and actions," F-Seconders maintained. Because, "if that's the explanation," then "why does illness strike an individual who has a keen mind and wants to do something?" Why did they "bring another kid up here yesterday—a little boy, nine years old? He hasn't even been born yet, really. He isn't old enough to have done anything really wrong, and he doesn't stand probably a hundred-to-one shot." Why did we have "several priests and a minister sick on this ward," and "why did a good man like Father Flynn have a heart attack and die so young"?

The "concern" that F-Seconders felt about these matters and their need to ask such questions were intensified by how seriously ill many patients were, the degree of suffering they underwent, the incurability of their diseases, their closeness to death. No matter "how bad the things you might have thought or done," did anyone "really deserve" to be ill in this way? patients wondered.

He [Paul] has a tough time moving around in the bed, and he has a—you know—the look in his eye is sometimes glazy; and when his eyes aren't glazy, they have almost a haunted look . . . The whole ward is very much aware of it, and it seems like every morning everybody is asking the nurse, "Well, how did Paul spend the night?" And although not a great deal is talked about it, you just have to know that they are thinking —considering him—and are aware of the difficulties he is going through —and wonder why . . .

Do you mean to tell me that with all that beautiful space we call the sky, and all the planets moving around without crashing into each other, and the sun that warms us, not too hot nor too cold, and the earth in which we can grow things, and the rain, and the miracle of birth . . . that there is no hand directing all these things?

If there was, F-Seconders wondered, then what was the meaning of their predicament?

These, then, were the stressful problems of illness which the patients of Ward F-Second shared: incapacity and inactivity; isolation from the well world; submission to teams of physicians, the apparatus of medical science, the routine of a teaching hospital, and the rigorous demands of experiments; uncertainty as to the nature of their diseases and the outcome of the studies in which they participated; incurability; close contact with death; and the problem of why they had fallen ill in the first place—what did it all mean?

When you first get sick and come to the hospital, you feel pretty much alone. You feel a good deal of self-pity and bitterness. "Why did this happen to me?" you know, and all that sort of thing . . . At first, you don't pay much attention to the other fellows on the ward, or care much about them . . . And you don't really understand the physicians— the staff, you know. Different groups of doctors come into the room . . . You don't know them by name, but you try to segregate them by face . . . Well, time passes. After you've been in for a while, your outlook on the hospital and your illness changes . . . You become part of a new little world. Instead of just lying in bed and thinking about your troubles, you get interested in the people around you and what's happening to them . . . You get to know the other patients. Many of them have more serious problems than you do, so, you begin to think you don't have any right to be self-pitying or complain, because you're pretty lucky in comparison . . . You find that F-Second is really a good ward—quite a place, in fact . . . The guys are a good bunch of sports . . . There's something doing all the time . . . A lot of laughs . . . So, in spite of everything you can have some swell times . . . You get to know the doctors . . . Very fine, very thoughtful, very nice fellows . . . You develop a lot of faith and trust in them . . . You even get so you can see the problems they have . . . And you feel you're helping them and medical science . . .[19]

Gradually, as they became more deeply involved in the "world of Ward F-Second," patients learned to cope with their problems in group-patterned ways. The next chapter will consider the ways of coming to terms which the men of F-Second evolved: their organized commitment to one another, "take up thy bed" credo and behavior, striving to attain medical "stardom," development of medical expertise and interest, humor, religion, and "game of chance."

NOTES FOR CHAPTER IV

1. Taking L. J. Henderson's classic article "Physician and Patient As a Social System" as his starting point (*New England Journal of Medicine*, Vol. 212 [May 2, 1935], pp. 819-823), Talcott Parsons has developed a body of theoretical ideas about the physician, the patient, and modern medical practice which have given impetus to the development of the sociology of medicine. Primary among the concepts which he has set forth is a definition of sickness as a social role. As indicated,

attributes of this role and its relationship to the values and institutions of the larger society are fully elaborated in Chapter X of his book, *The Social System*: "Social Structure and Dynamic Process: The Case of Modern Medical Practice" (Glencoe, Illinois: The Free Press, 1951). They are also more succinctly stated in an article entitled "Illness and the Role of the Physician: A Sociological Perspective," *The American Journal of Orthopsychiatry*, Vol. XXI, No. 3 (July, 1951), pp. 452-460. Recently, Parsons has further developed the basic ideas on which these two essays were premised in a still-unpublished paper entitled "The Definitions of Health and Illness in the Light of American Values and Social Structure."

2. For a statement of some of the possible latent functions of isolating sick persons from well persons in our society, and entrusting them to the care of medically-trained persons in a hospital setting rather than to the family, see Talcott Parsons and Renée C. Fox, "Illness, Therapy and the Modern Urban American Family," *The Journal of Social Issues*, Vol. VIII, No. 4 (1952), pp. 31-44.

3. Parsons, "The Definitions of Health and Illness in the Light of American Values and Social Structure."

4. *Ibid.*

5. What this patient said suggests that in addition to depriving F-Seconders of doing things they enjoyed and confronting them with domestic and financial problems "like who will take care of the wife and kids and pay the rent on the cottage," the enforced exemptions of illness threatened their conception of themselves as "normal men." For an excellent discussion of the importance of work and a job in giving men in an activity- and achievement-oriented society like ours a sense of self-worth, accomplishment, and a meaningful articulation with society as a whole, see Nancy C. Morse and Robert S. Weiss, "The Function and Meaning of Work and the Job," *American Sociological Review*, Vol. 20 (1955), pp. 191-198. This essay is based on an analysis of short "fixed question-free answer" interviews conducted with a random sample of 401 employed men in the United States.

6. This is not to imply that the patients of Ward F-Second were improperly persuaded or forced to participate in research. We already know that the physicians of the Metabolic Group obtained their voluntary consent for any experimental measures they tried. However, as we shall see, the serious, chronic nature of their diseases, along with certain characteristics of the ward community to which they belonged, and the nature of their relationship to the physicians of the Metabolic Group, made many patients feel that they "ought" to consent to experimentation, and others that they "very much wanted to."

7. John Lister, M.D., "By the London Post," *New England Journal of Medicine*, Vol. 258 (January 30, 1958), p. 235.

8. The patient was a thirty-two-year-old man, admitted to the hospital in the terminal phases of malignant hypertension and congestive heart failure. Because he was one of the first patients to undergo a complete bilateral adrenalectomy for his condition, he was interviewed daily by the psychiatrist who was Chief of the Medical-Psychiatric Group. The psychiatrist appraised Mr. Grimm's reactions to the tests he underwent in the following way: "This patient repeatedly expressed himself as 'holding it in,' which referred not only to his feelings of anger, but also to a primitive conception of his body as a highly vulnerable barrier between himself and the outside world of which he was unconsciously terrified. Further associations in later interviews abundantly confirmed this, and it became very evident that hypodermics which penetrated the skin, medication entering his

mouth, enema tubes penetrating his rectum, and the introduction of a catheter into his urethra, were all experienced as overwhelmingly powerful assaults with the implication that he himself was passively helpless."

9. The dialogue quoted here is an excerpt taken from an interview conducted by a psychiatrist with a patient hospitalized on Ward F-Second who, like Mr. Grimm, had undergone an adrenalectomy for malignant hypertension.

10. The instructions quoted above came from a metabolic endocrine research ward other than the one we studied. However, the same rules about food and fluid intake and collecting specimens governed the behavior of patients (and nurses) on Ward F-Second. Rather than being distributed in printed form, they were orally conveyed.

11. These remarks were made by Ray Woodham, the adolescent boy with chronic glomerular nephritis, whom we have already met and will meet again in later sections of the book. Ray was on a severely restricted, completely salt-free diet. If he had eaten some of the foods he cited, he would have become edematous and gained large amounts of weight due to the accumulation of fluids which his impaired kidneys could not excrete.

12. It is perhaps of some sociological significance that this delicatessen-nostalgic patient was Jewish. Although I did not collect systematic data on the relationship between the ethnic backgrounds of patients on Ward F-Second and the ways in which they reacted to their constant or restricted diets, it was my impression that Italian and Jewish patients were more affected by the regulation of their food intake than Irish patients, who comprised the third predominant ethnic group on the ward. For example, Italian and Jewish patients frequently "reminisced" about the foods they used to be able to eat, particularly traditional foods such as ravioli, spaghetti, lasagna, gefülte fish, smoked salmon, bagels, etc. Comparable discussions did not seem to take place among Irish patients. These observations are compatible with the well-known fact that food has special symbolic and socio-psychological significance in both the Italian and Jewish cultures. However, the observations made on Ward F-Second in this regard are no more than suggestive, and would have to be systematically carried out in order to be properly validated.

13. What this patient was describing were the difficulties that two members of the Metabolic Group experienced doing a venipuncture on him. Routinely, a venipuncture is performed with a hypodermic needle attached to a hypodermic syringe. It involves introducing the needle into the vein, and is one of the most important and frequently-used techniques in all branches of medicine. On Ward F-Second venipunctures were most often carried out in order to collect venous blood for subsequent laboratory examination or as the first step in administering an intravenous infusion of an adrenal steroid compound.

Some physicians are more technically skilled than others at doing venipunctures. However, irrespective of how skilled they are, most physicians are likely to have difficulty getting the needle into the veins of certain patients. For example, some patients have "poor" or "difficult" veins, which are not visible or are difficult to palpate; some have veins that have undergone a process of sclerosis and become "hard"; and still others have veins that tend to "slip around."

In addition, most physicians seem to have their "off days" when it comes to doing venipunctures: days on which they recurrently fail to insert the needle into patients' veins. Not only on Ward F-Second, but in other hospital settings as well, we have often seen physicians, who were still having trouble drawing blood from a patient after two or three tries, ask a colleague to do the venipuncture for them. Apparently, there is some recognition among physicians that "not succeeding puts you under extra pressure, so that you are even less likely to get into the vein the next time you try it." This is quite interesting to the sociologist, since it suggests that the ability of the physician to do a venipuncture is not only a matter of technical skill, but is also contingent on his relative confidence and equipoise.

In my studies of medical students, I have observed that they have some tendency to regard success or failure in doing venipunctures as an important indicator of their over-all technical competence as physicians. For example, one student told me that when he "fouled up on venipunctures" it made him "feel that [he] had chosen the wrong profession."

For our present purposes, it is interesting to note that "how good they were with the needle" was also one of the important bases on which the patients of Ward F-Second judged the relative excellence of the various physicians who were members of the Metabolic Group. A "really good doctor" was someone who "got the needle in on the first try"; and as the indignant patient quoted above indicates, a physician who recurrently had trouble doing venipunctures was judged to be a less competent physician, not only in this respect, but in others as well.

It would be interesting to know how important a role the ability to do venipunctures plays in the self-evaluation of physicians in general, and how common it is for hospitalized patients to judge physicians on this basis. It is my hunch that this kind of relationship between the venipuncture, the self-evaluations of physicians, and the way in which they are evaluated by patients has general significance. In fact, one of the elements which may go into making the venipuncture somewhat of an emotional challenge for the physician is his implicit or explicit awareness that he is being judged by the patient in terms of his proficiency with the needle.

14. Thorn *et al.*, "Clinical Studies on Bilateral Complete Adrenalectomy in Patients with Severe Hypertensive Vascular Disease," p. 975.

15. The long quoted passage above was pieced together out of a series of interviews conducted by a psychiatrist with one of the patients on Ward F-Second who underwent total bilateral adrenalectomy for hypertensive vascular disease.

16. This is not to imply that the strain of uncertainty was this severe for most patients, or the consequences as serious. Precisely because it is an extreme case, this psychotic incident points up in exaggerated form one of the kinds of stress to which many F-Seconders were more mildly and innocuously subject.

17. In the next chapter, we will hear more about this patient's psychotic episode. It was a source of amusement to other patients on Ward F-Second, providing them with "natural," *in situ* material for the counterphobic, impious joking which helped them to cope with the problems and stresses of their predicament.

18. Bronislaw Malinowski, "Magic, Science, and Religion," p. 15.

19. The long quoted passage above was pieced together out of comments which I heard patients make on different occasions.

CHAPTER V — How the Patients of Ward F-Second Came to Terms With Their Problems and Stresses

ONE OF THE PRIMARY WAYS in which the men of F-Second came to terms with their problems and stresses was by deeply committing themselves to one another, and to the ward community which had emerged from the predicament they shared.

There's an old saying that misery loves company, you know. Well, on a ward like this, you get close to people. You get to feeling associated with them . . . like members of the same club . . .

"Being close-knit together," F-Seconders said, "belonging to a group of guys who are in the same boat you are," is "one of the main things that helps [you] adjust to illness and strange hospital life." Even "just sitting on the porch or in one of the cubicles and talking to the guys helped," patients said. ("It makes you feel less alone . . . It takes your mind off yourself . . . It gets you interested in the problems of others . . . ")

Thus, the "feeling of unity" and identification with one another that the patients of F-Second developed lessened their sense of isolation and "aloneness" and their preoccupation with "just [their] own troubles." It also provided them with support and "encouragement." (In the words of one patient, it made them "feel cheered up.") For example, Mr. Flanders, one of the patients who had undergone an adrenalectomy for hypertensive vascular disease, felt "shaky" and "worried" about the fact that his blood pressure did not seem to have been lowered very much by the operation until he talked to another patient who "had also been adrenalectomized":

He's a chubby-looking, healthy-looking man, and he seemed very contented. I asked him if his blood pressure came down right after the operation, and he said not noticeably. He said it took a period of about six months before it came down . . . He was very encouraging without being overenthusiastic. It made me feel better about the operation . . . gave me hopes that it'll be profitable . . .

As this incident suggests, one of the specific ways in which F-Seconders "helped each other" was through the exchange of "medical information":

They cut in both sides of your back, up near your kidneys, and they either break the ribs or saw them, I don't know which. They take a piece out to get to the adrenal glands. And they tell me they're only about as big as your fingernail. No doctors told me this. This is information being . . . one patient knows what the other guy's stage is better than himself . . . Like I had a little edema evidently. I found that name since I came here. When you swell around the ankles and so forth, that's edema. I learned it not from the doctors, but from the guys around the ward . . . They sure give you an education!

As we shall see, this process of "education" by the "guys on the ward" had several different sorts of consequences for patients. One of the important positive effects it seems to have had for many patients is that it provided them with information and a "sense of knowing . . . and understanding" which helped to offset some of the stresses of uncertainty with which they were faced.

Encouraging their "fellow patients in need," "trying to make them feel good," and "passing information along to them" also gave F-Seconders the "satisfied feeling" that they were "doing something worthwhile":

Maybe you think it's unusual for a patient to roam around the hospital as much as I do. But it's my aim to be helpful to others if possible. I have found a little work that gives me much pleasure . . .

We had a party last night and it was very enjoyable. One of the fellows was gonna have a heart operation today, so we thought we'd have the party to make him try to forget the coming ordeal . . . I said I thought he'd do very well. I told him, I said, "I think you'll do fine." I said, "Well, look at me. I had an operation and I came through. My trouble," I said, "it wasn't nearly as bad as I thought it would be." He said, "Well, if you can do it, I can do it, too." I said, "Sure you can!" It made me feel good to think I might have helped . . .

The sense of accomplishment and purpose that helping each other gave F-Seconders to some extent seems to have counterbalanced the feelings of incapacity, helplessness, and futility that being seriously and often irremediably ill aroused in them.

F-Seconders were proud of the ward community to which they belonged and which they had helped to create. Many of them felt that the kind of "oneness" and "concern for the welfare of others" that characterized their ward made it morally superior in some ways to the "world of wellness" from which they had been removed. This conviction gave them some compensation for their enforced exemption and isolation from what they regarded as the gratifying aspects of activities and relationships in the "outside world":

You know, in all the time I've been here I've only seen maybe one or two men who I thought were disagreeable. All the rest were pretty wonderful . . . I've met some remarkable people on this ward. Like Mr. Willis. He went blind suddenly. He was a swell old gent—so cheerful and brave. Or Jackie Foote. He's a wonderful kid. Seventeen years old and sick all his life with a kidney disease. The things he does for people on this ward! I've seen him get up four times in a night to answer a patient's bell . . . Then there are Pat and Tony . . . What characters they are! They can make a joke out of anything . . .

You know, if we could get some of the people in the world who are stirring up wars to live on this ward—say, if Stalin and Molotov and people like that were to get real sick and come here for a while—maybe their being here would change them . . .

One group of patients—those with hypertensive cardiovascular disease who had undergone adrenalectomy—formalized their commitment to one another and their desire to "encourage others with similar afflictions" by organizing themselves into a club. "The first guy to have his adrenal glands removed is President of the Adrenalectomy Club," a patient who was a candidate for the operation explained.

He shook my hand and said I was a lucky fellow. He's really a rugged-looking guy. It perked me up. He said when he came in his pressure was 260 over 210. He thinks it's wonderful. He's really grateful . . . The second guy to have it done is Vice-President. God, he looks beautiful! If I come out half as good as him, I'll be satisfied. From what he says, you know, he drinks beer; and he eats pickled herring; and he goes fishing every day; and he's just as brown as the leather on a blotter pad. They say he's even got his hair back. Five things in one! . . . The third guy done is Secretary-Treasurer. Before the operation he had this edema. I mean, his legs were swollen and his face was puffed up . . . He told me I'll never be sorry . . .[1]

As a result of this visit from the officers of the Adrenalectomy Club, this patient felt "really informed" about the operation, "less worried," and "more optimistic" about its outcome for him. Their positive influence on him was so great that he began to hope that he would "walk out of the operating room . . . just for the record with the Adrenalectomy Club." The officers themselves felt pleased with what their visit seemed to have accomplished.

As some of these descriptive details suggest, F-Seconders' "education" of one another consisted of more than the transmission of "medical information [and] encouragement." In good part, it was a process of mutual socialization and social control through which F-Seconders evolved group ways of coming to terms with their shared problems and stresses, enforced them, and taught them to patients newly admitted to the ward. The following incidents illustrate some of the techniques F-Seconders used in order to "see to it" that new patients and patients who were inclined to "act a little different" learned to "take things" and conduct themselves in ways that the ward regarded as suitable.

Hey, Peters—Buck up kid! You looked real good when you came in here. But now look at you! Why don't you go comb your hair, and take a shave? You'll feel better if you get out of bed . . .

We were all sitting around one night tellin' stories. I said, "You know, if you donate a *cat* to the Medical School, they'll give you a dollar for it. But they wouldn't give you eight cents for any one of us!" A new fellow on the ward was upset by that. He didn't talk to me for days. But he came around in the end. He learned not to be so serious . . .

Mac's going to be presented at Grand Rounds this morning. He really ought to have a star over his cubicle! He's one of the *big* patients on the ward . . . He was one of the first to have the adrenalectomy . . . and all the doctors go to see him all the time . . .[2]

Mr. O.: Hey, Texas! How come you're moving down here? Didn't you like it up there on the other end of the ward?
Mr. T.: I did until they moved that guy Wolff next to me. He's im-

possible! Unpleasant, nasty, demanding, inconsiderate, bawling the nurses out every minute unnecessarily . . .

Mr. O.: We've had other people like that on the ward before. Ones that started out that way, anyway. But they changed fast. They stopped demanding things when they saw that wasn't the way others act . . .

(Later, when the patient under discussion began to complain in his characteristic way, this is how two of his fellow patients handled it.)

Mr. W.: I'm losing weight like mad in this place! Down to 160 now. I'm hungry all the time. They just don't give me enough to eat in this place. How do they expect me to get well without enough to eat? I need strength.

Mr. O.: We ought to put a sign on your cubicle saying, "Where does it hurt you today?" You're not in here to eat. You're in here to get well. The doctors know what they're doing. With your sickness you're not supposed to eat so much . . . Boy, when you leave the hospital, the nurses and doctors will really get a vacation! All day long you ask for juice. They can't get enough to fill you up. You ask for things like sausages for breakfast and steak and mushrooms for supper . . .

Mr. W.: Who me?

Mr. M.: The thing that burned me up was your calling the nurse at the top of your lungs this morning. It must have been about 6:15. Miss T. was giving out medications, and you were hollering for hot water to shave with. That's when I told you to wait because your shaving was a little less important than medicines . . . What's your rank in the Army anyway?[3]

Mr. W.: Pfc.

Mr. M.: When you get back to the Army Hospital, I'd like to see you try hollering for hot water like that!

Using cajolery, humor, praise, and criticism, as well as information and encouragement, the ward community taught patients to come to terms with illness and the hospital in certain patterned ways.

"Take up Thy Bed" Attitudes and Behavior of F-Seconders: Their Origins and Functions

It was such a flawless September morning that many F-Seconders had shuffled and wheeled their way out to the ward porch. Warmed by the sun, they talked feelingly and without restraint about many things. Suddenly, however, the porch became a silent place. An

elderly gentleman—a newly-admitted patient—was trying to propel
his wheelchair through the porch door. The other patients stopped
their conversation and silently watched him. The man struggled with
the chair for a while, but despite all his efforts, it stood obstinately on
the porch threshold, moving neither forwards nor backwards. Finally,
he got out of his chair, and looking very pleased with his decision,
triumphantly pushed it through F-Second's swinging porch doors.
The patients on the porch burst into laughter. "It looks like—like
'Take up thy bed and walk!' " Their laughter and what they said confirmed the special significance of this wheelchair drama. In a chance
incident, one of their shared ways of coming to terms had been acted
out.

In a sense, "take up thy bed" was one of the normative injunc-
tions that implicitly shaped the outlook and behavior of patients on
Ward F-Second. F-Second was *"not* a ward where you just sit in bed,
or lie around all day," patients said. "Usually about twelve out of
fifteen were up in chairs or walking around." F-Seconders "didn't
like to stay in bed unless they were so sick that they couldn't possibly
get out." The ward "wasn't a dead place either," patients declared.
"It was known as the Clubhouse of the hospital, because there was
something doing all the time . . . There was always a card game going . . . T.V. . . . people visiting . . . stories and jokes . . . and parties
that were really parties!" These were some of the things that made
F-Second "really a good ward," patients said. "Not too much like a
hospital . . . but a place where you could have a hell of a time."

F-Seconders were proud of the non-bedridden, convivial, gala
aspects of their "ward life," and they worked hard to maintain them.
We have already seen the jocular method they used to persuade patients who were "too quiet and did nothing but lie in bed all day" to
"climb out of the sack" comb their hair, "take a shave," and "join
in the fun and laughs."

The "take up thy bed" orientation of F-Seconders also found expression in the dramatic story-telling and heroic behavior in which
they engaged:

Last summer I was in here with a crisis . . . Three days before they
let me go home, when I was feeling swell and up and around all day,
they had me on the Danger List still . . . Just because no one bothered to

fix the chart, I guess . . . I was proud of that being on the D.L.—because that made me the healthiest, most walking around D.L.-er they ever saw!"

I was at least half-conscious during the whole operation. I could hear the surgeon's voice and the other doctors coming in and out. I didn't seem to mind it at all. And I ate scrambled eggs and toast for supper that same night . . .

After my operation, when I finally came out of the coma, I looked at myself in the mirror, and was I a sight! A week's beard, eyes glassy as blue blazes, hair greasy as blue blazes from the cortisone! So, the first thing I did was ask for a razor. And even though my hands were shaking all over the place, I shaved myself . . .

Illness had removed the men of Ward F-Second from the sphere of normal social activities and set them down in a "hospital world" where they were subject to the apparatus of medical science and the supervision of teams of medical personnel. Many patients were destined not to get better, or to get progressively worse. Death was an imminent probability for some of them. Further, the serious, chronic nature of the illnesses with which patients on Ward F-Second were generally afflicted, and the fact that numerous of them acted as subjects for experiments meant that they were likely to be hospitalized repeatedly for relatively long periods of time. F-Seconders responded to these conditions in a nonsupine way, by "staying out of bed"; being as active and mobile as possible; making their ward "more like a club than like a hospital"; and trying to demonstrate their physical prowess, stamina, and resiliency. In part, F-Seconders seemed to be asserting their desire and capacity to "do some of the things that strong, healthy, vigorous men are doing" in spite of the fact that they were constrained by illness, confined to the hospital, and subject to strict medical control. There was also an element of simulation in their active, non-bedridden behavior—something like an attempt on the part of F-Seconders to act as if they were well or getting better, even though realistically that might not be possible.

The tendency of patients to "stay out of bed" and their "clubhouse" activities were facilitated by the physicians of the Metabolic Group. As we have seen, the Group allowed and even encouraged patients to move freely about the ward whenever possible; they also provided them with the television set and arranged or financed some of the parties that were held on the ward. To some extent, this was a deliberate attempt on their part to make patients more willing and able to cooperate with them as research subjects. On more latent levels, it resulted from their emotional involvement with patients and their anxious desire to compensate them for the fact that they could not make them better and were subjecting them to experimentation.

The physicians of the Metabolic Group also contributed to the "take up thy bed" outlook and activities of their patients by showing that they approved of it. In the words of one of its members, the Group responded "like a bunch of blooming roses" to active, striving behavior on the part of patients which suggested that they had improved, or had been benefited by procedures they had undergone or drugs that they had received. For example, when they arrived on the ward one morning and found that "after 48 hours of ACTH, [a] patient was doing calisthenics!" (*sic*) they expressed their delight, and exultantly recorded the event in the patient's chart. Similarly, when the Group received a letter from a patient saying that "with the help of some extra cortisone he had been able to do a bit of hiking and climbing along mountain trails in the Rockies and Selkirks," their answering letter commended him for being a "real advertisement for the Addisonian group . . . and cortisone pills."

Finally, the fact that the "medical stories" of numerous F-Seconders were written up in newspapers and popular magazines also seemed to have exerted some influence on their "take up thy bed" behavior. For lay-press accounts of the new procedures and drugs which had been tried on F-Seconders focused on the active, energetic "feats" that such patients had been able to perform since receiving these experimental forms of treatment, and presented these as evidence that a "new cure" might be forthcoming:

Mr. Donald Brooks, who has suffered for 12 weeks from lupus, feels well enough to pack up and go home from the hospital. With his fingers, only a few weeks ago stiffened by arthritis, he has made a braided rug while under observation for the drug's effect on him. Now "bursting with energy," he got out of bed four days after his first injection . . .

Hope of new life comes to Louis Bontadini, who is receiving new treatment for gout and arthritis. Unable to work some eight years, Bontadini feels so good from his doses of ACTH, the experimental drug, that he hands his cane over to Head Nurse, Jane N.

One patient . . . who had his adrenal glands removed by surgery went ice-fishing . . . a few weeks after the operation. His only complaint was that he got uncomfortably cold . . . Another patient, who had been given only six months to live, responded so well that he got a job as a night orderly . . .

A complex set of variables contribute to the appearance and prominence of many such articles in the lay press and to their emphasis upon the amount of strenuous activity the patients featured in them are able to undertake as a result of a "new miracle drug" or a "hope-inspiring new procedure." The fact that advances in medicine are "front-page news" in our society, and that they are often presented to the public by journalists in a triumphant, achievement-oriented way, merits further study. Here we will only list some of the factors which seem to account for this: the high positive value placed upon activity, achievement, and health in our society;[4] our faith in the capacity of medical science to meet progressively the challenges of illness; interest on the part of the medical profession in informing and educating the lay public; the desire of pharmaceutical firms to publicize new drugs they are producing; the fact that journalists "attempt to convey an impression" of what a medical event "means" or the "mood" surrounding it rather than all the carefully-qualified details which are requisite for "scientific accuracy"; the "vying for space" characteristic of newspapers and magazines; and their goal of selling as many copies as possible to the public.[5] These are some of the factors that make medical developments newsworthy in our society, and contribute to the fact that in reporting them, the lay press often focuses upon the way in which new drugs and procedures have made it possible for patients to "get out of bed," "hand over [their] canes," carry out demanding jobs, and even engage in athletic activities.

The patients of Ward F-Second avidly read these popular medical articles; and as we know, many of them appeared in such articles. The fact that these accounts stressed the "throw away your cane" behavior of patients reinforced the predisposition of F-Seconders to act this way. In turn, this kind of behavior and "being written up in newspapers and magazines" were connected with another way the ward had evolved for coming to terms with their situation: becoming an "important research patient" and if possible a research "celebrity" or "star."

Medical Stardom as a Way of Coming to Terms

The achievement of prominence or "stardom" on Ward F-Second was based on the nature of a patient's disease, his participation in research, and the publication of such research. The quintessential "star" was a patient with a disease or condition which was "very interesting" to the Metabolic Group; who had taken part in a number of their "important" experiments; had done so cooperatively, intelligently and enthusiastically; and whose case had been featured in both professional and lay publications. For example, Walter Cousins, the "first patient [with hypertensive cardiovascular disease] to have his adrenal glands removed and live," and President of the Adrenalectomy Club, was such a patient:

Case 1 (W.C.) This 34-year old white male laborer was known to have had hypertension for 10 years . . . Initial physical examination showed a dusky white male in congestive failure, with an enlarged heart and a pulse rate of 110 . . . Basal blood pressure varied from 150/120 to 180/140 mm. of Hg. His heart was enlarged plus 40 percent . . . The adrenals were removed in two stages, each procedure complicated by wound infection . . . Blood pressure has fallen to the range of 130/90 to 140/100 mm. of Hg. . .

Summary: A 34-year-old laborer with long-standing hypertension and recent onset of congestive failure who has improved considerably following adrenalectomy.[6]

OPERATION ON LOWELL MAN
MAKES MEDICAL HISTORY

With the unconquerable combination of prayer, a new miracle drug, and his own willingness to submit to an operation in which his adrenal glands were removed, a Lowell man has played a major role in one of the most exciting medical stories of the age . . . Walter Cousins is the first person in this country and possibly the world to have his adrenal glands removed and live . . . The operation was performed to relieve him from an excessive high blood pressure condition . . .

When Cousins entered the hospital his blood pressure was 260 over 210—today it is normal at 130 over 90 . . . and he now has a job at the Hospital where he underwent this extraordinary procedure . . .

Operation on the patient became mandatory when the damage of the blood pressure to his entire system became so malignant that the only alternative was death—or the operation . . . The doctors told Cousins that it was a gamble, that it never had been tried before, and that if he agreed to it, he would be the first patient to submit to the operation. He was also told that in operating on him the doctors might discover a way to cure or at least relieve other victims suffering from high blood pressure. So, Walter Cousins agreed . . .

Encouraged by the miraculous success of America's first double adrenal removal, 11 more high blood pressure victims have undergone the same operation which Cousins consented to be the first to undergo. Four of these patients have died, and the others, including Cousins, have been kept alive by the administration of new miracle drugs, cortisone and desoxycorticosterone . . .

Feeling that it was too early to say what success the adrenal removals may have in treating extreme high blood pressure cases, Cousins said his famed doctor is remaining as conservative as possible in his claim of the real promise the present procedure offers to high blood pressure victims . . .

He consented to this interview only because he felt that in telling his story many high blood pressure victims may come to the realization that there is hope for an end to their sufferings. . . .

Whether or not a patient attained stardom was only partly within his control. He might or might not have a condition that was of special interest to the Metabolic Group, which would make him a candidate for one of their major experiments. He might agree to being interviewed by a reporter or not—but otherwise, he could not determine whether an account of the research in which he took part would be published. However, there were certain important respects in which a patient could influence the degree of research prominence he achieved. To begin with, he had the option to agree or refuse to participate in experiments when and if he was asked to do so by the Metabolic Group. If he consented to become a subject, he might fulfill his research role with exceptional cooperativeness and intelligence, in which case he was likely to be recognized and commended by the Group and asked to serve as a subject again—or he might do less well. He could maintain a relatively casual attitude toward his role as research subject, or he might become deeply committed to it. The latter would mean that he would be more inclined to consent to participating in studies whenever asked, might even seek out opportunities to do so, and in either case, would be highly motivated to be as "good" a subject as possible.

Not all patients on Ward F-Second were eligible for the status of research star, nor did they necessarily wish to attain it. However, even if they themselves did not achieve this kind of prominence or

want to, most F-Seconders "looked up to" patients who became research luminaries.

Functions of Stardom

What accounts for the fact that so many patients on Ward F-
Second considered becoming an important research subject an effective, rewarding, and admirable way of coping with their situation?

We have already indicated that participating in research was a
basis for achieving high status in the patient community. In addition,
providing that the studies they consented to undergo were at all pertinent to their conditions, patients had some hope that through these
experiments their physicians might evolve treatments that would help
them. Among those patients who had been told that this was not
probable and that their prospects for recovery were slight, there were
some for whom acting as a research subject was a way of "not giving
up." ("There was just a chance . . . ") Many patients conceived of
themselves as participating in experiments "for the good of medical
science, and for the humane benefit of others in the future":

I hope that my submission to these experiments will aid the scientific
advances to man, and restore men and women to normal living in years
to come . . .

Such patients had the conviction that they were "doing something important and worthwhile," and this seems to have helped diminish
their feeling that illness had made their lives "empty . . . unbusy . . .
and meaningless." Their hope that the experiments done on them
might "some day restore people to health and normal living" was
also a vicarious way of getting better, or at least, a substitute for it.
Perhaps they themselves could not expect to recover, patients felt,
but instead, they might help to make it possible for others:

A restaurant worker has offered himself as a medical guinea pig in
order that others may live healthier and longer lives because of his sacrifice . . . How does it feel to be a guinea pig? William Barber was asked.
Barber said it is the greatest contribution he has ever made or ever will
make to his fellowmen . . .

"Serving as research subjects" not only made patients feel that they were "greatly benefiting humanity"; it also gave them the more immediate "satisfaction of helping their doctors"—the physicians of the Metabolic Group:

> . . . If you need any details as to my symptoms, let me know, and I will report to you so you can keep your records up to date . . .
>
> My case is the reason Dr. T. started doing adrenalectomies. I had high blood pressure for many years, you see. And when I got Addison's disease, that cured it. It was my case that gave him the idea of doing an adrenalectomy to relieve hypertension . . .

> Dear Dr. S.:
>
> I was delighted to receive a personal letter from you . . . In regard to admission to the Hospital at a subsequent date, it would be most convenient for me to come directly after the first of the New Year. This would afford me an opportunity to stay longer if you should need me for study . . . I have received the package of medicine you sent me for which I am indeed grateful . . .

> Dear Jerry:
>
> This is to request once again your permission to use a photograph of you taken in 1948 in a textbook to which Dr. A. and I are contributing . . . In addition, it is highly desirable that we attain a photograph of your present status . . . Would it be possible for you to spend 20 minutes in the photograph department? This, of course, is old stuff to you, but I should like for you to know how grateful Dr. A. and I are for your wonderful cooperation in the research and teaching projects . . .

> Dear Dr. D.:
>
> I received your letter this morning, and will send this answer off in the next mail. I have had a very good summer, and hope to continue for many years. Of course, you have my permission to use my photograph. Due to some needed dental work I will be in the city on the 17th of August. Between 1 and 4 o'clock would be the time I could stop in for new photos. If this time is not convenient, I could stop in the morning . . .

In the words of still another F-Seconder, such patients welcomed the opportunity to "do whatever they could for the doctors who took care of [them], helped [them] . . . and were so nice to [them]." Patients also enjoyed the "personal relationship with the doctors" and the sense of being a colleague "working with the Group" that participating in their studies entailed.

By becoming research subjects, then, F-Seconders gained the approval and esteem of fellow patients; the attention and appreciation of the physicians of the Metabolic Group; a closer, more professional relationship with them; and a sense of making a contribution to their work, the advancement of medical science, and the health of other men and women (if not to their own). Achieving the status of "important" research patient or "star" brought patients greater recognition and gratification in all these respects, and also public notice and acclaim through the news stories in which they were featured. As a consequence, participating in medical research as subjects made F-Seconders feel that they were important to their fellow patients, their physicians, and to persons outside the hospital who would read about them and be benefited by them. This helped to lessen their feeling of isolation. It also gave patients a sense of purpose and accomplishment which made it easier for them to deal with the problems of incapacity, not being able to get well and meaning with which they were faced.

Finally, for some patients becoming a research subject seems to have been a counterphobic way of dealing with their fears of "experiments and doctors."[7] The case of Gene Gordon suggests this. "At the time of admission," his chart reads,

the patient was a very ill man, obviously in uremia, and in addition, suffering from a rather severe infection and also from the results of a penicillin sensitivity reaction. The patient was maintained on i.v. fluid therapy and was given chloramphenicol as an antibiotic. On the third hospital day an attempt was made to run the patient on the artificial kidney. After an hour's run a clot formed in the tubing and the run had to be discontinued. The patient refused to have any further dialysis performed . . .

At a later date, when he was approached by the Metabolic and Renal Groups with the prospect of undergoing a kidney transplant, the patient refused again, on the grounds that his "nerves [would not] hold up":

So, how would you like it if the doctors would come into your room one night and say, "Would you like to be operated on tonight?" Well, that's what happened to me. A kidney became available, you see . . . This guy was dying of heart failure, and there was a chance that my blood type being the same common type and all, the kidney might do well . . .
"Oh, no," I says to the doctors. "That's too much for me to take!" I told them that my heart and lungs would probably hold up, but I didn't think my *nerves* would . . .

One month later, in spite of the fear of this operation which he had expressed, and although the note in his chart said that he had "made a remarkably good recovery clinically" without it, this same patient was eager to undergo a kidney transplant:

> This bill all totaled, with my one from the other hospital, comes to something like $2000. But it isn't anything compared to what my bill will probably be in the fall when I want to come in to have that other kidney put in! If this kidney transplant's a success, you know, it'll be the first one, and I'll be a second Walter Cousins!

Partly because being a "famous research patient" (like Walter Cousins) had become alluring to him, this patient had come to terms with his fears of an experimental procedure by *volunteering* to undergo it.

Medical Expertise and Interest as a Way of Coming to Terms

Closely related to the pattern of submitting to research as a way of coming to terms, and partly a consequence of it, were the appreciable amount of medical knowledge patients acquired and the "great interest in medicine" which they developed.

The medical expertise and interest of F-Seconders took a number of forms. To begin with, a good part of their discussions with one another consisted of what one patient termed "medical talk." This "talk" was far more sophisticated and knowledgeable than the sorts of comments about symptoms, doctors, operations and drugs which lay persons typically make to one another. For example, the following discussion, devoted largely to the pros and cons of adrenalectomy for high blood pressure took place between patients in one of the cubicles on Ward F-Second. It sounds remarkably like a discussion cited earlier[8] about this procedure, which was held by the physicians of the Metabolic Group one evening in the course of their Rounds.

> Mr. O.: That Mr. Powers doesn't look like an Addisonian to me; his color's too good.
> Mr. S.: What is Addison's disease, anyway?
> Mr. O.: That's a disease you get when something happens to your adrenal glands.
> Mr. S.: Oh, that's what Mac's got, then.
> Mr. O.: No, he's an adrenalectomy. But it's practically the same in a way. Neither of them have functioning adrenal glands, except with Addison's disease at least your adrenal glands are there, and they sometimes do a little something for you. Adrenalectomy is when they remove your adrenal glands by surgery. Usually it's for high blood pressure.

Mr. M.: What an operation that's turned out to be! It's practically the same as cashing in your chips! It's just about like the batting average of the Sox.

Mr. O.: One thing for sure, if I had high blood pressure, I'd never let them do that operation on me. Or the Smithwick one either.

Mr. M.: Nah. I'd rather sweat the high blood pressure out any day. There are other things you can do for high blood pressure. Take pills, a special diet—stuff like that.

Mr. O.: There isn't even any guarantee after going through all of it that it's going to cure your high blood pressure. Take Mac, for instance. Here he is, after going through all the misery of the operation, having to take pills and needles and a special diet, and God-only-knows-what-else. And he hasn't even lost his high blood pressure. So, what good has it done him? It's only given him more trouble than he had to begin with.

Mr. W.: That there operation where they cut some nerves down your back is supposed to be good for high blood pressure. I know a woman who had it; couldn't even breathe before. Now she's much better.

Mr. E.: That's the Smithwick sympathectomy. Mr. Weiss's wife had it, and she's fine now, too, he says. But this adrenalectomy is supposed to be newer and better.

Mr. M.: How many have been done, Paul?

Mr. O.: About sixteen, I think.

Mr. M.: And how many are still livin'? About four?

Mr. O.: Let's see . . . There's Will and Mac and Abe and Hal. Yeah, four—I think that's all there are.

Mr. W.: Are they in good shape?

Mr. O.: Will and Mac certainly aren't. And I heard that Abe had a heart attack.

Mr. S.: What about Ernest Grimm?

Mr. O.: He's gone.

Mr. M.: He was a swell little gent.

Mr. O.: Yeh, he was. Only thirty two years old when he died.

Mr. M.: And he was comin' along real good, too, when I left the hospital the last time. I went down to the ward he was on to visit him after he had the operation.

Mr. O.: He had everything in the books wrong with him. He could hardly breathe, and he used to get hot all the time. He had to have a fan going in his cubicle . . . He seemed to be coming along there pretty well for a while, though. That operation really improved him. Even the night he died he seemed to be feeling pretty good.

Mr. W.: It happened all of a sudden?

Mr. O.: Yeah . . . Like with Walter Cousins. It really helped him. Before the operation his blood pressure was up to 300 over whatever it is. And afterwards, he used to tell us he didn't have high blood pressure any-more. It never went over 120 or 130. God, if it was going to work with anyone, I would have bet my chips on him! He was a husky looking specimen. Real strong with plenty of energy. He worked as an orderly in this hospital, and you should have seen him lift beds and everything! He got along wonderfully after the operation. In fact, he was on duty the morning he died. He'd just been examined the day before, too, and the doctors thought he was in terrific condition. He died the next day—of a heart attack, I think.

Mr. M.: Of a blood clot, I heard, Paul. That clot could have been travelin' for a long time . . . One thing, sure—I wouldn't have that operation 'til they're more certain about it.

Mr. O.: They're not going to get *my* adrenals, either. (*General laughter*)

On Ward F-Second, "even young boys" knew "as much about medicine" and were "as interested in it as [they were] in baseball." For example, the following discussion took place between Ray Woodham, the seventeen-year-old patient with chronic glomerular nephritis who was hospitalized on the ward, and Jimmy Furcolo, a fourteen-year-old patient with the same disease who came to F-Second to visit him after a check-up in the Out-Patient clinic:

Jimmy: What "hopponed" to you? Everything?

Ray: Yeh, everything! I've really had a rough time of it since I've been here. When I come in, I was feelin' fine. Oh, I was a little uncomfortable from the edema, maybe, and from the water on my chest. But aside from that, I was O.K. . . . So, right away they got to work on me, and they really fouled things up this time! Nothin's workin' right now! First they tapped my chest, and that give me a terrible cough. Then they doped me up with codeine and dicumerol [*sic*] and phenobarb. Then, last night my leg started to kick up, and I got phlebitis again, like I did last time. So, I was coughin' like mad, and the only way I could relieve it was by sittin' up. It practically killed me to sit up! The pain was awful! After that, they doped me up, and I've been sleepin' off and on since 10 last night . . . But I'm feelin' better today . . .

Jimmy: You can't fool me. You're feeling lousy. Your breathing's bothering you. You're puffing like mad.

Ray: No, it isn't. That's just from laying down so long.

Jimmy: I brought you some writing paper and some magazines. There's an article in the new issue of *Popular Mechanics* about the artificial kidney . . . Are you getting ACTH this time?

Ray: No, cortisone. I had it for five days. Dr. W. just stopped it today.

Jimmy: Have you diuresed yet?

Ray: No, you can't expect to this soon.

Jimmy: That's right. Not for three or four days. How did you get the cortisone—by I.V.?

Ray: Are you kiddin'? No, I had it in liquid form, and I had to drink it in juice. Boy, did that taste awful!

Jimmy: It's better than an I.V., though. At least you don't have to lie so still.

Ray: I don't know about that. It tastes hideous. And it affects your stomach. I don't even want to *look* at food at this point! After I get out of here this time, I'm gonna stock up on all the vitamin pills I can so I won't have to eat at all. Then maybe I won't swell up with water again.

Jimmy: Look, Ray, if you'd only stick to your diet like I've been doing, you wouldn't land back in here like this.

Ray: But I *did* stick to my diet this time.

Jimmy: No hot dogs?

Ray: No hot dogs—all except for the first week when I got out of the hospital. I will admit I busted my diet, then. I went to town. But after that, when I saw I had gained ten pounds, I didn't go off the diet again.

Jimmy: Look, Ray, in the past year and a half, do you know how many hot dogs I've had? Just one bit this big, and that satisfied me. Because the way I look at it is, if I stick faithfully to my diet, I'm going to get better . . . It would be much better for you, too, if you'd try to stick to your diet, and not overdo things, like taking long hikes the way you did last summer. They certainly didn't help you any!

Ray: Sure, I'll admit that I overdid it. But what the heck kind of summer would it have been if I'd stayed in all the time? I wanted to be out with the fellows. So, a coupla nights a week we'd all go out for some ice cream or a soda, and it was a hike of about two or three miles to the place. I don't think it was the exercise that did it, though. Because the time there when Jackie Foote and I were both on the ward, they put us both on bed rest. They wanted to see if it would help us. Well, Jackie started to lose a pound or two a day that way. But I just kept on gainin'. So, they took me off bed rest . . . No, I think it's my blood that's all fouled up. When they take samples, it's practically yellow it's got so much cholesterol in it. That's why I've got this trouble with my leg now. The blood's so thick and gooey it won't flow right . . . No, with me it's different than it is with you, Jimmy. I've tried everything there is to try: stickin' to my diet, not stickin' to it; bed rest, exercise. Nothin' seems to work anymore . . . But one thing I know, this time when I get out I'm not going to cheat at all. At least I don't want to have to be in here at Christmas. After that, no matter what I do, I know sure as heck I'll be back.

Jimmy: Don't say that, Ray. That's a long ways away. You can't tell what may happen by then.

Ray: In this business, old boy, you've got to face up to things—look 'em straight in the eye. I know I'll be back. But I'll try to do everything not to . . .

Many of the "medical discussions" between F-Seconders focused around the "medical reading" they did. The reading of "professional literature" and lay-press accounts of medical developments in which F-Seconders engaged was both an indication of their desire to "get a medical education," and one of the sources of the considerable knowledge they actually did acquire:

Mr. Powers' been studying up on his disease. He bought a copy of Dr. T.'s book on Addison's disease, and he's been reading it clear through. When he's finished, he's going to give it to me to read . . .

There was a big article on the kidney transplant operation in the Sunday paper . . . If they could only get that protein to take! You see, arterial and vein and bone grafts take. But according to that article, Dr. H. says the big problem with kidney transplant is that the body sets up a natural reaction, so that it throws the kidney off, instead of taking it on. So far the longest they've had a kidney live is for 101 hours. But if they can only lick that—What I don't understand is why they put the kidney here on the leg, instead of taking the bad kidney out and putting a new one in right there . . .

Some of the "medical talk" among patients was devoted to making comparisons between their own considerable medical knowledge and experience, and that of medical students, "young doctors" and mature physicians other than those of the Metabolic Group. Medical students and physicians were generally portrayed as "knowing less than they thought" and often, less than the patients themselves:

One of those who wear the long coats, you know—a medical student —was having a hard time getting the needle to go into my vein. So, I thought I'd give him a tip about how to treat a patient. I says, "Why don't you use another vein," I says, "and stick it in there?"

One time there I was takin' this medicine which Dr. C. explained would make my stools turn red. I had to save the stools for this test I was havin'. Well, one day a student came along and saw that I'd had a red stool. He went flyin' down the ward after that, thinkin' he'd really discovered somethin', or maybe that I was dyin' . . .

I get a kick out of watching these new young doctors and hearing them talk medicine. So often they think they're talking above the patient's head when they're not at all. Yesterday when I came in, for instance, several young doctors were in my cubicle examining me and discussing my case. They were trying to decide what to do to treat me; and I could have told them that from long experience. They were debating my diagnosis. Finally, they decided on mitral stenosis. And I said, "Yes, mitral stenosis *and* insufficiency." I think they were a little taken aback . . .

One time last summer, I was sitting in this drug store . . . and I heard some doctors talking about cortisone. So I turned around to listen to them. After a while they noticed me, and they asked me what I wanted. I told them I knew something about cortisone. They said, "How could you? Have you been reading the papers or something?" I said, "No, I'm just *living* on it!" They apologized then and listened to what I had to tell them . . .

In telling anecdotes of this sort the narrators may have exaggerated somewhat their medical knowledge. However, in their interchanges with the members of the Metabolic Group, F-Seconders demonstrated what their physicians regarded as a "very professional" degree of medical "understanding," competence, and interest:

Dear Dr. D.:
Perhaps as a result of not having had an injection on schedule (it's probably a coincidence), I have picked up a fine specimen of a cold. It has *not* put me in the sack, as colds used to in the days before cortisone . . .
Here is an observation which may be of interest to you. It seems to me that approximately three weeks after an injection of long-acting D.O.C.A., I definitely feel "let down." This continues for, say, a week, and then I begin to "perk up." This, mind you, before I have taken the next injection. Could this be by way of that "nubbin" of adrenal cortex which you think may still be alive, picking up, so to speak, where the D.O.C.A. has left off?

Dear Dr. P.:
Early Sunday morning (1 A.M.) I awoke with a terrible pain in my stomach. Shortly after, I began to vomit, and I had five violent attacks of vomiting. Then, after that, I began going at both ends, and had about six spasms of this at ten minute intervals. At the end of these spasms, I knew very little, and I had left a line from the bed to the bathroom.
My wife's niece was able to get her M.D. We told him he could call you at our expense, but it was at the height of the terrible storm, and he did what he thought was best and quickest. Following is his report and his treatment on arrival:
4:30 A.M.: Pulse 90 to 100. B.P. 90. Heart sounds faint. Muscle cramp with profuse vomiting and diarrhea. No abdominal tenderness, but slight tenderness left side of abdomen. Examination negative.
Given—1000 cc. Normal Saline Solution IV
        Lipoadrenal Extract 2 cc. IM
        Mild Sedative.

Dr. came again at 2 P.M. Temp. 102. B.P. 116 over 70. Pulse rapid. Had terrible pains in back and legs. Given another 1000 cc. Normal Saline Solution IV.
Demerol—IM.
Monday carried Temp. of 100, and had liquid diet.
Tuesday, Temp. normal.
Feeling better, but still very weak . . .

. . . Will you please send me the title and publisher of Dr. T.'s new book on Addison's disease? I understand he has just published a recent book. I have the other book published a few years ago on Adrenal Insufficiency. Also, if there is any other new literature available on Addison's disease, I'd love to have it . . .

Dear Dr. P.:

For one thing, I would like to know if a short treatment of ACTH would further stimulate my glands so that when put back on Testosterone I could regain my strength faster than at present. Or how about this substance called Adenosine-5-TriPhosphate (ATP)? I have read about all kinds of miracles performed with it . . . Now don't get the idea that I am displeased with my progress. On the contrary, I am well aware that I am lucky to be on my feet at all—in fact, lucky to be alive. It is just that if there is anything I can benefit from, I want to know about it . . .

Report on Effects of Long-Acting Desoxycorticosterone
February, 1952

Medication Daily: 1 cortisone   Total Diet: C182 — P91 — F 114
                     2 Polyvitamins   Daily   = 2118 Cal.
                     4 Iron
                     1 Rutin
                     1 Premarin
                 30 U. Insulin
Remarks:

Feel excellent, mind alert, appetite good, sleep well, and I am very active. Have made test four times a day and they usually run yellow at 7 AM, green at noon, blue at 5 PM, and green at 10 PM. No reactions. A few times when I had a no sugar test at bedtime I took from 10 to 15 extra grams of Carbohydrate. No complaints.

May, 1952
Medications: Total Daily Diet
Cortisone Pill — ½ at 7 AM — ½ at 8 PM   C. 182
NPH Insulin — 30 Units   P. 91 = Cal. 2118
2 Polyvitamins   F. 114
1 Rutin 60 mg.

Appetite very good, sleep well, mind alert, and I am very active. Rest one half hour after lunch and retire at 10 PM. No serious reactions. Some days when I am very active I take 10 grams extra—usually 4 lifesavers or half glass orange juice. Test usually contains 2.5% sugar. The last time I visited Dr. W. he advised me this was all right, as my blood sugar was 82 mg. and the non-protein-nitrogen was 28 mg.

Finally, as some of these letters from patients suggest, another form in which F-Seconders expressed their medical knowledge and interest was by "keeping records" of such things as their symptoms, treatment, medication, diet, fluid intake and output, temperature, weight, blood pressure, and their various hospital admissions. As we know, the physicians of the Metabolic Group taught and encouraged patients to keep notes of this sort for the purpose of periodically making accurate, detailed reports to them about their clinical status. However, in the words of an F-Seconder, to some extent, "keeping records was also the patients' own idea." Certainly the copious notes and elaborate charts of some patients went considerably beyond what the physicians of the Metabolic Group required or expected.

Three examples of records kept by patients follow. The first was produced by Ray Woodham, the seventeen-year-old boy with chronic glomerular nephritis, whose conversation with Jimmy Furcolo, a fellow patient, we have just quoted at length. The second example represents two pages taken from a notebook kept by "Mac," the third patient with hypertensive cardiovascular disease to undergo adrenalectomy, and hence, the Secretary-Treasurer of the Adrenalectomy Club. The third example of record-keeping by a patient is part of a huge chart drafted by a patient with Addison's disease who had systematically plotted out the history of his condition and its treatment over a period of ten years. (This chart was regarded as a valuable medical document by the physicians of the Metabolic Group):

Date	Symptoms	Medicine
Oct. 1	Cold	(Nothing) Gained about 16 lbs.
Oct. 23	Saw Dr. W.	Got Resodec
Oct. 26	Saw Dr. W.	Lost 5 lbs on Resodec
Nov. 8	Itching and rash	
Nov. 10	Upper Respiratory infection as a result of a cold injection. Penicillin 400,000 units discontinued. Resodec and A.C.	

Nov. 11 Fever. Injection 400,000 units penicillin. Also began aureomycin.
Nov. 14 Fever dropped and felt better.

MON. A.M. 7/10/50   Input constant
  weight 70.4 killograms [*sic*]   1700 cc.'s
     × 2.2
    ——————
    1408
    1408   Output: 500 cc.'s fluid
  ——————
  154.88 lbs.

MONDAY A.M.   *New Nurse*: Miss Pierson
Make Addis. Count:
Void at 1 min. of 9 A.M.
Void next at 1 min. of 11 o'clock
              Wed., 7/12 72.2 killos (158.2 lbs)
              Wed. A.M. 7/12/50 875 cc.'s output

TUESDAY A.M. 7/11/50   Special Bladder filtration tests of fluids to-
                    gether with blood tests.

WED. 7/12/50
Weight: 72.2 killos (158.8 lbs.)
Output 875 cc.'s (increase of 250 cc. output)
(gained 0.4 killogram or 8/10 of a pound from Tues. A.M. to Wed. A.M.)

THURS. 7/13/50   Weight 72.8 killos — 160.2 lbs.
                 Output 900 cc.'s (increase of 25 cc.)
                 (weight increased 0.6 killo, or 1.3 #)

FRIDAY 7/14/50   Weight 74.50 killos = (increase of 1.2
                 killos, or 2.6.#)
                 Output 675 cc. (decrease of 225 cc.)
                 Weight 162.8# this morning
                 (gain of 16.8# since arrived Hospital 15
                 days ago)

SAT. 7/15/50   Weight 74.2 killos. (increase of 0.2 killo,
                 or ½ lb.)
                 Total weight 163.2#
                 Output = 700 cc.'s fluids
                 163# (slight increase)
                 148
                 (17# increase since leaving home)

SUN. 7 A.M. 7/16/50	Output fluid 625 cc. (loss of 75 cc.)
	No B.M. this morning. (Yet)
	Input fluids (past 24 hours) 700 cc.
Weight	Weight Sun. A.M. (74.2 killograms)
Sat. A.M.	= 163.24 lbs.
Killos 74.2	increase in weight(0.2 = kills.
or	since yesterday AM) or
163.2 lbs.	0.04 = lbs.

MON. 7 AM 7/17/50	Input fluids (past 24 hrs.) 700 cc.
	Output fluids 575 cc.
	(1 small B.M. at 8 PM Sun. night)
	(1 small B.M. at 6:45 AM. Mon.)
	Weight Mon. 7 AM=74.2 killos=163.2 #
	(weight Sun. AM) 74.2 163.24 #

Oct, 1937: First Adrenal Crisis
Dec, 1940: Addison Disease Diagnosed
            Second Adrenal Crisis
Dec, 1940—April, 1942: Maintained on Cortate injections and Salt Tablets
            (Themotabs)

Treatment   *Symptoms*

Apr. 10, 1942—4 pellets DOCA implanted
June 4, 1943—3 pellets DOCA implanted
2nd implantation (lost one pellet)
Aug., 1943 to Feb 17, 1950—1 to 2 sodium
chloride enteric coated, 1 gm. tablets daily
Apr 1944—started 1 cc. percorten weekly
June 7, 1944—3 pellets DOCA implanted
July 10, 1945—3 pellets DOCA implanted

Mar 29 to Apr 19, 1945—
Sore throat and nose cold,
weakness, nausea
Nov 30 to Dec 10, 1945—
Home with flu, vomiting,
headache, weakness, nausea
Feb 2, 1946 to Feb 19—
Weakness, nausea, sore
throat, vomiting, headache
Third Adrenal Crisis
Hospitalized

April 18, 1946—3 pellets DOCA implanted

Treatment

Symptoms

Dec 14, 1946—Jan 3, 1947 —Sore throat, vomiting, weakness, nausea, chills Hospitalized

June 12, 1947— 3 pellets DOCA implanted (lost pellet Aug 28th) July 4 to July 13, 1947—5 cc. Eschatin daily and 1 cc. Percorten at intervals

July 4 to July 15, 1947— Sore throat and grippe, Weakness

Oct 8 to Dec 1, 1947—5 cc. Eschatin and ½ to 1 cc. Percorten 2 times a week

Jan 11 to Apr 29, 1948— Cold, cough, sore throat, weakness

May 4, 1948—3 pellets DOCA implanted May 6, 1948: started Methyltestosterone 2 a day—dropped to 1 a day July 7, 1948— discontinued Aug 4, 1948: Methyltestosterone 1 a day Oct 6, 1948 discontinued Feb 8, 1949 to Feb 28, 1949— 5 cc. Eschatin and 1 cc. Percorten almost daily

Feb 8, 1949 to Apr 17, 1949: Sore throat, cough, chills, weakness

Mar 11, 1949 to Feb 17, 1950 — 5 cc. Eschatin and 1 cc. Percorten 2 to 3 times weekly Apr 13, 1949—3 pellets DOCA implanted

Sept 9 to Sept 20, 1949— weakness, cold, cough

Feb 21, 1950—3 pellets DOCA and 2 pellets Compound E implanted; discontinued sodium chloride tablets (528 mg.) Feb 24 to Mar 29, 1950—5 cc. to 10 cc. Eschatin daily

Feb 24 to Apr 28, 1950— cold, sore throat, fever, weakness, Hospitalized 3 times

Treatment	*Symptoms*
May 30, 1950—started daily injections ½ cc. Cortisone—continued to Nov 24, 1950	
Apr 30 to May 21, 1950—2 cc. to 3 cc. Eschatin daily	
May 22 to May 29, 1950—2 cc. Percorten daily	
Sept 30, 1950—4 pellets DOCA implanted	
Nov 25, 1950—Started 25 mg. Cortisone daily (oral)	
Dec 13—Reduced cortisone to 12½ mg. daily	
May 29, 1951—Injection 3 cc. (90 mg.) DOC Phenyl Acetate	
July 31, 1951—Injection 2 cc. (90 mg.) DOC Phenyl Acetate	
Nov 21, 1951—Injection 2 cc. (60 mg.) DOC Phenyl Acetate	
	Oct 11 to Nov 5, 1951— Cold, cough, fever, weakness; carried on work from home
	May 5 to Nov 22, 1951— Still confined to home; carried on work from home
	Nov 23, 1951—Returned to office
Dec 13, 1951—Injection (60 mg. minus) DOCA Phenyl Acetate	

Not all F-Seconders acquired as much medical knowledge or became as interested in medicine as the patients who kept these elaborate records. There were some patients who disapproved of "so much medical talk," and tried to avoid "learning all that [they] could" about their own diseases, and other patients who chose to think about their conditions "as if [they] didn't know as much as they actually did":

There was a section in the book I was reading last night that really struck me. It was a description of how prisoners learn all they can about points of law that have relevance to their cases. That seems to me to apply to this ward, too. Patients here talk about so very little outside of illness and medicine, and so many of them make a study of their diseases . . . There's too much of that sort of thing to suit me . . . When Mr. Carver gave me a medical book to read the other day, I didn't do any more than glance at it, and I handed it right back . . .

The way I think of my disease is that it's just a problem of filling up with water. And so I think, "If I get rid of the water, I'll be all right." Of course, I know it's not scientific. Obviously, if there's water, there has to be something wrong with my kidneys that causes it. But in spite of that, I go on thinking about it the other way, anyhow . . .

Patients such as these who did not wish to know too much about illness and medicine or become too involved in thinking about them, and who took measures to keep themselves from doing so, were a small minority on Ward F-Second.[9] A high degree of medical knowledge and interest in the forms described characterized most F-Seconders. To some extent this knowledge and interest was a secondary consequence of their contact with the physicians of the Metabolic Group, the "crowds of doctors" who "went to school on" them, and the medically sophisticated veteran patients on Ward F-Second—all of whom directly and indirectly furthered their medical education. In addition, as we have seen, many F-Seconders actively sought "medical information," took pride in their knowledge and the "professional records" they kept, and showed a "very great interest in medicine." These aspects of their behavior grew out of the fact that "getting a liberal medical education" provided most F-Seconders with an accessible, appropriate, and effective way of coming to terms.

Functions of Medical Expertise and Interest

The expertise and medical interest which F-Seconders developed seems to have helped them to deal with their problems and stresses in a number of ways.

As we have seen, "medical knowledge and comprehension" enabled F-Seconders to live more safely and normally with their intricate, chronic diseases and the experimental measures they consented to undergo. Through "getting to know a lot about medicine," F-Seconders also gained the approval and admiration of many fellow patients, and at the same time became better equipped to help them by "passing medical information along to them." We have already observed that this gave patients a sense of achievement and unity that made it easier for them to cope with incapacity and isolation.

Their medical knowledge and interest "made [F-Seconders] feel closer to the doctors" as well as to their fellow patients. It helped them to "understand the physicians" of the Metabolic Group—"what they were saying and thinking . . . what they expected . . . what some of their problems were." It also gave F-Seconders a sense of being almost "on an equal par with them" professionally and personally:

Happy day-after-Washington's-birthday to you! I'm having a certain amount of stomach trouble. The symptoms, Dr. Oates (that's me!) tells me, are those of hyper-chlorhydria. And of course, he tells all, even if he doesn't know all. He also tells me that he once heard of cases wherein actual perforated ulcers had developed from too much cortisone, so I can't help but turn to you who I feel sure knows just a *bit* more about the subject than he does . . . To be more specific: the pains are not severe; they become worse perhaps an hour or two after I have eaten; they are relieved by eating; my stomach bulges even more than usual after I have eaten; quite a good deal of gas forms, and it causes me to "burp" quite often— mind you, in a very melodious fashion! Until I hear from you, Dr. Oates has put me on a bland diet beginning this evening, and cut my cortisone intake to two—to 12.5 mg. per diem . . .

Howard Oates.

F-Seconders also found that the various ways in which they showed their medical knowledge and interest "brought the doctors closer to them." They observed that physicians "appreciated patients [who were] intelligent about carrying out orders," and were "impressed by patients who knew a lot," and "kept good records."

Thus, as their medical knowledge and interest increased, F-Seconders became more identified with the physicians of the Metabolic Group. In turn, the members of the Group responded to patients' "enthusiasm" about medicine and their "understanding" and "skill" by treating them more like colleagues and friends. One of the consequences of this sequence for patients is that it made them feel less subjugated by the various forms of control physicians exercised over them, and less "at their mercy." In fact, as some of their boastful tales about what they taught the doctors indicate, the expertise which patients developed gave them a basis for asserting themselves. The theme that runs through all the anecdotes of this sort that patients recounted was explicitly stated one day by an F-Seconder (in another context): "A lot of us know as much about our sickness as many doctors do, and maybe more than some."

"In this business, you've got to face up to things—look 'em straight in the eye," Ray Woodham told Jimmy Furcolo in the conversation between these two boys with nephrosis reported a little earlier. For the many F-Seconders who shared this attitude, becoming medical experts and keeping precise, detailed records was a "look it straight in the eye" way of dealing with their complex, ill-understood, often incurable illnesses, and the changing, frequently experimental forms of treatment they underwent. Their expertise and interest also seem to have given patients a greater sense of certainty about "how they were doing" and "what was happening to [them]— for better or worse." Finally, their medical knowledge and interest, and especially the physicianly records they kept, made it possible for patients to "think more scientifically about [their] diseases" and some of the untoward things that happened to them, and as a consequence, "be more objective" about them as well.

February 2-19—Weakness, nausea, sore throat, vomiting, headache.
Third adrenal crisis.
Hospitalized . . .

Straightforward medical records of this sort were not the only kinds of documents F-Seconders produced. Sometimes they brought expert knowledge and humor together to create a satiric medical document, or a medical poem. Examples of three such creations follow. The first is a case history "written up" by a group of F-Seconders after they conducted a mock interview with a fellow patient. The second is a hospital "report of death" form that Ray Woodham made out for his then still very much alive nephrotic "buddy," Jimmy Furcolo. The third is a poem by a patient who had undergone adrenalectomy for hyperadrenalism. These three documents are written examples of the kind of joking in which F-Seconders continuously engaged. As such, they introduce us to one of the most important ways of coming to terms the ward community evolved: their "F-Second brand of humor."

ALMY, R. LEWIS.
Age: 20. Date of Birth: February 17, 1932.
Sisters: Two. Aged 17 and 14.
Marital Status: Single. (Thank God.)
Complexion: Fair. Color of Hair: Brown. Color of Eyes: Blue.

Diseases: Pneumonia at 9, Diphtheria at 11, Measles at 5,
Mumps at 5, Chicken Pox at 2.
Chronic Horse Radish, Dandruff, Crabs.
Insanity — Tests have proven this beyond refute.

Smokes 1 pack a day.
Drinks occasional beer.
Hobbies: Eating, sleeping, women, numismatism.
Pet Peeves: Doctors and nurses.

Trouble Upon Admission: None.
Present Illness:
1. Troubles of the heart.
2. Finds it hard when getting up in the A.M.
3. Starvation because of tests.

Good Features of Hospital
1. Good food when not forced to endure starvation.
2. Lovely nurses.
3. Sterling companions.
4. Good doctors.   (?)

Diagnosis: Not enough Love and Care.
Treatment: T.L.C. Starting at 8 A.M. Whenever necessary.

——— HOSPITAL — REPORT OF DEATH

Name ....Jimmy Furcolo....... Ward F-2................. Unit No.....9B256
Age ....14........... W[idowed] ....Sep. Service .... Medical..............
Date of Admission ....Nov. 6, 1951....... Hour of Admission....2:30 P.M.
Date of Death...........Dec. 1, 1951........... Hour of Death.......6:30 A.M.

Principal and related
causes of death, in ....He died 'cause he was too damn lazy to live.
order of onset
with dates ....

Nature and date of operations? .... none ....
Accepted by Medical Examiner .... Yes.......X...........No............
Who wishes autopsy? .... no one...............................
                     received by [crossed out] ....
Permission refused to .... Ray Woodham, M.D. ....

Every Report Must be Signed by
the Doctor

PATHOLOGIC DIAGNOSIS

Discharged to Ward X
December 12, 1951 at 9:00 A.M.
.... Ray Woodham, M.D. ....
                                    Pathologist

DIAGNOSIS: The following is an exact copy of the cause of death appearing on the death certificate.

Jimmy Furcolo died of self-inflicted gunshot wounds in the head. Reason for death: too damn lazy to live.

Ray Woodham, M.D.

AFTER AN ADRENALECTOMY

There upon my kidney,
Weeping and broken-hearted,
Sits a portion of one Adrenal
Who from his friend has parted.

In his mind he recalls
A memory of a clear September day,
When an instrument scooped down
And carried his friend away.

Here this lonely Adrenal sits
Thinking of days gone by,
And the intimate moments they shared
Bring many a tear to his eye—

For he longs so for the friendship
That through the years was spent
Doing the things he did
And going the places he went.

He confides in Mr. Kidney
Just across the way,
Whose cranium is now barren
Where an Adrenal once did lay.

There's a message from the Pancreas
Who is willing to help if she can,
But the "sweetest" message of all
Were from the Islets of Langerhans.

It was a message that gave him courage
To face the future alone,
Secreting the finest Adrenalin,
An essential body hormone.

He continues on with his duty,
But still, he feels quite sad
As he thinks of his life-long friend
In some far-off Pathology Lab.

True, he deserves much credit,
But even though he has tried,
He can't forget his companion,
In a jar of formaldehyde.

He can picture his "buddy"
Struggling on for his life
While probing needles dot toward him,
Then a forceps and a knife.

Finally, there's silence about him
As he is stripped of his cortical layer,
And a tear drop stains his cheek
As he quietly says a prayer.

Soon his prayer is answered
And he is back in his jar on a shelf,
Weak from the operation
And feeling sorry for himself.

He peers through the glass that surrounds him
And longs to be back home . . .
When he notices an encouraging smile
From a neighboring gallstone.

Laughter From the Cubicles: The Nature and Content of Humor on Ward F-Second

As these documents indicate, the humor of patients on Ward F-Second focused on "the important things [they] had in common"—especially, the problems and stresses they shared.

Patients joked about their inactivity, incapacity and isolation:

. . . He died because he was too damn lazy to live . . .

It looks like—like "take up thy bed and walk."

We're a bunch of Rip Van Winkles . . .

Listen, if they keep me in here much longer, by the time I go home, there'll be a sign on the door reading, "Cottage for Sale."

Let's see—my wife is thirty-six. Well, if she doesn't want to take me back, I'll trade her in for two eighteen-year-olds.

My wife is gonna love these casts I have on! Every time I turn over at night, I'll fracture *her* legs! I can see it now—O'Connor'll be sleepin' on the couch . . . Jesus, if they made these things any longer, they'd have to cut a drop seat in 'em or something!

A good deal of the joking and clowning in which F-Seconders engaged, and some of the events they regarded as funny, were concerned with the various ways in which they were subject to the apparatus of medical science, to the control and scrutiny of physicians, and to the regulations of the hospital:

I think the reason I'm so fouled up is because of all the gooey stuff they're always sticking in my veins. My veins must be coated an inch thick with all that sticky albumin and resin. What I need is an I.V. of Sani-Flush . . . They expect you to take all your medication straight, in its pure form, without a chaser. Like that resin. Drinking that stuff is like drinking a glass of cement! Not cement exactly—more like mortar. If anyone were given the choice between drinking that and being allowed to have salt in their diet, and not having salt at all and not having to take that stuff, I can't imagine their choosing the resin! My stomach feels as though *I* was in the fight the other night instead of Wolcott, and as though Marciano'd punched me in the belly a hundred times! I've got to handle my stomach with kid gloves—especially because I forgot to bring my cast-iron apparatus for my stomach and my intestines with me this time. I wear one of those every time I come to the hospital, eating what they give me here . . .

That Mac is a sketch! He was goin' along there real well. The lines on that chart the doctors put up in his cubicle, you know, were nice and steady—weight and chemistries and all. Then, all of a sudden, the lines on the chart went down like in the stock market crash! All the doctors started rushin' in. Dr. M. got all excited, and it takes a lot to get him excited. Well, in the end, they found an empty box of saltines in Mac's bed. What he'd done was eat a whole box of them the night before. What a character!

Two patients by the name of Hoffman and Kaufman were side by side on the ward in cubicles right next to each other. Well, one morning they were both asleep when the orderly came up to the ward. He had orders to take Mr. Hoffman down for one of those G.I. series—a barium enema and all that. He walked into Mr. Kaufman's cubicle and said, "Mr. Hoffman?" Well, Kaufman was half asleep, and the names sound sort of alike anyway, so he said, "Yes." They took him downstairs and he went through the whole test by mistake. It was only afterwards that they found out it was the wrong patient!

What the best-dressed patient on this ward ought to wear is a cellophane shirt, or a sign saying "Exhibit A" . . .

Dear Dr. E.:

Much as I would like to see the smiling faces of you and your fellow workers, I don't particularly cotton to the idea of spending any length of time in the Hospital. However, I suppose that is something I must do once each year, and inasmuch as it has been approximately one year since I last entered your sweat shop, I hereby make application to enter the sanctum sanctorum (that's F-Second, in case you're wondering), come Sunday evening, March 17th. You do prefer that your patients commit themselves on that day of the week, don't you? . . .

Your obedient servant,
Howard Oates, A.D.

As we know, the "sanctum sanctorum," F-Second, was also referred to by patients as "The Hall of I.V."—a place where the "Battle of the Bottles" was fought every day. In the same spirit, patients designed a "coat of arms" for the ward: two criss-crossed hypodermic needles, with a drop of blood suspended from the tip of each.

F-Seconders also made jokes about the experimental surgery some of them underwent, the "new wonder drugs" most of them were receiving, and more generally, about their role as human subjects:

When the dietician came in after dinner, I was standin' there and I was talkin' to some of the guys. I said, "I'm gonna have some fun with her—the dietician. I'm gonna ask her what I get Thursday. I'm gonna ask her if I can't have three steaks for breakfast, dinner and supper on Thursday." So, when she came back down the ward I says, "Miss C.," I says, "what do we get Thursday?" She said, "What do you mean, Thursday?" "Well, don't I have a choice," I says, "the last day?" She says, "What do you mean 'the last day?'" "Well, I get operated on Friday," I says. "I'm gonna have an adrenalectomy. After that, I don't know what I'm gonna eat," I says, "so I'd like to have three steaks . . ."

One F-Seconder tried to grow tomatoes in the flower boxes on the ward porch. Two of his plants bore fruit; but one produced much larger tomatoes than the other. Patients referred to the plant with the big tomatoes as "the healthy one," and to the plant with the small tomatoes as "the sickly one." They printed "Cortisone-Grown" on a tongue depressor blade and stuck that in the box with the healthy plant. For the sickly plant, they made a comparable sign which said, "*Not* Cortisone-Grown."

A group of F-Seconders inflated some of the rubber tubing ordinarily used for tourniquets, and constructed a "kidney" out of it. They presented it to a patient who was in the advanced stages of a serious renal disease.

Patients sometimes referred to themselves as "living drugstores" and, more frequently, as "glorified guinea pigs." They even found humor in the misconduct and untoward consequences of experiments for which they acted as subjects:

One time Dr. C. came to me and said they wanted to try two milligrams of this new stuff that they'd only tried one other place in the world. Dr. C. said, "It's supposed to be very good. Will you try it?" I said okay. Well, they brought this stuff in in a shot glass for me to drink—at 2:00, 2:30, 3:00, 3:30—every half-hour until 9:00. Finally, they came in with the last glass. I said, "I won't be able to hold it down." They didn't believe me, so I drank it finally, and brought it all up. I had to use the wash basin—the kidney basin wasn't big enough. Dr. D. and Dr. C. came running to find out what was wrong. Well, it turned out that they were supposed to have given this stuff to me every *four* hours. Instead, I got it every *half*-hour . . .

Remember that time when Mac was getting all that cortisone, and he kind of went off his rocker? He came prancing down the ward one morning, flowers in one hand, a urinal in the other, saying, "I'm dead, and I'm going to Heaven with these in my hands!" It was a panic!

F-Seconders found another rich source of humor in the signs and symptoms of their ill-understood chronic diseases. A group of patients with diabetes who were spilling a great deal of sugar in their urine dubbed themselves the "Four-Plus Brigade."[10] Two patients with excessive iron deposits in their bodies were given the title of "Iron Men."[11] F-Seconders with intractable ulcers were described as "living with a milk bottle" and "unable to look a cow in the eye." A garrulous patient with hypertension was accused of having "high blood pressure of the lips." And when F-Seconders "put the wrong shoes on the wrong feet" of the paralyzed Leo Angelico, this was considered humor in the best ward tradition. (". . . So, when I was sitting up in the chair, and looked down at my feet, they were going the wrong way. What a bunch of guys!")

Finally, there were the "death jokes" of Ward F-Second. These were perhaps the most frequently made and the most relished of all:

God, all those flowers Mr. Weiss got makes this place look like a funeral parlor!

One way or another you get out of this place eventually. But there's only one way to get out for sure . . .

Last time I tried to go out of here in my blue gabardine suit, it made me look worse than when I came in. God, I looked like Death warmed over!

Mr. M.: On this ward, we have what you might call a "rotating" population—the same guys coming and going all the time . . .
Mr. O.: Yeah, but a lot of them never come back. They go to Heaven instead.

He was too far gone by the time he arrived. You just can't expect to start when the runner is already somewhere between third and home . . .

Do you remember the night Mac did all that supernatural stuff on the ward? Turning all the lights down low, sweeping a broom around in a circle in the middle of the floor, and trying to contact spirits from the other world!

We played a joke on the orderly last night. I draped myself in a sheet and got John to call the orderly for a bedpan. When he came in and saw me standing in the middle of the floor with that white sheet on, he dropped the pan and went running down the ward!

I sure came close to those pearly gates, all right! I knocked on them. But Saint Peter told me to get the hell out!

The time I had the heart attack, I thought maybe I was getting asthma at first. But when I called the doctor and told him how I felt, he said, "You'd better come into the hospital right away." When I got there all these doctors were running around and came in to examine me. When they were finished, I sat on the edge of the bed and smoked a cigarette. Because I'd made up my mind that I wasn't gonna worry. The doctors stood around talking to each other and debating things. One doctor said I shouldn't even be allowed to shave myself; another said he disagreed. Finally, in a joke, I said: "You fellows better get together pretty quick. Can't you see I'm dyin'?"

Did you ever hear the story about the grave-digger who dug too far down? Well, it seems that one night there he shoveled such a big hole that he couldn't get out of it. Fortunately, a drunk happened to be passing through the cemetery and heard his cries for help. The "rescuer" finally groped his way to the digger, and stood at the edge of the open grave, looking sympathetically down at him. "You must be awfully cold down there," he said. "Here, I'll cover you up." And taking a nearby shovel in hand, the drunk buried the grave-digger.

*The Meaning and Functions
of the Humor of Ward F-Second*

> . . . They treat a joke as a serious thing, and a serious
> thing as a joke . . .
> —Sean O'Casey
>
> There is no humor in heaven . . .
> —Mark Twain
>
> The closest thing to humor is tragedy . . .
> —James Thurber

Earlier, we saw that humor was an important mechanism through which patients were introduced to F-Second and taught to cope with their situation in the ways the ward community prescribed. Like all humor, the joking of F-Seconders also helped to relieve tension, by providing patients with diversion and "comic relief." In this connection, the fact that humorous behavior on Ward F-Second was not simply a matter of joke-telling is significant. The humorous documents which patients created and the comic horseplay in which they engaged enabled them to write out and act out (as well as talk out) some of their tensions, in a form that was more expressive and less emphemeral than the succinct, ready-made joke.

The humor of Ward F-Second was not primarily a source of easy fun. In a sense, it was the inner emotional "language" of the ward: the highly patterned form in which patients expressed their deepest sentiments about "serious things" of importance to them. F-Seconders joked primarily about the deprivations, restraint, suffering, and uncertainty which illness, medical science, the doctors, and the hospital imposed on them; and also about the possibility that some day, with the help of new drugs and procedures, the efforts of physicians, and their own cooperation, they might "get well and go home for good."

Like the humor of their physicians, the humor of patients was antithetic in nature: counterphobic and inversely reverent. F-Seconders joked about things which especially disturbed or frightened them, and about those to which they were positively committed or about which they deeply cared. Through humor, then, they "made light" both of their painful feelings and of their beliefs and hopes. This seems to have helped them to cope with the difficulties they

faced, and feelings of being alone, helpless, afraid, worthless, disappointed, and angry evoked in them by their predicament. Laughing at
their hopes about getting well (and at themselves for entertaining
such hopes) made it easier for them to come to terms with the fact
that, actually, this might never be possible.

In part, the outlook which F-Seconders expressed through their
humor was a fatalistic one. The idea that they had been arbitrarily
cast as comedians in some absurd life-and-death drama over which
they had little control runs through much of what they considered
funny. The "world" they depicted through their jokes was tragicomic
and indifferent to men and their particularity. It was a universe in
which human beings seemed to be less valuable to the progress of
medical science than cats, and a Mr. Kaufman "went through a G.I.
series by mistake" because his name sounded like that of the patient
for whom it was intended.

In other respects, the world that F-Seconders described through
their jokes was a curiously literal place. Paralyzed legs were feet that
"were going the wrong way"; moribund patients "looked like death
warmed over"; human "exhibits" wore "cellophane shirts"; and some
of the phenomena and events of this world were identified by clearly-
lettered signs. ("Cortisone-Grown"; *Not* Cortisone-Grown"; "Exhibit A," and so on.) "Things are what they are," F-Seconders
seemed to be saying in some of their jokes—suggesting again a deter-
ministic point of view.

However, the fact that F-Seconders jokingly insisted on having
things this "clear and simple" seems to indicate more than the passive acceptance of fate on their part. In the serious, "real" world,
patients were confronted with problems of uncertainty and meaning;
but in the realm of their jokes, many things were either indubitable,
easy to decipher, or explained by a caption. This suggests that the
joking behavior of F-Seconders was an active attempt on their part
to make sense—or, at least mock sense—of their predicament.

A good deal in the humor of F-Seconders was not acquiescent. As
we have indicated, patients expressed feelings of chagrin, frustration,
disappointment, and anger through many of the jokes they made. In
some of their jokes they explicitly directed these feelings against their
physicians. Other jokes had the impertinent, devil-may-care outlook
of the patient who described himself as sitting on the edge of his bed

smoking a cigarette while the doctors tried to decide what to do about the severe heart attack he had just experienced. But the most defiant of all the jokes F-Seconders made were those about death. These represented gallows humor in its most outraged and impious form. F-Seconders did not simply make joking allusions to death. Their humor was a way of "looking [death] straight in the eye" and trying to overcome it. Patients wrote out mock death certificates; they jokingly "knocked on those pearly gates"; they played at summoning up the spirits of the dead, and at coming back from the "next world" to haunt those who were still alive. Engaging death in this way, and ridiculing it, helped F-Seconders to feel less afraid of it. It also seems to have given them some hope that like the drunk in one of the humorous stories they told, they might triumph over death and "bury the grave-digger."

The humor of Ward F-Second, then, provided patients with a medium through which they could express feelings of resignation and despair about their fate, and at the same time protest against it. This seems to have helped them to come to terms with these feelings sufficiently to reassert that there must be some meaning and order in the absurd predicament in which they found themselves, and some hope for a way out:

I sure came close to those pearly gates, all right! I knocked on them. But Saint Peter told me to get the hell out!

As this joke suggests, the humor of Ward F-Second and its religion overlapped to such an extent that it was hard to tell where laughter left off and prayer began.

Laughing Prayer: Religion on Ward F-Second

In a number of indirect and subterranean ways, Ward F-Second was a deeply religious community. Behind the drawn curtains of their cubicles, many patients read Bibles and prayer books, spelled out the beads of their rosaries, and listened to religious programs on their muted radios. These aspects of religion on Ward F-Second were so private that it took a long time to "discover" them: to catch a glimpse of a cherished crucifix, for example, or hear a snatch of a radio-borne sermon. It took even longer to realize that the special treatment given patients who were clergymen, the highly intellectual theological discussions among Protestant, Catholic, and Jewish patients, and some of the joking in which patients engaged were all oblique forms of worship. On Ward F-Second, feelings about "the Guy above" were usually not publicly expressed in an outright fashion.

Sometimes, however, a man's religious sentiments burst from him. Overwhelmed by the beauty of a spring morning, an F-Seconder praised God for the exquisiteness of His "handiwork":

It's all too perfect for there not to be a God . . . And the more you travel, the more evidence you see everywhere you go of God's beauty and handiwork . . .

With something like the fervor of an Abraham, another patient offered himself to God as a scientific sacrifice:

I hope that my submission to these experiments will restore men and women to normal living in years to come . . . If they do, I will have aided the scientific advances of man and repaid those who helped me, in the manner which I think God would expect . . .

Just as He spins the planets and regulates the sun, many F-Seconders believed, so God rules over the lives of men. In all that He directs, there is "order" and "purpose." The planets turn "without crashing into each other . . . the sun shines upon us neither too hot, nor too cold"; and men live out their days according to a superhuman plan.

Although they acknowledged His existence and divinity, F-Seconders also questioned and challenged God—and in desperate moments, they even cursed Him. The source of health, the giver of life, He desecrates his own miracles with disease and death. Why? F-Seconders asked. Because of "the lives [men] lead, and the thoughts" they harbor? Because "we don't know right from wrong"?

Why doesn't He tell us when we've done something wrong? Why doesn't He tell us you've committed a crime and you're going to be punished for it? Tell us right there and then so we'd know . . . God damn it! It's a wonder that *anyone* lives to be sixty, with all the things that can happen to you before then!

The religion of F-Second was both a bowing down and a defiance; and in their joking about it, they found a way of synthesizing reverence and blasphemy.

Remember that night Pete read that religious poem he'd written? It was a kind of religious poem that took place in the hospital—about Christ didn't have IV's and transfusions. Stuff like that . . . It was really a terrible poem, but I got a big kick out of hearing it . . .

Mr. C.: Remember the night before Matson was due to go up for his adrenalectomy operation? Mac started saying prayers over him. The poor guy was so nervous already that it was pitiful. And then, with Mac reading that Book over him! I had to tell him to cut it out . . .

Mr. A.: And on Sunday mornings Mac was a riot! He'd get the whole ward down here and read to them out of his Bible! And then we'd all sit around and sing hymns . . .

Mr. O.: Do you remember the night Mac did all that supernatural stuff on the ward? Turning all the lights down low, sweeping a broom around in a circle in the middle of the floor, and trying to contact spirits from the other world!

Mr. M.: Yeah. And remember that time when Mac was getting all that cortisone and he kind of went off his rocker? He came prancing down the ward one morning, flowers in one hand, a urinal in the other, saying, "I'm dead, and I'm going to Heaven with these in my hands!"

The praying Mac, F-Seconders agreed was a "riot" and a "panic": such a religious zealot that he could terrify a man, and set a whole ward to singing hymns. He was also an irreverent "character": a dabbler in the séance, and a man who would carry his urinal to Heaven. So pious and so profane! F-Seconders laughed at Mac's Bible-reading partly because they were abashed by the intensity of their *own* faith. And they exulted in his blasphemies because they, too, felt derision:

It all started with Adam, running around in that Garden—having a good time playing around with fig leaves and all. *He* didn't have to spend his days here like we do, sitting around with a bum knee or in a wheel chair!

A God who tolerates wards and wheel chairs—destroying the perfection that He Himself created—"ought" to be mocked.

On Ward F-Second, men laughed at their prayers—and prayed when they laughed.

A Game of Chance

Finally, along with humor and religion, the patients of Ward

F-Second had a "game of chance" way of viewing and dealing with their situation, which helped them to come to terms with the problems of uncertainty and meaning which they faced.

"Life is pretty much of a gamble," many F-Seconders felt—hazardous and unpredictable—like some huge game of chance.

> . . . In life you have to take a lot of chances, not all of them are going to come out the way you plan . . . It's pretty much of a gamble . . .

It sometimes seemed to F-Seconders that whether a man got sick or stayed well, got better or worse—even, whether he lived or died—were as much a matter of chance and luck as the outcome of a game of poker or dice:[12]

> I used to play poker with a group of my associates every Friday night, and we had a $3 limit. Well, that $3 limit never bothered any of us. We were all working, and we could afford that every week. We used to call it our amusement tax. If we lost it, why that was our tax. If you won, well, you were just lucky and that was fine. I never used to lose very often, nor did I win very heavily. Usually, I just about broke even . . . Sometimes I'd win. I'd win maybe $12, but over an average of time, why I don't think I ever came out ahead very much . . .
> (And how do you feel about the operation performed on you as a risk?)
> It, too, is a gamble.
> (A gamble.)
> Uh huh. I still don't know—the last few days I've been thinking—wondering how it will all come out . . .

> I was always lucky at dice. I never lost when I was shooting dice. Very lucky that way. I was—I was lucky in other ways. But I wasn't lucky when I got sick. I mean, I'm lucky to be alive right now, but I wasn't lucky when I got sick . . .

> You can't guess who's going to make it and who's not. For instance, there was this big fellow in the bed next to me who was going to have a heart operation. I heard him moving around in the middle of the night before the operation. I asked him if he was worrying, and he said yes. So, we talked 'til 4 in the morning . . . Well, that fellow went up to the O.R. and he never came down . . . But Mr. Green, who was so light you could have blown him over with a feather, he had the same operation, and he came through all right . . . Then, there was this little fellow from Maine who had the adrenalectomy. He didn't look as if he'd make it either, but he did. On the other hand, Walter Cousins went out like that! If the adrenalectomy was going to work on anyone, I would have bet my chips on him . . .

Was who "made it" and who didn't really just a matter of chance—or was there some pattern? Could they "figure it out"? If it was just a matter of luck, were the "odds for or against" them? Would their luck "hold up" or had it "run out"?

F-Seconders did not only ask these questions verbally; they also asked them through the game of chance they devised. They took bets on such things as "how [an] operation would turn out" for a patient about to undergo one, and whether a patient who was "very sick" would live or die.[13] ("[We] like to make little amateur predictions and see how they come out . . . ") Sometimes a "small wager" was "part of the game," sometimes not.

Their audacious betting, like their humor, provided F-Seconders with a way of expressing their feeling that the plight they shared seemed as amoral and undesigned as chance itself. This symbolic recognition of chance was also a kind of affirmation against it. Such lawlessness ought not to prevail, F-Seconders declared through their betting. Surely, the life and death of a man is part of some universal scheme of things. Turning to the wager—to the "little amateur prediction"—F-Seconders dared to believe that out of their willingness to meet contingencies head on in this way, some meaning and order might be found. Winning a bet gave them some reassurance that there was a "system," which they could "figure out," and which might "work in [their] favor."

Finally, the game of chance which F-Seconders played was also a petition. It was customary for the medical staff to move a terminally ill patient in the process of dying from his cubicle to a room just outside the entrance to the ward. When this happened, patients did not take bets on his chances for survival. "When they put you out there in that room," a patient explained, "you've had it! There's no use taking bets on you any more. You're too far gone by that time . . . " This means, then, that so long as patients were willing to "lay odds on whether that fellow down the ward would last much longer or not," they felt there was some chance that he might. In a way, their bets were ironic but hopeful prayers for his survival and welfare—and for their own.

Relationship Between Ways of Coming to
Terms of Patients and Physicians

These were the ways in which the patients of Ward F-Second came to terms with their shared problems and stresses: through laughter, prayer, and their game of chance; medical stardom, interest, and expertise; their "take up thy bed" credo and behavior; and their deep, organized commitme it to one another.

Some of the ways of coming to terms which the patient community developed were close facsimiles of those evolved by the physicians of the Metabolic Group. The counterphobic, impious joking which took place in the ward cubicles also occurred in the Metabolic laboratory and conference room; physicians and patients devised comparable games of chance; and both found support, reassurance, and guidance in the solidary group to which they belonged.

To some extent, the similarity in the humor of physicians and patients may have resulted from their influence upon one another, for a certain amount of joking characterized the letters they exchanged, and sometimes "you would hear the sound of doctors and patients laughing together coming from one of the cubicles." However, the fact that physicians and patients were faced with comparable problems seems to have been the basic reason for the congruity between their humor, as well as their games of chance and group solidarity. The physicians of the Metabolic Group and the patients of Ward F-Second were confronted with great uncertainty, serious, irremediable illness, and death. One might almost say that the nature and magnitude of the problems they faced were so important in shaping the ways of coming to terms which these two groups of men evolved, that irrespective of the differences between being a physician and a patient, and to a large extent independently of one another, they arrived at some of the same solutions for their difficulties.

Other ways of coming to terms which physicians and patients developed were complementary, rather than identical. The physicians of the Metabolic Group treated many of their patients as privileged, personal associates, taught them a good deal about their diseases and the experiments in which they participated, and made them feel that by acting as subjects they were contributing in a professional way to medical science. Conversely, many patients established an intimate, colleague-like relationship with physicians of the Group, developed into medical savants, and became professionally dedicated to the role of research subject. In these respects physicians and patients devised ways of coming to terms with their situation which implemented and reinforced one another.

Disadvantages of Ward F-Second's Ways of Coming to Terms

We have already indicated that the close relationship which existed between the Metabolic Group and their patients had at least one important dysfunctional consequence for these physicians. Sometimes their attachment to patients made it hard for members of the Group to carry out their clinical and research activities with the objectivity and equipoise of scientists. This close relationship also created difficulties for patients. Some F-Seconders became so identified with the physicians of the Metabolic Group, and so committed to "helping them with their research work," that when their participation in experiments ended, or when the time came for them to be discharged from the hospital, they felt neglected, disappointed, "lost," "afraid":

You doctors! How fast your demeanor changes! There was a time when you all considered my case interesting, and you'd come to see me one after another. Now I'm not an interesting case any more. So you all rush by like locomotives!

Well, I'm going out into the wide world today. Dr. J. asked me yesterday how I felt about leaving. I told him I was going to feel a little lost and scared, and somewhat like Adlai Stevenson did when he lost the election . . .

Dear Dr. D.:
I want to thank you for having me at the hospital for the recent tests . . . I do hope you will have an opportunity to use me again . . .

A member of the Psychiatric Unit of the hospital once described some of the patients on Ward F-Second as having "an intense transference relationship to the whole Metabolic Group, the Hospital, and medical science." He also referred to the elements of "countertransference" in the kind of relationship the Metabolic Group established with patients. In a sense, what we have been describing here are negative consequences of a social process through which "transference," "countertransference," and finding "secondary gains" in illness were made possible and to some extent encouraged by both physicians and patients.

The feeling of anxiety that many patients experienced at the prospect of leaving the hospital and their "lonesomeness" for it after they went home were also connected with the deep commitment of F-Seconders to one another and to their ward community. F-Second was a "place where day after day, men who were all sick and confined to one room lived together, talked together, and laughed together." Around their common predicament, they created a "different sort of world": a world in which men made jokes about death and religion, ran human lotteries, founded an Adrenalectomy Club, and took pride in becoming stellar "guinea pigs." Some of these "special" characteristics of the ward community which helped F-Seconders to come to terms with serious, chronic illness, "hospital life," the medical laboratory, and first-hand contact with death also had certain negative consequences:

This place keeps drawing you in toward itself, and the world outside starts to get smaller and smaller—farther and farther away. You begin to forget what the world out there is like . . .

As a consequence, many F-Seconders were reluctant to "leave the guys on the ward," "scared" to return to the "outside world" which had receded from them, and "unable to put Ward F-Second out of their minds after they got home." Thus, the mail that arrived on the ward often brought letters from patients who had been discharged from the hospital:

. . . Leo, I want you to know that you are the swellest guy I have ever met. Your outlook on life, your cheerfulness, your great help in helping others adjust themselves to strange hospital life—all this in spite of your own troubles—this contribution could not be greater than doctors, nurses, and even families. May God bless you.[14]

Dear Miss Fox,
  I would appreciate your arranging a Hallowe'en party for Ward F-Second, if you have the time and it meets with the approval of the doctors. I haven't any specific suggestions, as I don't know exactly what will be permitted. But I am counting on you—and please send me the bill . . . I suppose F-Second has changed a good deal by this time. Please remember me to any of my old friends still there . . .[15]

Many patients came back to visit "old friends still" on the ward, with whom they "reminisced about what F-Second was like in the old days" when *they* were hospitalized on it:

This place has kind of got Charlie. Sure, he has to come to the O.P.D. But he could just leave right after that. Instead, whenever he comes in, he goes all around to see everybody. It's that way with most of the fellows who were here for a long time. They all want to come back because they know what they've been through here. And they can never forget. It's always there deep inside them. So they feel for those who are still here. They want to know how the others are coming along.

These guys on the ward now are all so quiet. They do nothing but lie around in bed all day. You should have been on the ward when *I* was here! Why, one time there, for instance . . .

Some mornings, if you went out on the porch, you might "find this fellow there. He raised a little garden when he was on the ward. And he kept coming back to take care of the boxes on the porch he planted things in."[16]

To the extent that being "close-knit" and having the "world" of F-Second "deep inside" them made it hard for some patients to adjust to "life outside the hospital," and likely to "feel terrible when anything happened to an F-Second friend," coming to terms in the ways the ward community prescribed had disadvantages:

. . . It may interest you to know that as of June 10, H. Oates, the erstwhile slob, went back to work for the first time in 15 years. If I may coin a phrase to go along with the occasion, "mieux vaut tard que jamais," or, as the French say, "life begins at 41!" In good Oates style, I'm working in (and out of) a town 60 miles away. I must confess that I'm quite pooped after 4 days of this rat race, but even so, I don't sleep as much as I'd like to by way of worry and anxiety . . .

When I'm home, and all the people in the room start talking at once —even if they're my own family—I get nervous and tired. Like one night there last summer, my brothers got into this political discussion, and it wore me out just listening. That's why I feel I'm not made to be with strong, healthy people any more.

. . . This year I did not go back to the Hospital as I usually do in September . . . And I do miss it very much—so much that I am forever thinking about the Hospital and all the wonderful people I knew there . . .

Ray: You see, it's like this, Leo. You and me, we're very good friends. But if you were to have nephrosis, that would be a different thing. Because then when you got real sick like you definitely would with nephrosis, I'd feel terrible. That's why I don't think you should become good friends with nephrotics or people like them . . .

Leo: You mean to say then, Ray, that you would desert your fellow man when he's in need at a time like that? Look, I was a good friend of

Paul O'Brian's. He had Hodgkin's disease and we all knew he was going to die. But that didn't stop me from having a lot to do with him. I wanted to. And then there was Moscowitz. I knew him well, too, and I'm glad I did. And what about Walter Cousins? I was really shocked when he died because he was such a powerful man. He used to come up here nights a lot, and he'd talk to me about a little summer cottage he had, and how he got away week ends, and different things he liked to do—I felt terrible when he died. But I'm not sorry I knew him. I'm glad. Like your friendship with Dominic Adabbo. You're not sorry about that are you, even though he's gone now?

Ray: Look, Dom and me *were* very good friends. And when I came back to the hospital I wrote him a note, telling him I was here. I got a box of candy back with a note that wasn't in his handwriting saying: "This is from Dom Adabbo. Write to him often." Well, I didn't know what to make of that, but I wrote back to thank him. That same day I got a note saying Dom had passed away. I felt terrible. I was—well, I don't know—I was in a state of semishock for days . . . So, that's why I say, talk to 'em when they're that sick, yes—but don't get to be too good friends with them . . .

As this exchange between Leo Angelico and Ray Woodham indicates, the patients of Ward F-Second did not all come to terms with their problems in exactly the same manner. The ward community provided patients with certain patterned ways of thinking about their situation and dealing with it: preferred attitudes, values, and behaviors which were taught to new members and were to some extent enforced. However, this still left room for variation between patients, both with respect to how they felt about these recommended ways of coming to terms, and precisely how they made use of them. Such factors as the personality characteristics of each patient, the type of disease he had, his prognosis, age, marital status, occupation, religion, and ethnic background undoubtedly made for differences in the nature and intensity of the patients' commitment to the ward's designated solutions and the ways they combined them.

The differences in outlook and behavior of individual patients we have encountered suggest something of the variation that existed; and several times we have noted that differences in the ethnic origins of patients seemed to affect the ways in which they experienced and managed their problems. A detailed, systematic treatment of the bearing that such factors had on the ways in which patients responded to their situation falls outside the scope of this study, as does a consideration of patients in terms of their individuating life histories and special personality traits.

However, there are three patients among those we have met to whom we wish to devote the next chapter. These are patients who seem to have had symbolic importance for the ward community as a whole, primarily because each personified an archetypical mode of coming to terms with the problems and stresses which F-Seconders shared. Learning more about these patients, letting them speak for themselves, and hearing what other F-Seconders said about them will accomplish a number of things. It will quicken our appreciation of the fact that Ward F-Second was comprised of real persons, each of whom was an important and unique human being in his own right. It will deepen our felt understanding of at least three patients as individuals. At the same time, it will provide concrete, case-history examples of different ways in which patients evaluated, combined, and utilized the ward's patterned solutions, and of some of their functional and dysfunctional consequences. Finally, it will enable us to listen in as the basic question around which Ward F-Second was built is openly debated. What is a good adjustment to the situation we share? F-Seconders asked themselves—the "best way" of coming to terms? Two diametrically opposed answers came back: the reply of a Paul O'Brian and the response of a Leo Angelico.

Face up to the fact that you will probably never get well, and that death is imminent, Paul O'Brian advocated. Have faith; but protest against illness and death. Live as long and fully and deeply as you can in terms of the world outside and wellness. Stay out of bed as much as possible. Make jokes and laugh with the fellows on the ward. But don't become too attached to them, or to the doctors. And don't succumb to the allure of medical stardom by committing yourself to the laboratory or to the notion of furthering medical science.

Accept the fact that you are paralyzed and probably always will be, Leo Angelico maintained. "Try to take what the Lord has decided [and] make the best of it." Put out of your mind things like "walking on the street," going to work, being at home with your family. Don't think too much about leaving the hospital. Find solace, pleasure, inspiration, and important work to do for the patients and doctors, right here and now on Ward F-Second. Get up in a wheel chair as much as possible and try to help patients who are "having a hard time" by visiting them and talking to them. Beyond that, assist the doctors, achieve "fame," and accomplish the "mission" of bringing health and happiness to "thousands," by acting as a volunteer for the Metabolic Group's experiments.

Finally, standing midway between the rebellious acquiescence of a Paul O'Brian and the active resignation of a Leo Angelico—symbolizing the way in which they could be reconciled—was a patient we never came to know but "always heard about." This was Jackie Foote, the seventeen-year-old boy who represented Ward F-Second's image of the "ideal" adjustment.

Notes for Chapter V

1. The Adrenalectomy Club is not a phenomenon uniquely characteristic of patients on Ward F-Second. Other patients in other hospital situations have formed comparable clubs. Probably the most widely-known of such clubs is the "Half-Lung Club" which appears in Thomas Mann's *The Magic Mountain,* a novel which takes place in a Swiss sanitorium for patients with tuberculosis—a sanitorium which actually existed, and which Mann visited when his wife was a patient there. In the novel, Joachim, a patient in the sanitorium, explains to his cousin Hans Castorp, who is visiting him, that a pneumothorax (a surgically-effected collapse of the lungs) is "a risky business . . . Those people you just saw all have it . . . They have formed a group, for of course a thing like the pneumothorax brings people together. They call themselves the Half-Lung Club . . ." Thomas Mann, *The Magic Mountain* (New York: Alfred A. Knopf, 1948), p. 51. Many clubs of this sort exist in the United States, and some of these have acquired such a large membership, and become so highly organized, that they have evolved into voluntary health associations of national importance. Some of these clubs, and their relationship to certain generic characteristics of American society, will be discussed in Chapter VIII.

2. The phrase, "He really ought to have a star over his cubicle" was heard repeatedly on Ward F-Second. As will be seen, it provided the author with a way of conceptualizing a constellation of attitudes, values, and behavior patterns through which many patients came to terms with their situation: the phenomenon of "medical stardom."

3. Because he had a rare kidney condition, and might possibly need to undergo hemodialysis (a run on the artificial kidney machine), this patient had been transferred to Ward F-Second from an Army hospital.

4. Parsons, "The Definitions of Health and Illness in the Light of American Values and Social Structure."

5. See *When Doctors Meet Reporters* (Compiled by Hillier Krieghbaum from the record of a series of conferences sponsored by the Josiah Macy, Jr. Foundation) (New York: New York University Press, 1957), especially pp. 62-63 and 76-78.

6. Thorn *et al.,* "Clinical Studies on Bilateral Complete Adrenalectomy in Patients with Severe Hypertensive Vascular Disease," pp. 995-996. The basic

medical facts about the case of Walter Cousins presented in this article and in the account of his operation written up in a local newspaper which follows are essentially the same. However, the article written by the journalist differs from the one published in the medical journal in at least two respects: the writing style is dramatic and evocative rather than objective and neutral in tone; and it focuses primarily on the "human interest" aspects of the event (i.e., the man, Walter Cousins, what he underwent, how he feels, etc.), rather than on the impersonal medical findings. Newspaper reporting of medical events and the presentation of such events in scientific publications frequently differ in these respects.

7. An unpublished paper by one of the hospital psychiatrists, "A Note on the Motivation of the Experimental Subject," helped me to understand the case of Gene Gordon's "conversion" to the role of research subject. In this paper, the psychiatrist analyzes a series of intensive interviews which he conducted with two "normal college students" who had volunteered to act as subjects for the Metabolic Group. Like those performed on many F-Seconders, the experiments to which these young men submitted entailed receiving large doses of ACTH and cortisone via the intravenous route. Among the psychiatrist's major findings was his observation that the personalities of both subjects were highly counterphobic.

It is interesting to speculate about how pertinent another of the psychiatrist's findings may have been in motivating patients on Ward F-Second to act as research subjects. Both of the men he interviewed exhibited a need to pose a severe challenge to their bodies in order to assert their "invulnerability" over all "dangers." It does not seem unlikely that undergoing experiments may have served something like this function for some patients as well. Though they were physically incapacitated, certain F-Seconders may have derived a sense of greater intactness from the role of experimentee. One spoken piece of evidence supports this possibility. A patient describing his experience in receiving intravenous infusions of adrenal steroid compounds to another F-Seconder was heard to say: "I just sit and watch those drops and test my strength that way."

8. Chapter III, pp. 58-60.

9. The psychiatrist or psychologist would probably regard attitudes and behavior of this sort as indications of "denial" on the part of such patients. The defense mechanism of denial essentially consists of the individual behaving as though certain external dangers did not exist at all. Refusal to learn about one's disease, or to think of it "knowingly," then, can be ways of denying its perilousness, or even its very existence.

Although the ward community placed a high value on medical expertise and helped to effect the "medical education" of its members, there was one occasion on which we saw the men of F-Second conspire to keep a patient from "knowing" or "finding out." This was when Walter Cousins, the President of the Adrenalectomy Club, died. F-Seconders on the ward at the time decided to keep the news of his death from Mac, Secretary-Treasurer of the Club, for as long as possible. Ostensibly, this was because the sudden death of Walter Cousins—the "first" and the so-called "best" of the adrenalectomies—suggested that other patients who had survived the procedure might also die, and because Mac himself was quite ill on the ward at the time the death occurred.

R.: It was too bad about Walter Cousins. He was one helluva swell guy. And what a shock to see somebody that healthy-looking go all of a sudden.

M.: (*whispering*) Shhh . . . Don't talk about Walt in front of Mac. We want to keep the news from him . . .

Two things are of special interest here. First, it was only by virtue of a self-conscious plot on the part of the ward that some of the usual pressures toward encouraging patients to "learn as much as [they] could about what was going on" were held in abeyance. Second, according to the psychiatrist assigned to his case, Mac's primary defense mechanism was an extraordinarily well-developed capacity for denial. The ward community seems to have recognized this fact, and under the drastic circumstances of Cousins' death, supported it.

10. "Four-plus," in medical parlance, is a measure of the amount of sugar found in the urine. A normal individual would have a zero measurement, indicating no sugar in the urine; one-plus signifies a trace of sugar; and four-plus denotes the greatest amount of urinary sugar possible.

11. The disease referred to here is hemochromatosis.

12. The first interchange of comments quoted above took place between a psychiatrist and a patient on Ward F-Second who had undergone an adrenalectomy, in the context of a psychiatric interview. The comments enclosed in parentheses are those of the psychiatrist.

13. It seemed to me that the Irish patients on Ward F-Second were more prone to do this kind of betting and to make macabre jokes than other patients. Some substantiation for this impression can be found in Irish literature, which contains a great deal of "black humor." More particularly, there is a short drama, written by Oliver St. John Gogarty, which takes place in a hospital for incurable patients in Ireland in which patients joke and run sweepstakes on who is going to die next, in ways that so closely duplicate those of F-Seconders that I feel justified in suggesting that there may be a special association between being Irish and engaging in these forms of behavior. See Oliver St. John Gogarty, "Incurables," in *A Week End in the Middle of the Week, and Other Essays on The Bias* (New York: Doubleday and Company, Inc., 1958), pp. 44-64.

14. In the next chapter, when we become better acquainted with Leo Angelico, the patient to whom this letter was written, we shall see that particularly many of the new patients on the ward thought of him in this way—as a tragic, but radiant figure, who helped them to adjust to the hospital and their illness.

15. This was one of the kinds of things which the patients of Ward F-Second occasionally asked me to do. See Chapter VII for a detailed description and analysis of the role of the participant observer in the patient community.

16. The flower-tending patient was an Italian gentleman, as were most of F-Second's porch gardeners. Italian patients were the horticulturists of the ward. They initiated the porch garden and cultivated it. The F-Seconder who conceived of the "Cortisone-Grown" sign for the robust tomato plant was also Italian.

CHAPTER VI— Three F-Seconders: Paul O'Brian, Leo Angelico, and Jackie Foote

PAUL O'BRIAN

Hodgkin's Disease: a painless, progressive and fatal enlargement of the lymph nodes, spleen, and general lymphoid tissues, which often begins in the neck, and spreads over the body . . .
—*The American Illustrated Medical Dictionary*

I only know that one must do what one can to cease being plague-stricken, and that's the only way we can hope for some peace or, failing that, a decent death . . .
—Albert Camus, *The Plague*

Disease so adjusts its man that it and he can come to terms; there are sensory appeasements, short circuits, a merciful narcosis . . . But one must fight against them, after all, for they are two-faced. If you are not meant to get home, they are a benefaction, they are merciful; but if you mean to get home, they become sinister.
—Thomas Mann, *The Magic Mountain*

OUR FAMILY DOCTOR'S a good doctor, but he's not very good at handling patients in a social way, if you know what I mean. When I got sick, he told my father that I had only five years to live. If he had told *me,* I wouldn't have cared at all. But Dopey there had to go and tell my father and worry him half to death! That's why he won't believe my sister when she tells him how well I'm getting along in the hospital this time . . . Because this is the fifth year, you see . . .

With full knowledge of the nature of his disease, and the imminence of his death, Paul O'Brian, twenty-seven, lived out his days. From his doctors, he had demanded and received this merciless knowledge. ("I asked him whether he could tell me anything about the progress of Hodgkin's disease; how far it had gone . . . I asked

191

him how long he thought I had to live . . .") His ferocious drive to "find out" had made it imperative for him to ask these questions; and with a kind of savageness, he had come to terms with the unequivocal answers.

The coming-to-terms struggle had been a desperate one: a literal life-and-death battle. At first, a terrible void seemed to stretch before him:

> I wasn't working. And I was looking for a job, but not really very hard. I slept late every morning; went to bed late every night. And I had nothing to do . . . absolutely nothing to do. Nothing to look forward to . . . no one to see. I even went out one day and got drunk, thinking maybe that would help. But it didn't . . . You see, before I was sick, I was so active. I went to school, and to work. I had dates, and went dancing and to parties. I just never had a moment to spare, my life was so full . . . So to have my life so empty and so unbusy was a hard thing to get used to . . .

Paul's days were taken up by strenuous treatments, but they still seemed "empty" to him—without meaning, beginning or end:

> I don't know which of the two treatments they're going to give me this time: mustard or X-ray. I'd rather have X-ray, I think. No, I'd rather have mustard. I don't know . . . (*pointing to his upper chest*)—I guess I'd rather have X-ray if it's going to be from here up, and mustard if it's going to be from here down. Because X-ray goes on forever. Day after day they drag you down for your treatment, and you're as limp as a rag. Nitrogen mustard gas only lasts two days, and most of the time you don't know what's going on . . .

All of this involved "coming to the hospital, and going out— coming in and going out": a senseless repetition of arrivals and departures. There were days when Paul O'Brian longed for the ultimate certainty of his death:

> Listen, Dr. W., this is all stupid. What's the use of going on with these treatments? Just let me go home and forget about it. It's going to get me sometime or other, anyway.

> You know, if I thought I was going to have to go on like this for years—for more than five years, even . . . coming in and going out, coming in and going out—with only short intervals in between—I'd rather not live. Really, I'd rather die and get it over with.

And yet, Paul O'Brian refused to surrender himself. Move in

the pattern of wellness, he affirmed. And "keep endless watch . . . lest you join forces with pestilence."[1]

This time when I go home, I'm not going to wear a suit like I did last time. Last time, I sent for my favorite blue suit, and a special tie and shirt. And then, when I put them on, I discovered I'd lost so much weight that nothing fit and I looked just terrible. Like death warmed over . . . This time, I'm going to wear slacks, and a sport shirt, and a sweater . . . What I'd really like to do is drive my car home from the hospital. And when I finally do get to my house, I'd like to open the front door, run upstairs carrying my suitcase, and then rush downstairs again to the kitchen, and take a nice, cold beer out of the refrigerator . . . If I did all those things, then my family would really believe that I was well . . . and home to stay . . .

I hope I get out of this hospital mood before I get out of here, though. Like I'm sitting here now and saying to myself as I watch the people in the corridor and on the ward, "That's a nurse; and that's a dietician; and that's a famous doctor." I wish I didn't know anything about anything here—about who people are, and what's going on. I'd like it if I could feel and act as if I'd never been here . . . When I get out of here, I'll probably have to come back for a check-up once a week, for about a month or so. But do you know something? No matter how many times I have to come in for a check-up, I'll never come up to this ward. Never! Once I get out, I want to leave it all behind me . . .

Even when the ward claimed him, Paul O'Brian kept faith with nonappeasement. Every drop swallowed, every pound gained, he regarded as a triumph. For with each progression, no matter how small, he advanced his return to the outside world:

I remember when I was so sick for a while when I first came in . . . I'd lie there in bed and say to myself, "All I want for tomorrow is to be able to swallow a little tea." And when I finally succeeded in keeping that down, I'd say, "All I want now is to be able to drink a little tea, and eat a piece of toast, too." . . .

Paul had no tolerance for the supine. There was "something wrong" with a patient who "rested all day long," he declared. And when the whole of F-Second turned into a "stay-abed ward . . . with everyone in his cubicle by 9:30 at night"—that was the time Paul "really wished [he] could get out of the dump!" For him, a "quiet" ward was a "half-dead" place. And Paul O'Brian craved the "bustle," the clamor of life. As he envisioned it, the "perfect ward" would be a living defiance. "Graveyard roses" and "sickroom bonbons" would be outlawed. Beds and wheelchairs would stand empty. And "from every cubicle . . . you would hear all this laughter."

Death and disease would have no sovereignty in a world of Paul's making. They were his mortal enemies. Against all the ways in which they could seduce or overtake a man, Paul fought his never-ending battle:

So far as I'm concerned, Mac is a bore and a regular hypochondriac. Do you know, he keeps a record of everything that has happened to him since his operation? He writes it all down in that big fat notebook of his. His temperature, his weight, his headaches—even a pain in his toe. That annoys me to death!

When I look at Sam, I do more than wonder about that adrenalectomy operation. It certainly doesn't seem to have done him much good! All that trouble with his eyes. There's something terribly wrong with them. This morning he could hardly find his orange juice or his toast on his tray. His hands kept reaching in the wrong direction. His eyes must be all out of focus . . . So far as I'm concerned, it's just not worth having that operation. One thing for sure—they're not going to get *my* adrenals! . . . I don't see why anyone would want to be experimented on, anyhow!

This place keeps drawing you in toward itself, and the world outside starts to get smaller and smaller—farther and farther away . . . I wouldn't want to adjust perfectly to any place. And particularly not to *this* place.

10/22/51: *Discharge Note*
27-year-old white male with Hodgkin's disease known for four years. Entered hospital 21 days ago for sixth admission. Ran a progressive downhill course with increasing pulmonary difficulty and pain. For the past four days patient has been in severe respiratory distress, and during past 36 hours has required constant oxygen and large amounts of sedation. For the past 10 hours has been cyanotic, chest filled with large rhonci, gurgles, etc. Conscious until last hour when respirations became irregular, gasping and quite noisy. Patient finally stopped breathing, and some 30-50 seconds later heart sounds ceased. He was discharged to Ward X at 9:55 p.m.

Paul O'Brian's last days were a testament to his credo. He cried bitterly because he was "coming back to the hospital." ("The tears kept rolling down my face.") In spite of "a temperature of about a hundred-and-three," the morning of the day (October 1) he left home, he shaved himself. And he arrived on the ward resolutely determined to "do nothing but get well and go home again." ("This is the Jewish New Year, isn't it? Well, maybe things will start afresh for me.") Feverishly, he battled narcosis. ("I don't even know if I slept last night. That's how befuddled I am. It's all that dope I'm getting. It's changing my personality so that I hardly know myself. And I don't like it one bit. I'm just not going to take any more medication.") With unblurred contempt, he looked out on the ward. ("This place is dead! No one on the ward is funny any more. And everyone's in bed all the time. It's awful! A bunch of mourners, that's what they are. Take Mr. Kaye, for instance. He looks as if you could hire him to cry.") Shattering the funereal silence, Paul's voice rang out: "Come on, somebody! Make a little noise, won't you? Talk! Laugh! Do anything! But don't just lie there like a bunch of mummies!"

On October 13 Paul was still not "bedridden." On October 15, he launched himself on a "rehabilitation program":

They're going to try to rehabilitate me—Miss P., and the others. She's going to get someone up here to show me how to make a wallet. And she's going to bring me a book of funny stories. And I've asked her to get Father Mac to come up and see me . . . All that's to get me out of the apathy I'm in . . . Because it's not natural to feel as hopeless as I do now . . .

On October 19, Paul was put on the Danger List. ("My sister told me that I was on it, and I couldn't take it. I shouldn't care about dying. But I do . . .") On October 22, Paul O'Brian was "discharged to Ward X."

The day he died, Paul held fast to consciousness. (Dr. L.: "I've never seen anything like it! Most people aren't aware of everything happening to them like Paul is.") Through his oxygen mask, in a loud unmodulated voice, he talked on and on. ("How's everyone on the ward? Go see if my bed in the cubicle is made up, will you? Because I intend to get back there.") His family arrived. ("Hi. I had a pretty good night, last night . . . Why did you all come? It wasn't necessary. That means you had to leave work and everything. How did you get here? Did you take the car . . . ?") Paul lapsed into unconsciousness, and then aroused himself with a bitter reproach. ("You can go on talking to me, you know, even when I can't talk to you! I can hear every word you say! What's new in the outside

world?") The O'Brian family departed. ("They're too sentimental.
I don't want consolation.")

Paul had a choking spell. ("Open the windows! All the way
from the top!") He said he felt "very hungry" and wanted "something to eat." ("Chow! I want some chow!") In spite of his difficulty in breathing and swallowing, Paul downed a glass of orange
juice, a poached egg, and a cup of coffee, in huge, frenetic gulps.
("Hurry, hurry! The next bite!") The nurse arrived with the medicine tray, and Paul swallowed three pills at once.

Before he became unconscious for the last time, he asked for his
"square crucifix with the special blessing"; and he made a deadly
joke with the newspaper boy who appeared in the doorway. ("No,
I don't want a paper! I'm dying!") Reverence-and-blasphemy.

At 9:45 and-a-half, Paul "finally stopped breathing." At 9:55 p.m.
when his "heart sounds ceased" and he was "discharged to Ward X,"
the battle Paul O'Brian had waged ended.

LEO ANGELICO

This 40-year old male developed progressive muscular weakness of both lower
extremities and left upper extremity leading to evaluation and operation in 1943.
Exploration of the cord revealed a reddish-grey mass which was thought to be an
intramedullary spinal cord tumor at the level of C-4 to C-6. Resection could not
be carried out. There has been no progression since that time; both lower extremities and the left upper extremity are paralyzed. The right upper extremity is func-
tionally intact. Since 1950, this patient has been admitted every year to the
Metabolic Ward as a volunteer for metabolic studies. As a rule, he has been
discharged for two to three months every summer, and has usually spent this
time with his family.

A well-developed, well-nourished, healthy-appearing, young-looking, middle-aged
male who shows no abnormalities other than paraplegia of the lower extremities
and flaccid paralysis of the left arm. On the ward, he stays in a wheelchair during
the day, and requires the help of an orderly to be put to bed at night and in his
wheelchair in the morning. He is pleasant and seems to be well-adjusted . . .

Although he has found a fairly satisfactory solution to his problem by serving as
a permanent volunteer for metabolic studies, this is a solution which is only secure
on a year-to-year basis. It depends entirely on the availability of funds for his support and the support of a research ward. This has been pointed out to him every
year, and he and his family have been encouraged to use at least the summer
months for an attempt at vocational rehabilitation, taking advantage of his general
good health, his adequate mental faculties, and his intact right arm. This has never
been carried out to any satisfactory degree . . . As a result of this, he has spent his
summers going from relative to relative for one to two weeks at a time. This is an
unsatisfactory solution . . . It should be kept in mind that this man is now 40-years
old, that his condition has been essentially stationary for ten years, that his general
health is excellent, and that he will have to try to find a solution for twenty years
or so . . .

—From the medical chart of Leo Angelico

Disease so adjusts its man that it and he can come to terms; there are sensory appeasements, short circuits, a merciful narcosis . . .

The day routine . . . so piously observed, had taken on in his eyes . . . a character of sanctity. When . . . he considered life as lived down in the flat-land, it seemed somehow queer and unnatural.

—Thomas Mann, *The Magic Mountain*

I'm a realist . . . not an idle dreamer [Leo Angelico claimed]. And I don't kid myself into thinking that I'm going to get out of this chair and walk out of here. Because that's a lot of baloney, and I know it.

Of course, I've gotten worse as time has gone on. I can remember when it was only my foot that wouldn't work right. When I first went to the General Hospital, I was getting along very well with a cane. Over there, they put me through all sorts of tests, and gave me all sorts of pills, and put me in casts, and recommended that I use crutches—and God only knows what else. And they didn't find nothing.

But no matter what I did, I kept getting worse. Finally, I went to ———— Clinic. And there, Dr. P. wanted to operate on me. He thought that maybe as a kid I had a fall or something, that had injured my spine and made my brain slip down too far over my spinal cord. He thought if by operating he could put the brain back where it belonged and removed the pressure, why, it might be all right.

So, I went home and thought about it for a while. And I decided to go through with it—by this time, I was desperate, because there didn't seem to be anything else I could do. So he operated, and in a couple of days I come out all right. But he didn't find what he thought he would. All he found was a greyish-red mass on the spinal cord. At first he thought it was a tumor. But the biopsy said it wasn't.

So there I was . . . up against a stone wall. They couldn't do anything about removing that mass, because they figured if they started fooling around, they might paralyze me completely . . .

This, in Leo's own words, was the story of his disease—a mysterious illness that had run its course. Like the swellings in Paul O'Brian's neck, Leo's paralysis could not be reversed. Although he had been spared the ultimacy of death, Leo Angelico faced another finality—the walls and the bars of an inexorable, imprisoning condition:

Just suppose there were a brick wall over there, and you made up your mind you were going to walk right through it. Do you think it would make much difference to put mind over matter? That's how the idea of making up my mind to walk is. You know how my legs feel? As though there were twenty-five-pound cement blocks on the end of each of them!

No matter who you are, you never really get adjusted to being in the hospital all the time . . . A man wasn't made to stay inside in one place all his life. Does a canary ever feel completely happy in his cage? Does a lion enjoy being in his cage?

It was in rare instances, however, that Leo Angelico decried his fate. The days of bewilderment were over for him; the angry protest had been put aside:

I'm forty. So, obviously things happened to me before I came in here . . . I was married—I had a wife, and I had a son. But my wife divorced me. I was served with the papers the day I went to the hospital for the operation. My son will be twelve this October, I guess. I've never seen him since.

In the beginning, I was bewildered-like. I didn't know what the hell was happening to me. I didn't know what was wrong. And I kept going from doctor to doctor—and getting worse all the time. Slipping and slipping. I was like up in a cloud—and I was cross then. And bitter. I couldn't see why God had made such a big decision on me. I saw my brothers and sisters walking around so healthy-like—and I couldn't understand why it had happened to me and not to them. Things like that . . . But, after a while, I decided you've got to take what the Lord decides, and make the best of it . . .

Give up the fight, Leo advocated. Smilingly, acceptingly, "take things as they are," and live in terms of the present:

I made up my mind long ago that I wasn't going to be grumpy or cranky if I could help it. Because if you have a long face all the time, people get pretty tired of you . . . I made up my mind that I was going to take things as they are, and get as much good and benefit from them as I can. There's no point in being any other way. You're only hurting yourself . . . I just don't think very much about what could have been or what might have been if this hadn't happened. Like one fellow I know. He's always talking about what he was cheated of—what he would have been able to do that he can't now. I told him . . . he should try to make the best out of this . . .

For if you win out over rage and self-pity, the world of F-Second becomes a "wonderful" place:

You know, in all the time I've been here I've only seen maybe one or two men who I thought were disagreeable. All the rest were pretty wonderful . . . I've met some remarkable people on this ward. Like Mr. Willis. He went blind suddenly. He was a swell old gent—so cheerful and brave. Or Jackie Foote. He's a wonderful kid. Seventeen years old and sick all his life with a kidney disease. The things he does for people on this ward! I've seen him get up four times in a night to answer a patient's bell . . .

Then there are Pat and Louis. What characters they are! Pat can make a joke out of anything—and Louis's even better at it . . . Or Paul O'Brian —so young! He was planning on so many things when he left last time. Like driving his car, and going to dances . . .

The "Pauls" of the ward—Leo maintained—they're part of the reason "you can't spend time feeling sorry for yourself":

> When you see people suffering like that, you feel you're lucky. There are so many worse things than what I have, for instance. Being born blind, or an idiot. Or man-made things—like being shot up in the war. Compared to that . . . compared to a lot of guys here on the ward, I'm really well off . . . The boy down the ward is having a rough time. He had an I.V. running all night. And the one across the way's been suffering something terrible. He threw up all night. Billy's a little better, but he's far from his old self. And they say that J.W.'s a pretty sick boy . . . But as for me, I don't have any pain. My physical condition's good, and I feel well most of the time. Except for a little aching in damp weather . . . In a place like this, you always see somebody worse off than you are. So, how long can you go on thinking about your own troubles?

Wheeling himself from bed to bed, Leo made physicianly calls upon suffering and dying patients:

> Sam: Oy, oy. Leo, Leo.
> Leo: Hello, Sam. How are you?
> Sam: I feel lousy. How are you?
> Leo: I'm pretty good, Sam. I wish you felt as well as I do.
> Sam: I feel lousy. Oh, God, oh God. Oh, dear, oh, dear.
> Leo: I would have been down to see you before this, Sam. But I've been busy up there with the I.V.'s, you know.
> Sam: Oh, well, oh, well. Poor Sam, poor Sam.
> Leo: I'm sorry you're feeling so lousy, Sam.
> Sam: How is your friend, Leo?
> Leo: Who do you mean, Sam? Do you mean Will? He's fine. He comes in a couple of times a week to the clinic and to see Dr. J.
> Sam: How's Mr. Flanders?
> Leo: You know what happened to him? He's fine. Was out of the Hospital for a while and then went home to California.
> Sam: That's good.
> Leo: Have you been eating, Sam?
> Sam: Not yet.
> Leo: Are you trying?
> Sam: Yes.
> Leo: That's good. Because it's very important—Look, Sam, you get some rest, and I'll be back to see you later.
> Sam: Okay, Leo. Thanks.

Like Hans Castorp in Thomas Mann's *The Magic Mountain*, Leo Angelico concerned himself with "the severe cases and the moribund" because he did not wish to take flight from the world of disease. This is a community of sickness and death, he asserted, and we ought not to "act as though we had nothing to do with it."[2] Rather, it is our moral responsibility to draw close to our fellow patients in their time of greatest need. Nor is this the only humanitarian service we can perform as F-Seconders. There is also the "job" of experimental subject, through which we can aid our "fellow-men in need."

In the realm of the laboratory, Leo Angelico had achieved ward supremacy. Three years as "standard human assay subject"; a record of hundreds of I.V.'s; a personal I.V. pole (adapted for wheelchair use); a stop watch for timing and regulating ACTH infusions; a stack of reprints from the *New England Journal of Medicine* ("We are much indebted to Mr. Leo Angelico, whose unfailing cooperation enabled us to work out the fundamentals of intravenous administration of ACTH . . .")—all these attested to Leo's stardom. Like the "young man" in the projective story he related to a psychologist, Leo was one of Ward F-Second's "main attractions":[3]

> This is a young man . . . who has dreams of attaining great fame. As he ascends the swings above . . . he is thinking about how some day he will get the center ring . . . Finally, after working very hard, he does get to the main attraction and great fame in which we find him . . . which makes him very happy because he brings great joy to thousands . . .

Though he was doomed to a wheelchair existence, Leo's participation in "research" gave him the sense that he had "ascend[ed] . . . above" his paralyzed state, was a "main attraction," and was bringing "great joy to thousands."

> Having received IV ACTH on several hundred occasions, he shows no evidence of resistance to the material when administered by this route. Although there has been some variation in his control 17-ketosteroids, this response is still essentially predictable.

Hours of submission to his task had made Leo a "perfect research patient." "No evidence of resistance . . . response . . . essentially predictable"—Leo had become as synchronized as his stop watch:

> Where are those damn doctors? I was supposed to give them a urine

specimen and they were supposed to start at 10:30 on the button. Here it is a quarter to eleven now. Well, if they want to spoil the experiment, that's their business.

When the doctors were "off schedule" and the I.V.'s did not "run on time," Leo was very disturbed. For his certitude depended on the "daily round." There was always the possibility that at the completion of each series of assays he might be permanently discharged because his services as a research subject were no longer needed or wanted. Thus, a deferred I.V. could mean the beginning of no I.V.'s at all. And Leo Angelico wanted to "make sure" that such a day was not close at hand:

I want to keep these veins as good as I can for as long as I can. Otherwise, I'll be out of a job!

I just asked Dr. D. how long I could go on taking ACTH without overloading my adrenal glands. He said the way they did it, spacing the I.V.'s and all, it wasn't too likely to happen . . . Dr. D. said so far as they're concerned I'm still having a normal response to it. So he says maybe I could go on five years or more taking ACTH like this . . .

Unlike Paul O'Brian, who dreamed of "leaving the ward behind" and "going home for good," Leo Angelico looked with fear upon the prospect of such a journey:

Poor Paul. He was planning on so many things . . . Like he was going to a dance when he got out, he said. I don't plan like that any more. I'll tell you the truth, I get a nervous stomach every time I have to make a change. Even a little one . . . For me, this hospital and this ward are like no other hospital and no other ward I've ever been in . . . I get cold chills when I think of leaving it . . .

For Leo was a stranger in the world outside F-Second:

When I'm home and all the people in the room start talking at once—even if they're my own family—I get nervous and tired. Like one night there last summer, my brothers got into this political discussion, and it wore me out just listening. That's why I feel I'm not made to be with strong, healthy people any more.

"Seeing my brothers come in full of vim and vigor," Leo said, "listening to them going real hard at discussions—I can't really believe I ever did all the things I see them doing." The Leo Angelico who "used to go deer hunting," play an instrument and parade in a marching band, and romp with his baby son existed only in the faded snapshots he kept in a night-table drawer. "All I know now is what goes on in here."

> Paul: If Leo were suddenly to get well . . . if he were to discover that he could walk and get out of that chair . . . they'd have to do a terrific job of rehabilitation on him . . .
> Leo: If it should happen in the middle of the night that suddenly I was well, I'd get up in my pajamas and bare feet, and no matter how crazy it looked, I'd walk home just that way . . . But after that—well, I haven't really gotten much farther in my own mind . . .

Paul Versus Leo

Around the smiling immobility of Leo Angelico, a controversy raged.

For Paul O'Brian, so fiercely enamored of wellness, Leo symbolized all the "adjustments" to disease that he so bitterly opposed. "Worse than anything, I'd hate to be like he is," Paul avowed. "Not physically. I wouldn't mind that so much. But mentally, I mean . . . Such a goody-goody. So nice and sweet about everything . . ." A man ought to "get mad," Paul felt. Years of paralysis should not deaden his anger, or silence his protest against the sick-day:

> Emptiness. Nothing but emptiness. You would think that with all the years that he's been sick, and the fact that he's still a pretty young man, and that he's never been in pain . . . You would think that he would have studied something, learned something during that time. But he's never tried to. As it is, day after day passes for him in exactly the same way . . .

Life in the outside world, Paul declared, is not attuned to such a "fixed pattern." What is more, it is a ceaseless round of activities:

> At home, we just don't live in that set, routine kind of way. Like on Sundays . . . we just get dinner whenever one of us feels like starting in. And sometimes, after dinner is over, we'll sit around the table talking and smoking and drinking coffee 'til maybe 9 o'clock, or something like that . . . We don't have a fixed pattern about anything. Why, do you know, when I drive to work every morning, I try to take a slightly different route so I can see something different . . .

> Before I was sick, I went to school, and to work. I had dates, went dancing, and to parties. I just never had a minute to spare, my life was so full . . .

Illness excluded you from activities such as these. But the alternative, Paul maintained, did not lie in bondage to the sick world. Rather than offering his arm to the laboratory, Leo Angelico ought to use it for *healthy* pursuits:

> You know, I know a girl as bad—worse off than Leo is. Because she can't even sit in a wheelchair. She had only the use of one hand, too. But she taught herself to paint. And she paints these wonderful flower pictures and trays. My sister used to go to classes she taught in that sort of thing.

Taking a paintbrush in his hand, turning his head to face the window, a man should keep the well world alive within him. "But Leo doesn't really know what the outside world is like any more," Paul claimed.

> He's forgotten . . . I know a fellow at home who's completely paralyzed. Even more so than Leo. He's been in bed for years with just one tiny window to look out of. But he's not like Leo . . . He's interested in lots of things outside that one little sickroom . . .

Not Leo—He admitted that all he "knows now is what goes on in here," and that for him, "this ward and this hospital [were] like no other ward and no other hospital" on the face of the earth. "But I know for a fact," Paul argued, "that everyone on this ward isn't as nice as you think they are."

> Take Mac, for instance. I don't see what's so swell about him like you were just saying. So far as I'm concerned, he's a bore and a regular hypochondriac . . . And what about that guy from Dorchester who has the cubicle across the way from mine? He used to send his wife running to the kitchen all the time. "My Henry would like another piece of toast," she'd say . . . Me, I think there's a lot of bad things in the people here, as well as the good ones. You make it sound too rosy . . .

> Paul: Did you hear what Leo just said to me? He said, "You ought to be here at Christmas time; it's really nice then." Be here at Christmas time! That's all I need! I'm sure sorry I'm not going to be here to enjoy it!
> Leo: I didn't mean it that way, Paul. I just meant it's really pretty here. Last year they had a silver tree in the middle of the ward—and they decorated every other cubicle—and all the nurses sang carols . . .

Silver trees and singing nurses—these, Paul contended, were some of the real "dangers" of F-Second. For in the "rosy" aspects of ward life, seduction lay. Unless a man took active precautions, the hospital would "pull you in toward itself":

Leo: Why didn't Jackie come up to visit if he was in the hospital, I wonder?

Paul: Why should he have?

Leo: I don't see why he wouldn't. He liked it here in the hospital.

Paul: Well, there are ways in which I've liked it, too. But I can tell you right now, that even though I'll have to come back every week for a check-up, I'll hardly ever come up here . . . I just don't believe in it.

Paul did not "believe in" visiting the ward often or in maintaining a great deal of interest in how patients still on the ward were "coming along." These were Leo-like ways—ways of surrendering to the sick world. "I wouldn't call that the perfect adjustment by any means!"[4]

How Other Patients Regarded Leo Angelico

Many F-Seconders reacted more favorably to Leo Angelico than Paul O'Brian did. Particularly for the new patients on the ward, Leo was a "guiding light"—a tragic and radiant figure. Totally paralyzed, confined to a wheelchair, he seemed to them the very incarnation of the suffering world they had just entered. Twelve years of illness, and "no hope of recovery!" The new F-Seconder had "never dreamed of a sickness so terrible":

You take Leo. He's been sick for twelve years, he tells me. You don't realize how lucky you are until you encounter something like that.

That sickness of Leo's is a terrible thing. There's not much hope for him getting better, is there?

Believe me, he's got it rough! His back's up against the wall.

And yet, over his bleak and paralyzed fight, Leo's cheerfulness shone forth:

He's such a sweet boy, with such a good disposition. He smiles all the time.

He certainly deserves a lot of credit for the way he looks at his illness. He's very good about it . . .

The neophyte was awed by such serenity. To a man who had "never been in a hospital before . . . never been sick," an attitude of smiling acceptance seemed a "real accomplishment."

Leo Angelico was also "admired" by many F-Seconders because

"he had a sense of vocation about being sick." He was not simply reconciled to his illness. He was "doing important work" by acting as one of the "top subjects" for the Metabolic Group's experiments, and he was "very dedicated to his job."

Because he seemed to be at peace with illness, "at home" in the hospital, and to have found meaning in his predicament, Leo was "a great help in helping others adjust themselves to strange hospital life."

Although most patients "liked Leo very much," some were less enthusiastic about the kind of adjustment he had made. A number of veteran F-Seconders who had graduated beyond the turbulent first stages of illness, and who, like Paul, had come to terms with their situation in a more active, unresigned, well-world-oriented way than Leo felt that his "outlook" was too docile. "Out of the mouth of babes . . .," the old saying goes. It was a boy-patient who put this feeling into words when he was "kidding around with Leo one day":

Leo: Ray has another bright idea. This is *really* a good one!
Ray: I think if we took Leo's legs off, and got him two artificial limbs like the veterans have—Well, then, maybe he could walk.
Leo: It wouldn't work.
Ray: You know, Leo, I don't think you really want to leave here. I guess you never had it so good! But to give up, and to stop trying— that's the easy and scared way out . . .

JACKIE FOOTE: THE "PERFECT" ADJUSTMENT
("Angel with a Baseball Bat")

. . . Patient is at home now . . . He goes to baseball games for recreation, but exercise has been limited by doctors' orders. He seems very well adjusted to his illness, cooperative, cheerful, and from the stories of his previous admissions, a great favorite around the ward . . .

—From the hospital chart of Jackie Foote

Ward F-Second's most uncontroversial, luminous figure was an "angel with a baseball bat." "Sick all his life with kidney disease . . . practically raised in the hospital," Jackie Foote, a seventeen-year-old towhead, symbolized the "perfect adjustment." "*Everyone* loved Jackie. No one," it was asserted, "could be more wonderful, more perfect than he."[5]

He usually arrived at the hospital "all swollen up something terrible—his whole face, his arms, his legs." And yet, "no matter how sick he was, he was always doing something to help other patients or cheer them up." Many times, he had been known to "get up at night and help a patient, when he felt worse himself than the patient who was calling for help." Not only that, but "he was very precocious. He could reel off the names of those drugs, one after another, without any effort at all." In short, Jackie could cope so well with the challenges of illness and the hospital, that he was always ready and equipped to reach out a helping hand to others less well-adjusted than he.

"But Jackie was not an angel, by any means. He was all boy . . . He had a swell sense of humor . . . He was a happy-go-lucky kid, always joking . . ." Most characteristic of all, "he just loved baseball." He "went around all day long swinging an imaginary baseball bat." He was "natural," had "lots of interests," was "vigorous," and "thoroughly alive."

Thus, in the eyes of Ward F-Second, Jackie was more than a "hospital angel." He was a "normal," mischievous, baseball-enamored adolescent, as well. Ward F-Second's all-perfect boy stood poised between the sick world and the well world—exquisitely adjusted to the demands of both.

At the time this study was made, "for the first time in many years Jackie [had] managed to stay out of the hospital for months." "He still comes in to the O.P.D. from time to time, but the doctors now have the feeling that maybe he'll get well," patients said. They were not in favor of "having him come up and visit the ward." ("It's not a good idea . . . It just might jinx him . . .")

"Jackie ought to get well," patients felt. "He deserves to." If, in fact, he had, it would have been a triumph for "everyone" on Ward F-Second.

"Follow-Up"

The last entries in Jackie Foote's chart, and a letter from Leo Angelico tell us what subsequently happened to these patients:

This was the sixteenth admission of this 18-year-old boy who has been suffering from terminal glomerular nephritis for the past 9 months. Under medical management, the prognosis was hopeless. The homologous kidney transplant was offered as a possible therapeutic measure after the risk of the operation and the limitations of the procedure were explained to his parents . . . Before the operation . . . Jackie became quite an analgesic problem . . . Following a visit by his brother who was full of summer plans of all his friends, Jackie became very despondent, and then agitated. He slept not at all one Saturday night, and got out of bed many times, requiring someone at the bedside . . . He was unsedated, and allowed to get up in a chair . . . On July 20th, a homologous kidney transplant was performed . . . On the 27th postoperative day, after 6 days of steady downhill course despite hemodialysis, the patient became increasingly lethargic, and finally unresponsive . . . Discharged to Ward X, 10:45 a.m.

November 22, 1957.

Hi, Renée,

At last here it is. I do write once in a while. Well, how are you? I do hope everything is just fine with you. I have been thinking about you and the book you are going to write, or are writing. And how is it progressing? This year I did not go back to the Hospital, as I usually do in September. I feel a need for a change from research for a while anyway. But I do miss the Hospital very much—so much that I am forever thinking about it and the wonderful people I knew.

Four weeks ago I left my brother and family and am now in a nursing home for a while. You see, this month and next the hunting season is on for deer. And the men in our family, well, they just have to get out and into the woods and look for game.

Where are you on these lovely fall days? . . . When your story on F-Second is finished and in book form, please let me know about it. I'd love to have and read what you thought about that grand gang we knew. If I can be of help in finding addresses of people, I'd be happy to. When you have the time, please write. I'd love to hear.

My best wishes to you and yours, and happy Thanksgiving.

Your F-Second friend,

Leo [Angelico][6]

Some of the patients on Ward F-Second got well and went home to stay. But for patients like Leo Angelico, Jackie Foote, and Paul O'Brian, what *would* have been the "perfect adjustment"? There was a time when this sociologist would have been more inclined to offer a simple and somewhat partisan answer. However, partly as a consequence of the kinds of experience and learning that participant observation on Ward F-Second and in the laboratory and conference room of the Metabolic Group entailed, such pat answers and personal judgments now come harder and seem less satisfactory.

The next chapter will be devoted to the "story" of the participant observation on which this book is based: its life history, looked at from an autobiographical, methodological, and sociological point of view. I have several reasons for including this chapter.

An account of what the actual research process was like may have some humanistic value in its own right. It also will provide the reader with a basis for judging the reliability and validity of the materials which have been presented, as well as the accuracy of the interpretations which have been made. Furthermore, I hope that the attempt to describe systematically how the research was actually done, and to examine the role and way of thought of the observer, will further understanding of the relatively uncodified method of participant observation. Perhaps more systematic knowledge of what participant observation actually involves may increase the fruitfulness of research premised on this method. The next chapter is offered as one contribution to that end. Finally, since participant observation involves the assumption of a rather intricate social role, and a complex process of interaction with the individuals who are part of the social situation being studied, I hope that this account of the relationship between Ward F-Second, the Metabolic Group, and the sociologist will have some "basic" sociological value.

Notes for Chapter VI

1. Albert Camus, *The Plague* (New York: Alfred A. Knopf, 1950), p. 229.
2. Mann, *The Magic Mountain*, p. 295.
3. Card Number Seven in the Thematic Apperception Test: administered to Leo Angelico by the clinical psychologist affiliated with the Psychiatric Group of the Hospital.
4. The "tropistic" nature of the relationship between Paul O'Brian and Leo Angelico suggests that, psychologically speaking, they may have represented two sides of the same ambivalent motivation: the one rebellious, the other acquiescent. It may have been partly because Paul was involuntarily drawn toward Leo's solution that he felt compelled to attack him, and thus to strike out against all those things in Leo that he battled within himself (compliance, passivity, dependence, fixity). Analogously, Leo may have drawn close to Paul, out of his own inner needs for rebellion. ("I wanted to have as much to do with Paul as I possibly could," Leo once said.)
5. I only caught a glimpse of Jackie Foote once, during a short visit he made

to the ward one morning. Therefore, I have no way of distinguishing reality elements from projective elements in the ward's image of Jackie. Though some of the attributes ascribed to him may have been mythological in nature, it does not seem as important to try to establish this fact as to understand the symbolic meaning which they had for the patient community.

6. Since Leo Angelico and I have had no more than a Christmas card correspondence since 1952, this letter which I received from him in the Fall of 1957 came as a surprise. Perhaps one of the most interesting things about its contents is that it suggests that Leo regarded helping me with this book as a substitute for contributing to the research of the Metabolic Group. In the next chapter I will discuss my relationship to Leo Angelico in greater detail, and also indicate how patients and physicians defined my research and the book which would be based upon it.

CHAPTER VII — Ward F-Second, The Metabolic Group, and the Sociologist

... The researcher, like his informants, is a social animal. He has a role to play, and he has his own personality needs that must be met to some degree if he is to function successfully. Where the researcher operates out of a university, just going into the field for a few hours at a time, he can keep his personal social life separate from field activity ... If, on the other hand, the researcher is living out an extended period of time in the community he is studying, his personal life is inextricably mixed with his research. A real explanation, then, of how the research was done necessarily involves a rather personal account of how the researcher lived during the period of study. This account of living in the community may help also to explain the process of analysis of the data ... To some extent my approach must be unique to myself, to the particular situation, and to the state of knowledge existing when I began research. On the other hand, there must be common elements in the field research process. Only as we accumulate a series of accounts of how research was actually done will be be able to go beyond the logical-intellectual picture and learn to describe the actual research process.

— William Foote Whyte, *Street Corner Society*[1]

O N SEPTEMBER 5, 1951, announced but unprecedented, I made my first appearance on Ward F-Second. "This is Miss Fox, a sociologist, who has come to do a study on our ward." In the manner that was customary for introducing new nurses, interns, and residents to the ward, I was taken from cubicle to cubicle by the head nurse, and presented to each of the eleven patients who were hospitalized on F-Second at that time.

Later, in my borrowed white coat, I stood alone on the threshold of the ward. Before me stretched two rows of glass booths—their pink curtains drawn back to reveal a line of empty beds and a series of I.V. poles. My eyes came to rest on the furthest end of the ward, where, crowded around a card table, six men sat talking and laughing. I can remember thinking: "Why, they all look and act almost as if they were well!" I stood there wondering exactly what a participant observer "ought to do," and feeling rather intimidated by the fact that I was a woman about to make a study of an all-male community. Suddenly I found myself moving down the ward, past the cubicles, straight toward the group and their laughter. The men around the card table looked up. I was asked to join them. And, in this way, my study began.

But perhaps it really started a long time before—in August of 1945, to be exact, when I contracted poliomyelitis and became a patient myself. A severe case of polio, in both its bulbar and spinal forms, kept me in the hospital for months, and, after a long convalescence, left me with a moderate degree of residual, right-sided paralysis. At the time that I began making observations for this study, I was still an ex-patient, not only literally, but also with respect to some of the conceptions and attitudes I had. The reader should know this, so he may question and judge. For this study was not accidently conceived or undertaken. In part, it grew out of my illness: out of a hope that my personal experience and the training in social science that followed upon it would some day equip me to make the world of the hospital more feelingly and precisely understood.

It was extraordinarily opportune, then, that the hospital should have launched its Metabolic-Psychiatric Research Project at a time when I was about to embark on my thesis. Focusing their initial observations upon severe hypertensives who were undergoing adrenalectomy, research physicians and psychiatrists had designed a bold venture in the working integration of the medical and social sciences. Metabolic experts, psychiatrists, psychiatric social workers, a psychologist, and a sociologist would attempt to pool laboratory methods and clinical observations in the hope that a broader understanding of the "human organism's response to life stress" might be achieved. Adrenalectomy patients were chosen as a point of departure because they were faced with the challenge of a terminal illness, with the danger of an experimental operation that entailed the removal of vital organs, and with the fact of ultimate dependence upon adrenal extracts for their very survival.

Correlative studies were also planned. The core of the Metabolic Group's research lay in their work with diseases of the adrenal system, and in their biochemical studies of the effects of adrenal cortical extracts (artificially synthesized and exogenously administered) upon the human individual. As a consequence, there would be a rich spectrum of cases for the joint investigation at hand: primary disorders of the adrenal cortex (such as Addison's disease and Cushing's disease) and, in addition, a wide range of other maladies upon which ACTH, cortisone, and related compounds were being tried (for example, rheumatoid arthritis, gout, kidney dysfunctions, allergies, skin diseases, carcinomas, and so on). What is more, the Psychiatric Group was engaged in studying persons with heart disease who were being subjected to mitral valvuloplasty. Several such patients had developed postoperative depressions; and out of an emergency consultation, cardiologists and psychiatrists had evolved a plan for interviewing all heart surgery candidates. Though the mitral cases were not of adrenal relevance, the psychiatrists regarded them as a kind of control group. For, whereas (in contrast to the patients who had undergone adrenalectomies) they were not dependent upon artificial substances, these heart patients, like those with malignant hypertension, were afflicted with a progressive illness of special severity, for which they were undergoing an experimental operation, on a vital organ.

The first adrenalectomies had been performed, the first psychiatric interviews had been conducted, when I was asked to join this collaborative enterprise. What the function of the sociologist was to be, however, had not really been ascertained, for this was the first time that these two groups of physicians had ever had the occasion to work with an academic social scientist. Since the established role of the psychiatric social worker in the hospital was to counsel the families of patients, it had been hazily assumed that the sociologist might study the cultural milieu of the family. However, it was my special hope that some place might be found for a sociologist intent on making a study of a ward as a dynamic social system. In the course of my first meeting with the Psychiatrist-in-Chief, I expressed such a desire. His response was both enthusiastic and provocative.

At the time, the psychiatrist was conducting interviews with a patient (hospitalized on F-Second) who was bringing a great deal of ward-oriented material to his daily sessions.[2] Mr. Grimm had been admitted to the hospital because of hypertension and congestive failure. Cardiovascular and renal studies had revealed that he could not be expected to live for more than a few months; and so, as a last desperate measure, the Metabolic Group had proposed him as a candidate for total bilateral adrenalectomy. In Mr. Grimm's own words, the doctors had told him "you haven't got a chance without the operation . . . If you don't get it, boy, you're a dead duck!" And yet it was not the imminence of death that seemed to monopolize his thoughts, so much as the "Hospital" and the "Tests." For Edward Grimm, who had "never been in a hospital . . . never been sick . . . never saw none of this" was frightened by the proceedings of the strange new world in which he found himself. The therapeutic relationship he had established with the psychiatrist made it possible for him to express these fears freely—and his outpourings included vivid accounts of his life on Ward F-Second. Edward Grimm referred to himself as a ward "recruit"; he spoke of the activities of the Adrenalectomy Club; he reported on the comings and goings of some of his fellow patients. By virtue of these descriptions, the psychiatrist had gradually become aware that Ward F-Second was a kind of community. It was this growing realization that made him so receptive to my proposal to study a ward.

We agreed that F-Second (the ward on which the Metabolic Group's most important research patients were housed) should be my site of operations. But it was left to me to decide how I would present myself to that community; and to plan out my "daily round." Recalling the openness of the sick world from my own patient days— its candor and its remarkable grapevine—I felt that it would be wiser to appear on the ward as the sociologist I actually was than to assume a form of camouflage. "Passing" as a volunteer, a ward maid, a clerk —all might have their advantages, perhaps. But it seemed to me that given the knowing tendencies of the patient world (along with my own lack of talent for subterfuge), the probability of my being found out ran very high. Rather than risk the consequences of such a disclosure, then, I was willing to pay the penalties of nonconcealment. (The losses of such a frank approach, I imagined, might consist in increased restraint on the part of the patients, and in their reluctance to grant me access to certain ward intimacies.)

However, it was not purely as a classroom sociologist that I planned to make my appearance. To certify my presence in the eyes of both the patients and the medical team (I determined) I would adopt a white coat. I would be introduced to the F-Second world by those medical team members who had the closest firsthand relationships to it—the nurses. And I would make myself visibly useful by undertaking those ward tasks that did not interfere with my observations. By participating in the life of the ward in this way, I felt, I would gain more rapid and complete acceptance into the ward community. My decision to be a relatively active observer was also influenced by my inner need to do something more than just watch, listen, and take notes in the presence of such urgent human situations as one finds on a hospital ward. Thus, the role that I chose to play was one which would not only involve attributes of a thesis-writing graduate student making sociological observations but also those of an ancillary member of the medical team, helping the doctors and nurses with some of the work which had to get done.

Though my ex-patient status was an important and relevant fact, I did not intend to include it in my self-presentation. To be sure, it was a part of my inner equipment—both prejudicial and enlightening. However, because I hoped to understand the ward as a living totality—from the point of view of physicians as well as patients—I did not wish to be overly identified with either. Discretion about my former illness, I felt, would be a precaution against too closely aligning myself with patients.

But I had not accounted for a Leo Angelico. Sensitized to walking impediments by his own wheelchair plight, Leo took instant note of my subtle limp. In the outspoken way of a veteran patient, he asked me if I had been a "polio"; and with the same frankness I answered affirmatively. By the day's end, the "news" of my patienthood had traveled the length of the ward. From that time on, I was known as Miss Fox: ward sociologist and ex-patient. In the months that followed, whenever my ability to "really understand" the ward was questioned, the answer of the old-timers was always the same: "But Miss Fox *does* understand—because she was a patient herself!" In this respect, then, it was my own experience of illness and hospitalization (more than any other single fact) that speeded my acceptance by the men of Ward F-Second and validated my study in their eyes.

What this demonstrates is a basic property not only of participant observation but of social interaction in general. The roles that a person assumes—the ways they are defined, structured, and played out—are never completely self-determined. Rather, they emerge as the joint product of the dynamic relationships between an individual and other persons with whom he or she is interacting.

To the best of my knowledge, the patients of Ward F-Second saw me in the following ways. I was an ex-patient: one who had gotten well enough to "go home for good." Nevertheless, I had returned to the hospital to make a study. In this respect, I was like "most of the fellows who [had been] on the ward for a long time":

> They all want to come back, because they know what they've been through here. And they can never forget. It's always there deep inside them. So they feel for those who are still here . . .

I was a "nice girl," a "sweet person" who did many things to help patients. "Just talking to [you] really did [us] some good," patients said. I "worked hard" on the ward, cranking beds, carrying trays, distributing linen and mail. In addition, I could be counted on to arrange parties, write letters for patients, and make small purchases for them in the "outside world." Because I did all these things, was serious about my work, and "cared" about patients, F-Seconders commented, the hours I worked were as long, if not longer, than those of the doctors and nurses. I was "not a doctor exactly," but I was professionally connected with them: I wore a white coat, I made rounds with the doctors, and I attended some of their meetings. Above all, like the physicians of the Metabolic Group I was "doing research"—a "new kind of study"—out of which would come a "scientific" and "understanding" book, which would "tell the story of Ward F-Second" to many other patients and physicians, and to "people who don't know what the hospital is like, because they've never been sick."

In good part, the ways in which the patients of F-Second conceived of me were determined by the system of roles which existed before I appeared on the ward, and by some of the attitudes and values on which the patient community was founded. My role was compared to those of patients, physicians, nurses, and social workers —and perceived by F-Seconders as having something in common with each. The fact that I was a veteran patient returning to the hospital, and that I was conducting research, fitted the approved ways of the ward. Thus it was possible for the patients on F-Second to place me in a social context which had positive meaning for them. This was more important in gaining admission to the inner life of Ward F-Second than any personal qualities I may have possessed.

On the whole, the way I was identified by patients worked in my favor, both in the sense that patients seemed to like and approve of me, and that they were inclined to share most of the intimacies of their ward life with me. There was one notable exception. Because the men of F-Second regarded me as a "nice girl," they excluded me from what they called their "torrid sessions." ("We had a pretty hot one last night. The three of us sat around talking and telling jokes until about twelve o'clock.") On the grounds that this kind of "male talk and joking" primarily "about sex" was too masculine and obscene to have "ladies present," these sessions were defined as off bounds for me.[3]

It is significant to note, however, that although patients did not allow me to be present when such sessions took place, they did tell me when they occurred. So far as I know, this is not a confidence which they shared with other members of the medical team—male or female. This suggests that I was no more impeded by being a woman on a male ward than other female personnel, that patients did not exclude me from events which they shared with other members of the medical team, and that they granted me at least partial access to certain aspects of their ward life that they did not divulge to other non-F-Seconders.

As I reread the notes I took during my first days on the ward, I am surprised to discover that there is a sense in which I recorded most of what I eventually came to know about the men of F-Second. In the earliest pages of my field notes a "new" patient, who is undergoing the acute stresses of initiation into the sick world, pours out his troubles. ("I'm not like the other fellows. I can't act the way they do: happy and making the best of everything. I just haven't been able to take all this . . .") Paul O'Brian and Leo Angelico are deeply engaged in their mortal combat:

Paul: Do you know what Leo said to me? He said, "You ought to be here at Christmas time." At Christmas time! That's all I need!

Leo: I didn't mean it that way, Paul. I just meant . . .

And Jackie Foote, the ward's most "perfect" boy, is eulogistically noted: "You should see that kid . . . He comes in all swollen up something terrible . . . Yet, no matter how sick he is, he's always doing something to help other patients, or cheer them up . . . And he's such a happy-go-lucky kid, too. Always kidding around and swinging a baseball bat."

What is more, F-Seconders are hard at work trying to coerce "that Peters kid" out of the "sack." "Every night until eleven or twelve o'clock," there is a "session in one of the cubicles." The "joke" is omnipresent:

Pat: My wife is going to love these casts I have on! Every time I turn over at night, I'll fracture *her* legs! I can see it now—O'Connor'll be sleeping on the couch . . . Jesus, if they made these things any longer, they'd have to cut a drop seat in them, or something!

Mr. A.: Where are they wheeling him? Is he dead?

Mr. O.: No, he couldn't be dead. The bottle wouldn't be over his bed, if he were!

In the bright sunshine of the ward porch, the laughing prayer is heard:

It all started with that Adam . . . running around in that Garden having a good time, and playing with that fig leaf and all! He didn't have to spend his days here like we do . . . sitting around with a bum knee, or in a wheel chair . . .

And one morning, a human "raffle" is held.

Finally, the notes I took during my first days on the ward refer time and again to the unforeseen death of a certain Walter Cousins. A stunned patient community talks on and on about Walter's blood pressure and his adrenalectomy—about his feats of strength, his knowledge, his press clippings. If death can come to the President of the Adrenalectomy Club, the ward members decide, then this operation they're doing "isn't going to work for anyone!"

From the very start, then, my notes contain almost all the components of the ward picture I was ultimately to assemble. However, at the time that I recorded these observations, I was not yet aware of the patterned interconnections between them. At what point did I begin to see the ward in a coherently structured way? In the sense of month-and-day, I cannot really answer that question. But I do know that the so-called "understanding" of F-Second which I eventually attained was not simply the result of coming to know more about the ward in a cognitive sense. It also involved a process of attitude-learning (very much akin to what social scientists mean when they refer to the process of "socialization").[4]

As I look back on my experiences as a participant observer, it seems to me that I underwent an initiation like that of a new F-Seconder. For, in spite of my own prior experiences as a patient, I was not fully prepared for the challenges of a Ward F-Second. Plunged (albeit as an "observer") into a world in which serious, chronic illness, experiments on human subjects, and even death were common occurrences, I had to learn to come to terms with the same stresses that confronted the patients. A patient who was hospitalized on the ward at the time that I began this study once told me that he can remember how "serious" I was at first. "Once or twice there I was even afraid you'd bust out cryin'," he said. "After a while, though," he continued, "you began to understand and take things, so you were able to laugh and make jokes like the rest of the fellows."

As these comments suggest, my ways of coming to terms with the stresses of F-Second were not very different from the ones patients had evolved. When the ward was faced with an emergency, for example, I would find myself wheeling carts, carrying trays, answering bells for all I was worth. (Certainly, my "busyness" and the "take up thy bed" behavior of the ward are closely related.) I became so skilled at macabre humor that when Paul O'Brian lay dying, I was the only person on the staff (with the exception of one nurse) who was "able"[5] to joke with him in the way he so desperately needed. By day, I read medical charts; by night, medical books—and my expertise grew. I assembled a folder labeled "The Press," in which I stored an expanding collection of articles about F-Seconders. And—like the patients who kept elaborate records and charts—I was forever "writing things down." The studying, the collating, the chronicling, of course, were all essential to my role as researcher. At the same time, I feel, they also helped me to achieve and maintain equanimity in the face of the stresses of the ward. To some extent, the comparability between my ways of coming to terms and those of patients is probably attributable to the fact that the men of F-Second implicitly taught me to deal with the strains of their "hospital life" as they did.

The procession of F-Seconders who appear in my field notes include just about every patient who was hospitalized on the ward during the period over which I made observations. (When I checked the names of F-Seconders in my field notes against the daily hospital census of patients admitted and discharged, I discovered that the only patients I "missed" were several who arrived on F-Second *in extremis,* were placed in one of the rooms adjacent to the ward, and died within one or two days' time.)

Although almost every F-Seconder found his way into my field notes, some patients contributed more to my understanding of the ward than others. For example, patients like Leo Angelico and Paul O'Brian were obviously very important in shaping my view of the ward, and I established an especially close relationship with them. However, this was not simply or primarily because I felt a greater personal affinity for these patients at the outset, or they for me. As we have seen, Leo Angelico and Paul O'Brian were "important patients" in the patient community—two of its chief spokesmen. Partly as a result of their special statuses and roles they were somewhat more inclined to talk to me than other patients were, and, conversely, they attracted my particular attention.[6]

In addition to individual F-Seconders, there were also certain groups or classes of patients who significantly affected my conception of Ward F-Second—its stresses and ways of coming to terms:

—Veteran patients of considerable seniority and status, because they personified, articulated, and enforced some of the predominant norms of Ward F-Second.

—New patients, because in the process of undergoing the strains of socialization into the sick role and the ward community, they gave voice to the stresses of Ward F-Second.

—Boy patients, terminally ill patients, and patients undergoing acute psychotic episodes, both because they were less inhibited about expressing some of the underlying sentiments of the ward, and because their presence on F-Second elicited deeply-felt reactions from other patients.

A great deal of what I have said about participant observation implies that this method of research entails two problems in particular. These are the problem of the observer's emotional relationship to what he is studying (the kind of balance between involvement and objectivity or detachment which he strikes); and the problem of "observer effect" (the extent to which the observer modifies what he is attempting to understand in its "natural state"). These problems, of course, are not unique to the participant observer. They are relevant to scientific observation of any sort. However, because the method of participant observation consists of interacting with human beings for the purpose of studying them, it raises these problems in an especially acute and difficult form.[7] Before moving on to consider some of my experiences as observer of the Metabolic Group, I would like to try to give a systematic account of the problems of involvement and observer effect which I experienced in relation to the patient community, and some of the ways in which I attempted to resolve them.

I have already indicated that I feel there were certain aspects in which my own experiences as a patient helped me to attain an empathic but relatively objective understanding of Ward F-Second, and other respects in which these experiences made it more difficult to reach such an understanding. On the one hand, I arrived on Ward F-Second with a greater amount of sympathetic knowledge of "what it was like" to be a patient on a ward like F-Second than I would have had if I had "never been sick [or] seen any of this before" I began my study. To the extent that I had succeeded in coming to terms with my own analogous experience, illness and hospitalization probably gave me emotional resources for dealing with the stresses of Ward F-Second that I might not otherwise have been able to mobilize. On the other hand, the fact that I was an ex-patient made me more susceptible to becoming overly identified with patients, and deeply affected by what happened to them. It also inclined me to react in a somewhat partisan manner to the various ways in which patients came to terms on Ward F-Second. Initially, I had a tendency to approve of the active, defiant, well-world-oriented patterns of a Paul O'Brian, and to react somewhat less favorably to the compliance of a Leo Angelico, and to his sense of vocation about serving as a research subject.

This contributed to a sort of crisis through which I passed in the process of acquiring greater objectivity. It occurred in connection with the death of Paul O'Brian, for whom I felt "natural" sympathy, with whom I had a close relationship, and by whose bed I stood for hours on the day that he died—holding his hand and joking with him. Paul's death not only shocked and grieved me. It also brought me face to face with the disquietude I had been feeling about the meaning of what I was doing and its justification.

As an observer on Ward F-Second, I had been granted access to some of the "most private acts that [men] can perform,"[8] and to some of the deepest feelings they can experience. In return for this privilege, it seemed to me, all that I was doing was looking, listening, and taking notes, with the vague hope that, someday, a Ph.D. dissertation still to be written might become a book. Paul O'Brian's death brought these feelings to a head, with the result that for a while, my role as participant observer was very disturbing to me, emotionally and morally. At this particular time it seemed to me that if there were any kind of book at all that ought to be written about the ward, it should be a novel: a work that would feelingly portray the predicament of F-Seconders, rather than dehumanize it as a conceptualized, academic social science study was sure to do.

I have described this critical point in my research for several reasons. First, in their published accounts of "what it was like" to be a participant observer, a number of other social scientists report comparable incidents and feelings.[9] This suggests that such occurrences represent a common, if not inevitable, phase in this kind of research. It might help other participant observers to know this in advance of undertaking a study, as it helped me in retrospect. Second, what I have described dramatizes the fact that the degree and kind of objectivity that a participant observer needs in order to carry out a valid piece of social science research are not ready made and perfected when a study begins. Rather they are progressively achieved as the study unfolds.

In spite of the way that I felt at the time of Paul O'Brian's death, I did not abandon the study I had undertaken, or recast it in the form of a prospective novel. The professional training through which I had come to think in terms of sociological concepts and theories, my commitment to the field of social science and its advancement, the value I placed on striving to meet the norms of scientific objectivity—all helped to carry me over this difficult period.

I continued to observe, to take notes, and to think sociologically about what I was seeing, hearing, and recording.

Keeping field notes was not only a technical necessity. It also enabled me to achieve a more detached kind of perspective on the events which I observed. No matter how wearying my day on F-Second, or how profoundly it involved me, every night I attempted to reproduce it on paper. That writing process was a cathartic experience; it required a certain amount of intellectualization; and it forced me to make observations on my observations.

The passage of time was also conducive to the development of greater objectivity. My first unbroken, five-months-long period in the field gave me ample time to undergo the process of cognitive- and attitude-learning (or socialization) through which I acquired a more detached understanding of Ward F-Second. My subsequent withdrawal from the field made it possible for me to achieve greater emotional as well as physical distance from the ward. The second continuous period of five months which I spent on F-Second had something like the value a genuine restudy of the ward might offer. A more objective and equipoised observer returned to the ward at a later time to do a follow-up study and to see which of her earlier perceptions and interpretations still held, and which no longer seemed to pertain.

In the course of these two sustained periods of observation I was exposed to so many points of view that it became increasingly difficult for me to take an opinionated stand on the things I saw, heard, and experienced. For example, as time went on, I became less inclined to feel that the adjustment of a Paul O'Brian was in any way "better" than that of a Leo Angelico. For both Paul and Leo told me the story of their illness in the context of many details about themselves and their life-histories. I heard each discuss the other. I was witness to their many encounters and debates. I was exposed to the comments of the patients who glorified Leo, and to the rejoinders of those who were more skeptical about his adjustment. In the face of such diverse points of view, my original perspective came to seem too simple. I began to realize that Paul O'Brian's refusal to surrender could bring much added suffering to a man who would never get well. Gradually, I also came to see that the alternatives to Leo's

I.V.-taking were all as ungratifying and meaningless as "painting flowers on a tray."

It seems to me, then, that as time goes on, the observer becomes more litmus-like—capable of registering without judging most of what occurs. Perhaps I never actually achieved what would be considered an ideal degree of dispassion. However, I do feel that the process which I have described (along with the data independent of my observations which I collated from hospital charts, correspondence files, published articles, and reports) enabled me to attain sufficient objectivity to make the picture of F-Second set forth in these pages an accurate and true one.

It is harder, of course, to determine the effect which my presence on F-Second as an observer may have had upon patients than to account for the impact they had upon me.

Some of the things patients said indicate that simply by being an interested listener I occasionally made a therapeutic "difference":

Talking to you helps . . .

Why, my headache seems to be gone completely now! That talking to you really did me some good!

You cheer the whole ward up . . .

You spread light . . .

As already indicated, I was not merely a passive observer who listened, looked, and recorded. In many ways I played an active role in the life of the ward. My chief form of participation consisted of talking with patients, individually and in groups. Most of the conversations in which I engaged were initiated and directed by the patients themselves. Often they were already in progress when I appeared in a cubicle or on the porch, and I was asked to join "the gang" in much the same way that another F-Seconder would have been. My general policy was to intervene as little as possible in what patients said to one another in my presence, and to allow the remarks which patients specifically addressed to me at such times, as well as the confidences they privately shared with me, to occur spontaneously.

However, there were many occasions on which I engaged in a more active and purposive kind of talking with patients. Here my role as interested listener changed to that of interviewer: questioning patients in order to obtain a point of information or an explanation, probing for below-the-surface feelings, attitudes, and beliefs. Thus, a great deal of my active participation and intervention on Ward F-Second took the form of *in situ* focused interviewing.

The issue that remains is: to what extent and in precisely what ways did my looking, listening, questioning, and various ward activities modify the community I was trying to study? How greatly did the F-Second which I observed differ from the ward community which existed before I arrived, and to what extent could such differences be attributed to my presence? Truthfully, I cannot definitely answer these questions. I can only point to the following pertinent facts. My role as participant observer was compatible with the system of roles and values which existed on Ward F-Second before I appeared. I spent a long enough period of time on the ward so that I became a familiar, accepted (one might almost say "institutionalized") part of the ward. Many patients seemed to feel that I "really understood" what it was like to be an F-Seconder. These are scraps of evidence which suggest that in spite of the differences my presence on F-Second may have made in the life of the ward, I did not disrupt or change so greatly as to invalidate my findings, the community of which I became a part.

Though my knowledge of the patient community grew out of my presence on F-Second, this was not the case with the physicians of the Metabolic Group. Their work was not restricted to the ward. Only Morning and Evening Rounds brought them to F-Second as a body—though from time to time during the day, individual members of the Group would appear to issue personal orders to the ward staff, to administer experimental procedures, or merely to make a physicianly call on a patient or two. On such occasions, along with other F-Second personnel, I followed these physicians into the cubicles and about the ward. Not until I had spent a whole month on F-Second, however, did I become more than a Metabolic Group shadow.

On October 5 the Metabolic and Psychiatric Groups held their first joint meeting. The personnel of both teams were presented to each other, and plans for the year's collaborative research were drawn up. Along with all the other introductions, it was stated that Miss Fox, who had probably been noticed up on Ward F-Second, was a sociologist—and that her part in the joint program being launched would be to make a study of the ward as a community. That announcement excited an immediate response. After the meeting, several members of the Metabolic Group stopped to talk with me. To my great surprise, it was not curiosity about my project that they wished to express, so much as enthusiasm for it. Research physicians don't know their patients as "people," they assured me; a study like yours is "needed."

This was the kind of opening for which I had been waiting. As I have indicated, my first month on F-Second had not brought me into meaningful contact with the Metabolic Group. My view of the ward had been almost exclusively confined to the world of the patient. The fact that I was only assembling a half-picture had begun to concern me. But it was not until after the first joint conference that I found a way of correcting my bias.

Encouraged by the response of several members of the Metabolic Group to the idea of a "ward sociologist," I approached Dr. D., the young physician who supervised the Group, and told him about my research difficulties. Though in some respects my study was progressing nicely, I explained, I felt that its conspicuous weakness lay in the fact that it was too patient-slanted. What I needed most of all, I said, was the help of his Group, so that I might come to see F-Second from their point of view, as well. Without any reservation Dr. D. granted me full admission to the activities of the Metabolic Group— though he warned me that it would take "spiritual fortitude" to "spend any time at all" with them.

It was understood as a result of our conversation that I should not hesitate to ask the members of the Group questions, to call upon them, or to join them at any time. And it was with special enthusiasm, I felt, that Dr. D. invited me to take part in the Group's Evening Rounds. These meetings, as he described them, were a kind of workshop, at which cases were reviewed, research discussed, and future plans laid out. "All according to how incendiary they get," he added, "the meetings can last anywhere from half an hour to half the night."

I was pleased by Dr. D.'s general receptivity, of course, and the importance he seemed to attach to the Group's evening meetings excited my particular interest. These sessions represented one of the only occasions when the members of the Metabolic Group were all assembled in the same place at the same time, I reasoned. Dr. D.'s description of the nature of these meetings suggested that they would include a significant amount of discussion about daily clinical and research developments in the cases of patients on Ward F-Second. He also implied that these meetings characteristically involved an animated, and often controversial, exchange of opinions and ideas. For all these reasons I decided to attend Evening Rounds as faithfully as the members of the Metabolic Group did.

Perhaps more than any other single event, these sessions provided the sort of "medical education" I had been seeking. They helped me to develop an informed, sympathetic understanding of some of the problems which the Metabolic Group faced, and gave me an opportunity to observe directly some of the important ways the Group had evolved for dealing with these problems. For I soon discovered that Evening Rounds were not simply devoted to the official business of the day. To be sure, the members of the Group reported on every patient, and summarized all laboratory findings. But the meetings served other purposes as well. At these gatherings— through the debate, the gripe, the frank admission of discouragement, the joke, and the wager—the physicians of the Metabolic Group expressed their feelings about the problems they collectively faced, and tried to deal with them. As a consequence, when they left their conference each evening, they were better prepared emotionally, as well as intellectually, to meet the challenges of the next day of their "laboratory life."

Certainly it ought not to be taken for granted that the physicians of the Metabolic Group would permit, and even encourage, me to be present at their Evening Rounds. I was not a medical professional of any sort. I was a woman, and the members of the Metabolic Group were all men. No physicians (male or female) other than the members of the Group themselves were invited to attend these meetings regularly. And, as my description of these sessions indicates, in the privacy of their conference room, the members of the Metabolic Group expressed some of their most intimate feelings about their professional activities and responsibilities. This special privilege the Metabolic Group extended to me, their general cordiality, and their manifest interest in the research I had undertaken were all related to the ways in which they conceived of my role.

To begin with, the members of the Metabolic Group thought of me as a person with some expert knowledge and technical skill—a fellow scientist—who was conducting what they regarded as an "original and independent study." Because they were young investigators themselves, they were very receptive to new ideas and inclined to react favorably to any person who was seriously engaged in research of any sort. The particular nature of my study and my method of research (active, face-to-face observation) contributed to my positive reception by the Metabolic Group in a number of additional ways. Apparently "[my] kind of study" made these physicians feel that they were "doing something" about the nonlaboratory, "human aspects" of their problems as clinical investigators, and also helped to make their concern about these problems and the ways they had evolved for coping with them seem more legitimate in their eyes.

As we have seen, the members of the Metabolic Group were troubled by "the business of not being able to make patients better," and by some of the conditions and experiences to which they had to subject patients on whom they conducted research. To be sure, they joked with one another about their concern. ("The trouble with you is that you worry about all sorts of inconsequential things like the welfare of patients . . .") But the real proof of their "caring" lay in the fact that by making friends and colleagues of their patients, confiding in them, celebrating them, and according them privileged treatment, the physicians of the Metabolic Group tried to compensate patients for not being able to make them better, and for some of the discomforts and risks they underwent as research subjects. The members of the Metabolic Group were proud of some of the "extra things" they did for their patients. ("A good bed, wonderful food, fantastic medical care, and everything that goes with it, for only $12 a day—and sometimes free . . .") However, they were also somewhat uneasy and embarrassed about these indications of their solicitude. The physicians of the Metabolic Group were inclined to feel that it was inappropriate to be so concerned about patients. As men of science, they ought to be cool, objective, and detached as they went about their work.

Having a sociological investigator in their midst helped these physicians to deal with their concern and disquietude about it in a way that made it more acceptable to them. I was perceived as making a "scientific study" of some of the "human problems" that disturbed them the most. Thus, in supporting my research, the members of the Metabolic Group found a way in which they could show—and still be thoroughly "scientific"—how much they really cared about their patients. In the context of furthering my study, both directly and indirectly, they admitted to "caring a lot." They also invited me to "notice the humor in [their] meetings" and the "betting" they did. "Very unscientific ways of acting," they termed them. However, so long as I systematically observed these nonrational ways they had evolved for dealing with some of their problems, these means had greater legitimacy for the members of the Metabolic Group. For the physicians could think of these aspects of their behavior as objective data, which were "interesting" and had research importance.

The physicians of the Metabolic Group were even more enthusiastic about my study of the patients on Ward F-Second. In a way, they seemed to regard me as their representative on the ward: an affiliate of the Group whose specific research task was to study the problems of the patients. The mere fact of my presence on the ward and the existence of my study signified to the physicians of the Metabolic Group that the problems of their patients were being dealt with scientifically. Not that I instituted any measures. But one of the values underlying the Metabolic Group's own research was the belief that scientific investigation is a form of action in its own right, as well as a means of finding more effective ways of solving important problems. This made it possible for the physicians of the Metabolic Group to regard my study of their patients as a scientific way of implementing the concern they felt about them, and was one of the major reasons for which they supported my observations on Ward F-Second as wholeheartedly as they did.

Thus, my relationship to the physicians of the Metabolic Group, like my relationship to their patients, was facilitated and structured by the system of roles of which they were a part, the attitudes and values to which they subscribed, the problems they faced, and their established means for dealing with these problems. However, whereas the primary attitude-learning challenge I faced as participant observer in the patient community was one of achieving greater detachment, the reverse was true of my relationship to the Metabolic Group. It took me a while to develop a sympathetic understanding of their problems, and to appreciate how deeply they felt about some of the difficulties which confronted them.

There are at least three sets of factors which account for this fact. First, there was the problem (already described) of finding a suitable physical base from which the very busy and mobile physicians of the Metabolic Group could be observed. Second, as a graduate student in a field other than medical science, I felt somewhat constrained at first about questioning and interviewing the members of the Group. This was both because their professional status was greatly superior to mine, and because I had to acquire a considerable amount of medical knowledge before I understood enough about the various things I saw the physicians of the Metabolic Group do and heard them say to ask meaningful questions of them. The fact that the Group was not engaged in "ordinary medical practice," and that their research was based on very sophisticated biochemical, physiological, and pharmacological knowledge, as well as intricate laboratory methods, meant that the process of learning I had to undergo was an intricate and protracted one. It took even more learning and a longer period of time before I acquired enough knowledge to realize that many of the technically-phrased discussions of the Metabolic Group were as much concerned with moral problems connected with their research on patients as with its metabolic and endocrinological aspects. Once I had made the Metabolic Conference Room the primary site of my observations, and had acquired enough confidence and medical knowledge to ask members of the Group questions and to penetrate their technical discussions sufficiently to "hear" the attitudes and values they were expressing in this way, my sympathetic identification with them grew as rapidly as my intellectual grasp of their problems, stresses, and ways of coming to terms. Thus, the passage of time and the acquisition of knowledge (two of the factors which enabled me to develop a more objective understanding of their patients) also made it possible for me to attain a more feeling kind of understanding of the physicians of the Metabolic Group than I originally had.

The effects which my observations had upon the Metabolic Group have already been suggested. Talking to the sociologist provided these physicians with an additional channel for expressing the tension and concern they experienced in connection with their work as research physicians. Defining some of the ways they felt and acted as data for my study increased the objectivity with which the members of the Group regarded their own attitudes and behavior, and thus made them seem more appropriate to them. Supporting my study of Ward F-Second also gave the physicians of the Metabolic Group another acceptable way of showing they cared about their patients, and a sense of doing something remedial about those problems and stresses of their patients of which they were aware and for which they felt partly responsible.

Although my presence and activities as a participant observer affected the physicians of the Metabolic Group in these various ways, I do not think, on the whole, that this impaired or distorted my understanding of their problems and their means of coping with them. However, there are two concrete respects in which my effect upon the Metabolic Group may have prejudiced my findings. To the extent that "telling the sociologist about it" became an acceptable way for the physicians of the Metabolic Group to deal with their stresses, my presence may have stimulated expressions of concern on their part. It is also possible that by serving as "scientific justification" for their humor and game of chance, I may have been responsible for their more frequent occurrence. On the other hand, it was chiefly because of these ways in which my study helped the physicians of the Metabolic Group to come to terms with their situation that I was able to learn as much as I did about their problems and stresses. Thus, it is my feeling that the degree and kind of "observer effect" which I had on the Group yielded research advantages which were greater than the disadvantages it may also have entailed.

A detailed, systematic account of the processes by which a participant observer gradually makes organized sense out of what he sees, hears, and becomes a part of is a worthy subject for another whole book. However, before concluding this chapter, I would at least like to mention and illustrate some of the components which I think were essential to the ordered picture of Ward F-Second and the Metabolic Group represented by this book. One of my primary reasons for doing so is to take a stand against the nonanalytic, almost mystical way in which many social scientists, as well as lay persons, regard the processes by which a participant observer makes inferences and gradually builds them into meaningfully interconnected findings. There is a general tendency to think of a study based on participant observation as largely the product of an esoteric, personal kind of clinical talent on the part of the field worker, who is conceived to be endowed with qualities usually referred to as "sensitivity," "intuition," and "empathy." We have already indicated that "sympathetic understanding" is certainly one of the important constituents of participant observation. However, as we have shown, this is not merely an inborn, subjective characteristic of the observer. It is just as much a role attribute which he progressively learns in the course of making a study. This is not to imply that coherent, sociologically relevant observations follow automatically from role-patterned "methodological sympathy."[10] These can result only from the ability of the observer to "think sociologically" about what he is seeing and hearing: a capacity which he develops through professional training in the theories, concepts, facts, and methods of the field of sociology.

It is rather interesting that some of the ways in which my participation in the life of Ward F-Second affected my attitudes and behavior brought me my earliest insights. It was because through my vicarious experiences as observer some of the same things happened to me as to the patients themselves that I was able to forge my first links between the events I recorded. The manner in which I "discovered" the humor of F-Second, for example, beautifully illustrates this process. At a nonhospital gathering one evening, I caught myself in the act of making a macabre joke, and I can remember speculating on the source of my unlikely new talent. The next morning, as I moved about F-Second, for the first time I noticed how much of the Ward's conversation was phrased in the language of the grim joke, and how often I responded in kind. Without realizing it, I had learned to speak to the men of F-Second in the same way that they talked to each other. Long before this insight occurred, my field notes contained many samples of ward humor. But it was only by virtue of a self-observation that I became sufficiently aware of its prevalence to regard it as a phenomenon central to my study.

What is involved here is the observer's conscious recognition of the fact that a recurrent, patterned form of behavior characteristic of a group of individuals is significant. Self-observation is only one of the means by which such recognition is achieved.

Occasionally, a patient on F-Second or a member of the Metabolic Group would explicitly direct my attention to a phenomenon which he felt ought to be part of my study. ("I wonder if you've noticed the humor in our meetings," Dr. D. once asked me, "or the betting game we play.") More frequently, a particularly vivid or apt phrase which a physician or patient used to describe an event or type of behavior "caught my ear" and indirectly helped to make me aware of a patterned and significant phenomenon:

We celebrate our patients . . .

Mac ought to have a star over his cubicle . . .

Leo has a sense of vocation about being sick . . .

Statements like these were especially audible to me. This was not simply because they involved a colorful or interesting use of language. More importantly, they were *ad hoc* concepts: succinct descriptions and interpretations of a whole series of observations which had been made by the physicians or patients who uttered them. As such, they helped me to find patterned interconnections between some of the discrete observations I had been recording, to recognize new constellations, and to begin to understand their meaning.

However, I would not have been able to hear what physicians and patients explicitly and implicitly told me, observe things on my own, record such events as data in my field notes, or interpret their significance, if I had not had working ideas to guide me. As a trained sociologist, I was able to draw upon established theories and concepts of social science for such ideas. For example, conceptions such as the following were essential to my study:

—Physicians and patients comprise a social system.[11]

—Sickness is a social role with certain patterned attributes which like those of all roles have to be learned.[12]

—Magic (of which gambling is a functional equivalent), science, and religion are a "three-cornered constellation." They are distinct but interconnected modes of adjustment which enable men to meet uncertainty, attain rational mastery of their environment, and deal with problems of meaning respectively.[13]

These ideas and many others derived from the social sciences constituted my basic equipment and endowed me with a kind of inner architecture. They sensitized and alerted me to the occurrences and phenomena I have reported in this book. They gave order and structure to what I was seeing and hearing. And (sometimes almost simultaneously with the making of an observation, sometimes in retrospect) such working ideas enabled me to analyze and interpret the significance of what I perceived.

Along with such theories and concepts, a number of other factors helped me to understand and assign meaning to what I witnessed. To a great extent, of course, my interpretations were influenced and shaped by the direct testimony of the persons whom I observed:

> Our humor is a kind of protective device. If we were to talk seriously all the time and act like a bunch of Sir Galahads or something, we just couldn't take all this . . .

This highly conceptualized explanation of one of the important functions of the Metabolic Group's humor was spontaneously offered to me by one of its members. This kind of testimony was exceptional. More typically, I learned what various events and ways of acting meant to physicians and patients more indirectly, by listening to what they said to one another, or more actively, by asking questions of them at the time when a particular incident took place, and by conducting semiformal, intensive, ex post facto interviews.

I also relied on various kinds of nonverbal evidence. For example, I noticed that many patients kept records of their symptoms and medications, and that they enjoyed using graphs and hospital forms for such records as well as for less serious jottings. Several times I saw patients borrow a stethoscope from a physician and with interested, proud expressions on their faces, listen to their own hearts. I noticed that a number of patients had pictures of members of the Metabolic Group in their night-table drawers. In reading the correspondence between Howard Oates, a patient with Addison's disease, and the physicians of the Metabolic Group, I was struck by the fact that he often signed his letters, "Howard Oates, A.D." and that he devoted almost a whole letter to jokingly describing how "Dr. Oates" (himself) had diagnosed and treated a G.I. upset which he had experienced. Taken together, along with many things I heard patients say, such behavioral indicators gradually led me to the conclusion that the patients of Ward F-Second were deeply identified with the physicians of the Metabolic Group.

I also found that a close appraisal of the context within which certain behavior occurred (and the circumstances under which it did not) was another important aid to interpretation. For example, observing that the "game of chance" which the physicians of the Metabolic Group played was most likely to take place when an experiment was important and the degree of uncertainty connected with it was high, and that such betting was usually accompanied by joking banter, gave me important clues regarding its functions. It also helped me to see that it was closely related to the characteristic humor of the Group.

Finally, self-observation and analysis contributed to some of the interpretations at which I progressively arrived. For example, once I discovered that like the physicians and patients I was observing, I frequently made grim jokes, it was possible for me to ask myself how this had come about and why, to notice the sorts of occasions on which I was inclined to make such jokes, and to observe what such joking seemed to "do for me" emotionally. This sort of introspection gave me provisional insights into some of the possible meanings and functions humor might have for patients and physicians: interpretations which I then tried to rule out or verify through observing them.

In sum—what I have tried to suggest is that participant observation is a rational method of research based on specifiable techniques of observation, highly patterned, carefully controlled social interaction with the persons being studied, and the dynamic application of social scientific knowledge and reasoning to what is being observed.

An "old" F-Seconder once introduced me to a new arrival on the ward in the following way: "This is Miss Fox. She's not a doctor exactly. She's not a patient exactly. But she falls somewhere in between." This is the most succinct, final description of participant observation on Ward F-Second and in the laboratory and conference room of the Metabolic Group that can be offered.

NOTES FOR CHAPTER VII

1. Enlarged edition. (Chicago: University of Chicago Press, 1955), pp. 279-280. The quotation which makes up the epigraph to this chapter was excerpted from a richly detailed and very enlightening essay on the process of research which went into "The Evolution of *Street Corner Society*," which comprises the Appendix to the enlarged edition of Whyte's book (pp. 279-358). In addition to this essay, the following accounts of participant observation helped me to better understand my research experiences observing the Metabolic Group and Ward F-Second: Benjamin D. Paul, "Interview Techniques and Field Relationships," in A. L. Kroeber, ed., *Anthropology Today: An Encyclopedia Inventory* (Chicago: University of Chicago Press, 1953), pp. 430-439; Morris S. Schwartz and Charlotte G. Schwartz, "Problems in Participant Observation," *American Journal of Sociology*, Vol. 60 (January, 1955), pp. 344-354; Arthur Vidich, "Participant Observation and the Collection and Interpretation of Data," *American Journal of Sociology*, Vol. 60 (January, 1955), pp. 354-60; William Foote Whyte, "Observational Field-Work Methods," in Marie Jahoda, Morton Deutsch, and Stuart W. Cook, eds., *Research Methods in the Social Sciences* (New York: Dryden Press, 1951), II, 393-514. On a more introspective and less analytic level, "Elenore Smith Bowen's" book-length account of how she was affected by her experiences as a participant observer of an undisclosed bush tribe of Africa was also very illuminating. See "Elenore Smith Bowen" (pseudonym), *Return to Laughter* (New York: Harper and Brothers, 1954).

2. Mr. Grimm was the patient discussed earlier who gave the psychiatrist a detailed, vivid account of his reactions to the numerous procedures and tests he underwent prior to adrenalectomy. (See Chapter IV, pp. 120-121.)

3. There is some similarity between the conception of the observer as a "nice girl" which the men of F-Second held, and the way in which a street corner gang in a slum area thinks of the "good girl." As William Foote Whyte's study of such a gang revealed, corner boys make a sharp distinction between "good girls" and "lays." "Good girls" are the kind one marries. The slum sex code dictates that they ought to be treated with respect and propriety. There are strong sentiments among corner boys that the virginity of such girls ought to be upheld and protected, and severe institutional sanctions are brought to bear upon anyone who violates this code. The corner boys also expect that the good girls will behave in ways that conform to certain standards of respectability. For example, good girls are not expected to "hang on the corner." See William Foote Whyte, "A Slum Sex Code," *Class, Status and Power: A Reader in Stratification,* eds. Reinhard Bendix and Seymour Martin Lipset (Glencoe, Illinois: The Free Press, 1953), pp. 308-316.

4. Stated in more formal sociological terms, "socialization" consists of the processes of learning through which an individual acquires the knowledge, skills, attitudes, values, and behavior patterns which will enable and motivate him to perform a role in a socially acceptable fashion. For a precise, well-conceptualized discussion of the processes of socialization, see Robert K. Merton, "Some Preliminaries to a Sociology of Medical Education" in *The Student-Physician,* pp. 40-42; also, Appendix A: "Socialization: A Terminological Note," pp. 287-293.

5. Some of the members of the staff did not know enough about the patient community and Paul O'Brian to understand the necessity of such humor; others simply did not feel emotionally capable of making deathbed jokes.

6. In these respects, Leo Angelico and Paul O'Brian conform to what anthropologists call "informants": "articulate members of the studied culture who enter

into a more or less personal relationship with the investigator for a relatively long period of time." (See Benjamin D. Paul, "Interview Techniques and Field Relationships," p. 443.)

7. This is a problem which the social scientist shares with the physician, particularly the psychiatrist and the clinical investigator. In the final chapter we shall discuss this aspect of the Metabolic Group's situation in greater detail.

8. Bronislaw Malinowski, *Magic, Science, and Religion,* p. 30.

9. For example, see "Elenore Smith Bowen's" moving account of the crisis she faced and the "sea change" in herself which she underwent as the result of the death of one of her closest informants in childbirth. (*Return to Laughter,* pp. 169-276.) William Foote Whyte describes the "serious trouble" his conscience gave him when he discovered that he had gotten so emotionally involved in a political campaign he was observing in Cornerville that he voted twice. This represented a moral and emotional crisis for him. (*Street Corner Society,* pp. 312-317.) Finally, in his essay on "Interview Techniques and Field Relationships," Benjamin Paul lists a number of instances in which social scientists conducting studies based on field observations underwent such crises as a result of their over-involvement or under-detachment with respect to the persons and situation they were studying (pp. 440-441).

10. Lionel Trilling used this phrase in his essay on *Freud and the Crisis of Our Culture* (Boston: The Beacon Press, 1955), p. 37.

11. L. J. Henderson, "Physician and Patient as a Social System"; Talcott Parsons, "Social Structure and Dynamic Process: The Case of Modern Medical Practice"; "Illness and the Role of the Physician: A Sociological Perspective"; "The Definitions of Health and Illness in the Light of American Values and Social Structure."

12. Parsons, "Social Structure and Dynamic Process," "Illness and the Role of the Physician," and "The Definition of Health and Illness."

13. These distinctions among magic, science, and religion were originally made by Émile Durkheim and Bronislaw Malinowski, and further developed by Talcott Parsons. See Emile Durkheim, *The Elementary Forms of the Religious Life,* trans. by J. W. Swain (Glencoe, Illinois: The Free Press, 1947); Malinowski, *Magic, Science and Religion;* Talcott Parsons, *Religious Perspectives of College Teaching in Sociology and Social Psychology* (New Haven, Connecticut: Edward W. Hazen Foundation, 1951).

CHAPTER VIII — General Significance of "Experiment Perilous"

THE SIGNIFICANCE OF what we have learned about the physicians of the Metabolic Group and the patients of F-Second extends beyond the conference room, laboratory, and ward cubicles in which they experienced their mutual problems and arrived at ways of coming to terms with them. And so, in this last chapter we will not merely summarize what has gone before, but will also deal with some general implications of the "experiment perilous" in which these physicians and patients participated. We will indicate how their problems, stresses, and ways of coping with them seem to be pertinent to the situations of other physicians and patients, other scientists, and perhaps to any group of men confronted with life stress of magnitude. In so doing, we will also suggest implications which some of the findings of this study may have for the further development of conceptualized knowledge about interrelated social and psychological aspects of medicine, science, and human stress.

The first substantive chapter of this book (Chapter II) was concerned with the problems that the physicians of the Metabolic Group faced. These included problems of uncertainty, of therapeutic limitation, and of experimenting on human subjects. Such problems are not unique to the physicians who comprised the Metabolic Group; nor are they characteristic only of physicians engaged in clinical research. Rather, to some extent, these are problems which all physicians encounter.

As we have said, physicians are confronted with two basic types of uncertainty. One of these derives from limitations in the current

237

state of medical knowledge. There are many questions to which no physician, however well trained, can yet provide answers. The second type of uncertainty results from incomplete or imperfect mastery of available knowledge. No one can have at his command all the information, lore, and skills of modern medicine.

In turn, these forms of uncertainty to which all physicians are subject are connected with another set of problems which they also inevitably face: problems of therapeutic limitation. Since the knowledge and skills of the physician are not always adequate, there are many times when his most vigorous efforts to understand illness and to rectify its consequences are of little or no avail.

What the physician *can* do to help a patient, then, is often limited. What he *ought* to do is frequently not clear. And the consequences of his clinical actions cannot always be accurately predicted. Yet, in the face of these uncertainties and limitations, the physician is expected to institute measures which will facilitate the diagnosis and treatment of the problems the patient presents.

Largely because what the physician decides to do (and not to do) on behalf of a patient is generally based on less than perfect knowledge, it has been said that "in a sense [his] every clinical act is an investigation,"[1] and that "medical experimentation on human beings, in its broadest meaning and for the good of the individual patient, takes place continually in every doctor's office."[2]

The rapidity with which new diagnostic and therapeutic procedures and new drugs have been appearing in the last few swiftly-moving decades is also responsible for the fact that the practicing physician is often cast in the role of experimenter. It is hard for the physician simply to keep abreast of these developments, and even more difficult for him to appraise them. The available reports about their benefits and dangers are tentative and far from consistent, since only gradually, and to a considerable extent on the basis of a trial-and-error empiricism, can relatively definitive judgments about a new procedure or drug be reached. Thus, although typically, the physician in practice has published literature and the informally-transmitted opinions and experiences of colleagues to inform him about the properties of new technics and drugs,[3] the degree of uncertainty about their benefits, limitations and hazards which still remain is often large enough to warrant calling "experimental" some of the clinical trials he conducts on patients. Before he carries out such trials, the practicing physician, like the research physician, has the problem of trying to determine whether the dangers of the contemplated procedure or drug are sufficiently less than the hazards of the patient's disease, and its potential benefits sufficiently greater than both, to justify asking the patient to undergo it. If they seem to be, and he therefore decides to carry out such a procedure on a patient or administer such a drug, the practicing physician, like the clinical investigator, sometimes finds himself in a situation where the measures he employed fail to benefit the patient clinically, or have negative effects on him. Thus, physicians in practice, as well as research physicians, experience some of the uncertainties, limitations, moral ambiguities, and untoward consequences connected with the application of advanced medical knowledge and techniques to the medical problems of patients.

Not only medicine, of course, but all scientific activity has social consequences, harmful as well as beneficent. However technical or abstract, the experiments which biological and physical scientists conduct in their laboratories and field stations may seem, ultimately they may affect the lives of men and women in powerful ways—both for good and for evil. The "pure" scientist, however, is in several respects further removed and better insulated from the ultimate outcome of his actions than the physician is. On the whole, his attention is confined to the test tube and microscope; his research is conducted on lifeless matter or on animals; and the social implications of what he does are for the most part indirect and long-range.

The special difficulty of the physician—the problem that distinguishes him from most other scientists, be they in the fields of pure or applied science—is that the material on which he works is the disease-stricken human being. Thus, the decisions the physician makes, the procedures he carries out, the drugs he prescribes have a proximate, visible, flesh-and-blood impact on the patients under his care. To a significant extent, whether patients get better, get worse, or whether their conditions remain stubbornly fixed is contingent upon what the physician is or is not able to do for them. Because the welfare of the patient is thus directly associated with his actions, the human consequences of his uncertainty, limitation, and fallibility are more apparent to the physician than to most other scientists. It is harder for him to forget or systematically ignore the fact that what he does as a scientist makes an impact on people. Furthermore, the people whom he affects are not remote, anonymous entities. They are his patients: the individuals whom he sees, to whom he talks, and on whom he carries out various procedures, in his office, in their homes and in the hospital.

Although some of their problems were not different in kind from those of practicing physicians, the physicians of the Metabolic Group probably experienced such problems more frequently and to a greater degree. As clinical investigators, it was their special role to try new procedures and drugs on patients who were ill with diseases that lie outside the understanding and control of modern medicine. This meant that very few of their patients had simple forms of relatively common diseases which could easily be identified and treated successfully. A majority of their patients were ill with disorders which presented especially intricate diagnostic problems and had limited or poor prognoses. A great many more of the diagnostic and therapeutic technics and agents which they employed were very new and not yet standardized than those generally used by practicing physicians. In fact, it might be said that the Metabolic Group conducted preliminary experiments with new methods and agents *for* medical practitioners. The Group not only devised a certain number of new methods, but also evaluated them, improved them, and recommended how they ought to be used by their colleagues in practice. For all these reasons, the physicians of the Metabolic Group were probably more consistently faced with diagnostic, therapeutic, and prognostic uncertainties of magnitude—particularly those inherent to the field of medicine in its present state of knowledge—than most practicing physicians. They also more frequently had to deal with the problem of determining whether trying a new procedure or drug on a patient was justifiable, and more likely to be confronted with situations in which the methods which they had employed in order to benefit their patients clinically proved to have contrary effects.

There was at least one qualitative, rather than quantitative, respect in which the problems the physicians of the Metabolic Group experienced differed from those of practicing physicians. No matter how conjectural the measures to which a practicing physician may subject his patients, or how deleterious their consequences may be, he can find some security in the knowledge that his primary, and usually sole, intention was that of benefiting the patient by trying to diagnose his problem and treat it. This was not the case with the physicians of the Metabolic Group. As clinical investigators they were not only obligated to protect and further the welfare of their patients, but they were also responsible for advancing general medical knowledge. Usually, when they conducted a new procedure on a patient or gave him a new drug, they did so in order to acquire information as well as to help him. And sometimes their aim was primarily or exclusively that of advancing knowledge. Thus, their decisions about whether or not they ought to undertake a certain measure generally involved a rather complicated moral titration process. In some cases they had to balance the potential risks of the technic or agent they wished to test against its presumed significance for the welfare of the patients who acted as subjects and for the furtherance of knowledge. In other cases, where the patients on whom it was tried could not expect to be helped by it, they had to weigh the possible contribution such an experimental procedure or drug might make to medical science and the "good of society" in general against the suffering and hazards it might involve for these patients.

Because the physicians of the Metabolic Group were not solely, and sometimes not predominantly, oriented to benefiting patients, they often felt morally uncertain about the measures they essayed on patients, and about how they reconciled the dualistic requirements of their professional role. In a certain number of cases their responsibilities as clinicians and as investigators were compatible. But the physicians of the Metabolic Group were also confronted with many cases in which their obligations conflicted. In such instances they had to make a relative choice between them, in order to commit themselves to a definitive course of action. Particularly if something subsequently "went wrong," the physicians of the Metabolic Group could never quite be sure that they had struck the proper kind of balance. On the one hand, it was possible that they had unnecessarily impeded an experiment because they had been too concerned about the welfare of their patient-subject; on the other hand, they might have exposed a patient to an undue amount of risk and suffering because they had been too zealous about the investigation they were conducting. This was one of the aspects of their situation as clinical investigators which the physicians of the Metabolic Group experienced as stressful.

One of the major findings which emerged from our systematic observations of these physicians is that the problems of uncertainty, limitation, and experimenting on patients which their activities as clinical investigators entailed imposed a considerable amount of stress upon them. Despite the detachment and equanimity expected of them as medical scientists, and the professional training and experience which enabled them to live up to these norms to a greater extent than lay persons, the physicians of the Metabolic Group often felt quite disturbed over the inadequacy or uncertainty of their knowledge, their inability to diagnose or definitively improve the clinical status of many of their patients, and the difficulties they experienced in trying to reconcile their clinical responsibilities with their responsibilities as investigators. In the privacy of their laboratory and conference room, chiefly through the "serious joke," these physicians often expressed feelings of tension, frustration, and disquietude over these problems of their "laboratory life."

In order to meet these stressful problems with the degree of objectivity and equipoise which would enable them to adequately fulfill both their clinical and research responsibilities the physicians of the Metabolic Group needed and actually devised a series of mechanisms. In Chapter III we described and analyzed some of these. The organized unity of the Metabolic Group, their humor, game of chance, and intimate privileged ways of treating patients all partly served this function.

There already exists [Robert K. Merton has written] a vast literature on "scientific method" and, by inference, on the "attitudes" and "values" of scientists. But this literature is concerned with what social scientists call ideal patterns, that is, with ways in which scientists *ought* to think, feel and act. It does not necessarily describe, in needed detail, the ways in which scientists actually do think, feel and act. It is at least possible that if social scientists were to begin observation in the laboratories and field stations of physical and biological scientists, more might be learned, in a comparatively few years, about the psychology and sociology of science, than in all the years that have gone before.[4]

Our study of the problems, stresses, and ways of coming to terms of the physicians of the Metabolic Group is based on the kind of first-hand observation which Merton advocates. What emerges from such observation is a picture of a group of medical scientists who actually think, feel, and act in ways which are considerably less "cool, impartial, detached"[5] and rational than would be the case if their attitudes, values, and behavior patterns conformed perfectly to some of the ideal norms of science. The physicians of the Metabolic Group not only experienced a significant amount of stress in carrying out their responsibilities as clinical investigators. In their laboratory and conference room, where they could not be seen or heard either by their patients or by professional colleagues, they expressed a great deal of emotion about their shared difficulties. And among the ways in which they came to terms with their problems and feelings about them were three nonrational forms of behavior: joking, wagering, and the establishment of a countertransference relationship with their patients. In these respects, the attitudes and behavior of the research physicians of the Metabolic Group were not in keeping with the graven, aloof, logical-rational ideal image of scientists widely accepted as an accurate portrayal of how they actually feel and act.

Since there is almost no published literature which presents a systematic, firsthand account of the expressed sentiments and observed actions of other groups of scientists, we do not know to what extent and in precisely what ways the thoughts, feelings, and behavior of the Metabolic Group are like and unlike those of other clinical investigators, practicing physicians, biological and physical scientists. However, there are fragmentary empirical data and reasonable social psychological grounds on which we can venture the guess that some of the patterned ways of thinking, feeling, and acting exhibited by the Metabolic Group might be characteristic of other groups of scientists as well. We refer specifically to the nature of the relationship the Group established with their patients, their humor, and their game of chance.

In the only four published descriptions of research units we found (three articles and a book),[6] some reference is made to the unusually close relationship between medical staff and patients. In two of these publications the medical staff and patients are depicted as comprising something like a "family."[7] Another mentions the "homelike spirit on the ward" resulting from the fact that "every possible means is taken [by the staff] to make [patients] happy and comfortable and show them that we are interested in them as individuals rather than as just interesting cases."[8]

There is evidence in three of these publications that the medical staff and patients on these research wards also had a mutual tendency to identify with one another as colleagues. The patients on one ward are described "not only as possessors of diseases worth studying, but as active members of the research team":[9]

Patients no less than investigators have shown both loyalty and devotion to the cause of research . . .[10] Certainly it can be said that the patients in Ward 4 have had closer and more understanding relations with their doctors than most. Their devotion to a common cause and the study of disease for the good of man draws them together . . .[11]

In this same book about a research ward written by the physician who was its founder, a laudatory chapter is devoted to the man he considered the archetype of many patients on the unit who collaborated with members of the research group, and made an active, knowledgeable contribution to clinical investigation:

Patients on occasion have made more than passive contributions to the scientific understanding of their cases during their sojourns in Ward 4. None, however, has promoted more dramatically and forcefully the conduct of research than did the late Captain Charles Martell, master mariner in the United States Marines during World War I . . .

Established in Ward 4, the Captain quickly fell in with its strict routine and became its most colorful occupant . . . His cheerful mien and wonderfully good adjustment to his illness were inspiring. He took a keen interest, intelligent but not in the least morbid, in the researches being made in his case. He longed to be cured, of course, but also had high hopes that the studies done on him might be helpful to others. Most of the patients treated in Ward 4 through the years have had something of this spirit . . .

The group of people involved in the studies of Martell and the other patients with hyperparathyroidism numbered at least fifty! There were internists, general surgeons, genito-urinary surgeons, orthopedic surgeons, dentists, pathologists, chemists, dietitians, nurses, and, not least, the patients themselves who cooperated in these investigations . . .

The reason I have included Martell's case in some detail is to dramatize the role of the patient in clinical research . . . There are scores in the long roster of patients of Ward 4 that have presented problems of great variety and challenge to the medical investigators, and have themselves taken part in their solution . . .[12]

An article about another research ward reports with some pride that the "little-girl patients" on that unit "wear white caps which have been devised for them by the nurses [whom] they like to follow on their rounds," and that "the sick little boys have worn-out stethoscopes which were given to them by their current heroes, the white-coated doctors."[13]

Another of these articles mentions the fact that the physicians and other members of the medical staff connected with that particular metabolic research ward "encouraged patients to visit the laboratories and to help with minor chores with which they could be safely entrusted" and that the laboratory staff responded by "spending part of their lunch hour in the patients' rooms chatting or sharing a television program."[14] The research physician who wrote this article goes on to describe in an approving manner some of the other ways in which being hospitalized on this metabolism ward "enriched the lives" of patients:

... The initial resentment [of patients] over being ill was gradually attenuated by their recognition that they shared their disabilities with others. Our policy of studying a variety of disease entities in one unit was found to have an unsuspected advantage which stemmed from the inclusion in one group of different types of disabilities. A patient with one defect came to feel that she might well regard herself fortunate not to have been struck down with the disability characteristic of another type of disease; thus, the absence of a defect became a positive asset. Then, out of an understanding of what it means to be less than normal, came the desire to be mutually helpful and with it, an admiration for the courage of others in coping with their disabilities ...

A very appreciable contribution is made by our former ward patients who continue under observation in our out-patient clinic, which is located on the same floor. During their out-patient visits, they not only meet those with whom they had been previously hospitalized and cement the bonds which had grown up between them, but they never fail to return to our metabolism ward. The fact that they have returned to their homes improved in varying degrees and sometimes entirely cured is an enormous encouragement to those under hospital study for similar conditions. Firm friendships have grown up and it is very evident that a sense of belonging to a group and to an organization deeply interested in their welfare has enriched their lives.[15]

These accounts not only suggest that other research units which sound remarkably like Ward F-Second exist, but more specifically for our present purposes that the research physicians (and other staff members) connected with such units responded to the situations of which they were a part by dealing with their patients in some of the same ways the members of the Metabolic Group did. They treated them as cherished "members of the family" and celebrated professional colleagues, and proudly helped to foster the sense of commitment to medical science, the research group, and to each other which patients tended to develop in this setting.

In our discussion of the counterphobic, impious grim joking which helped the Metabolic Group to come to terms with the most stressful aspects of their situation—particularly those connected with the death of patients and the dangers of the experiments they were asked to undergo—we indicated that this kind of joking seems to be generally characteristic of physicians. Our observations of medical students suggest that in their earliest years of their training physicians learn to deal with the stressful situations they encounter as professionals and with their emotional reactions to such situations through "medical humor." There are no published studies which help us ascertain whether or not this kind of joking is also prevalent among groups of scientists other than physicians. However, we do have one piece of evidence which suggests that grim humor may be used by physical and biological scientists as well as physicians to cope with the difficulties and perils of their professional situation. The evidence to which we refer is a mock diploma which one of the physicians of the Metabolic Group had received from the Oak Ridge Institute of Nuclear Studies (and which he had framed and hung on the wall of his office). Apparently, all scientists who complete the course in radio-isotope procedure given at Oak Ridge receive this certificate, which is very much in the spirit of grim humor:

Greetings

To whom these presents come, be it known that
[Name of Recipient]

having been successfully bombarded in the Oak Ridge Institute of Nuclear Studies, presenting a favorable cross-section of several barns, and retaining a normal leucocyte count is entitled to the degree

Dabbler in Radio-Isotope Procedure

with all the innuendos and privileges pertaining thereunto. This degree confers the privilege of absorbing one-tenth roentgens per day and radiating neutrons of traceable knowledge.

Fifth year of the neutron
William G. Pollard, Executive Dabbler
Ralph T. Overman, Chief Dabbler

As for the game of chance which the physicians of the Metabolic Group played, we do not have any concrete data from which to speculate about whether this kind of wagering might also be characteristic of other groups of scientists. However, on theoretical grounds we would guess that betting of this sort, or its functional equivalent, probably takes place in many laboratory situations. We base this guess on the social-science conception that when men are faced with a situation in which the empirical end they wish to attain is emotionally important to them, and there is great uncertainty about whether they will succeed in achieving that end, they usually devise non-empirical or magical techniques to "enable them to carry out their . . . tasks with confidence and poise."[16] We have seen that the physicians of the Metabolic Group were continually faced with un-certainty situations of this type in connection with the outcome of the experiments they conducted on their patients. And, as we have indicated, taking bets on how their most "chancy," important experiments might turn out, provided the Metabolic Group with a non-empirical means of expressing some of the tension they felt as a consequence of this uncertainty, and a way of reassuring themselves that the results they predicted and hoped for would actually come to pass. We assume that all scientists experience this sort of uncertainty, and that because their knowledge in such instances is not sufficient to insure rational control and predictable success, they, too, feel some need for a nonrational means of adjusting to it. It seems to us that wagering is a particularly appropriate and likely technique for scientists to employ in this regard, since it simulates the rational way in which they make their more knowledgeable predictions. For these reasons, we would expect to find something like the Metabolic Group's game of chance occurring in numerous laboratories.

In sum, we have suggested that although there were certain respects in which the problems, stresses, and ways of coming to terms of the Metabolic Group were rather particularly and exclusively characteristic of them, in other respects they were probably very much like those of other scientists. We shall have to wait for social scientists "to begin observations in the laboratories and field stations of physical and biological scientists"[17] to determine how close a resemblance there is between the physicians of the Metabolic Group and other scientists.

In Chapter IV, we shifted our site of observation from the laboratory and conference room of the Metabolic Group to the ward on which their patients were hospitalized. Here, we came to see that in a number of respects illness was a shared, socially-patterned experience for the men of F-Second.

To begin with, although the physical conditions of F-Seconders varied considerably, and although in personality terms individual patients could differ as radically as Leo Angelico and Paul O'Brian, they nevertheless all faced what one patient termed the "common problems of illness." Primarily this was because illness is not simply a biological condition which each man suffers alone in his own idiosyncratic way. It is also a social role, which imposes certain patterned conditions and requirements on all persons who are defined as sick. Thus, in keeping with the stipulations of the sick role, the men of Ward F-Second were all exempted from many of their normal social activities and responsibilities. They were also exonerated from moral responsibility for having gotten sick and for making themselves better. As expected, they had put themselves under the supervision and care of physicians. Admission to the hospital had removed them from the "well world." As hospital patients they were expected to submit to the scientific procedures and agents which their physicians brought to bear upon the diagnosis and treatment of their conditions, to cooperate with them and other members of the medical staff, and in every possible way help to effect their own recovery.

The common problems of F-Seconders derived from these socially prescribed exemptions and obligations associated with illness. Being released from their usual tasks and duties and from moral responsibility for their state confronted F-Seconders with problems of incapacity, inactivity, uncertainty, and meaning. Their confinement to the hospital subjected them to problems of isolation and of subjugation to the control of physicians, other personnel, and the organized technical facilities of modern medical science.

The problems which F-Seconders faced, and the degree of stress which they experienced as a consequence, were compounded by two special features of their situation. First, most F-Seconders were ill with serious chronic diseases, which in some cases were progressively debilitating, or even fatal. Second, many patients had consented to act as research subjects for the physicians of the Metabolic Group.

This meant that a considerable number of F-Seconders were not able to achieve the ultimate goal of the sick role: that of recovering sufficiently to graduate out of it. In conjunction with their status as research patients, the incurability of many F-Seconders increased the magnitude of some of their other problems. They were more severely incapacitated, isolated from the world of normal activities for longer periods of time, and subject to more surveillance, supervision, and control by physicians than patients who are less seriously and inexorably ill. The fact that many F-Seconders had diseases which are still not well understood and as yet cannot be cured, and that they were subjects for experimental procedures and drugs, also enhanced their uncertainty about the nature and outcome of their illness, and intensified their moral concern over the meaning of their predicament. Why are we ill in this irreparable way, F-Seconders wondered. What have we thought or done to "deserve" it?

We have stated that most of the problems which the physicians of the Metabolic Group experienced were not different in kind from those of other physicians, but, rather, greater in degree. The same thing might be said about the relationship between the problems of F-Seconders and those of other patients. As we have said, because illness is not only a biological happening, but a socially patterned experience as well, it confronts all patients with certain problems. On the whole, the serious, chronic nature of their illness and their status as research patients merely seems to have enlarged and intensified these problems for F-Seconders.

The magnitude of their problems and stresses and the open nature of their ward community may have made F-Seconders more articulate about their shared difficulties than other hospitalized patients. However, we assume that the sentiments we heard F-Seconders express in connection with these problems are at least felt by most patients in hospital situations, and that there are probably many other wards on which patients discuss them with one another in much the same way that the men of F-Second did. The fact that an increasing number of hospitalized patients are ill with chronic diseases, and that in recent years more clinical research units like F-Second have been created,[18] makes this all the more likely. For this means that there are more patients such as those of Ward F-Second:

chronically ill veterans of the sick world, who in some cases have undergone research. The one systematic, detailed study of patients in a general hospital with which we can compare our findings ("The Role of the Patient in a Hospital Ward," by Rose L. Coser)[19] lends some support to our reasoned guess that the problems of physically ill patients on other wards, and even some of the things they feel and say about them, are comparable to what we observed on F-Second. Here again, we need a series of observational studies of patients in various hospital contexts in order to ascertain the patterned similarities and differences between the problems and stresses of F-Seconders and those of other patients.

In Chapter V, we found that the ways in which the patients of F-Second came to terms with their shared difficulties were also socially patterned. Their humor, laughing prayer, and game of chance; desire and efforts to attain medical stardom; development of medical interest and expertise; take-up-thy-bed attitudes and forms of behavior; and club-organized commitment to one another were the ways which the men of F-Second collectively evolved for coping with their predicament. The ward community also had effective means for teaching and enforcing these preferred attitudes, values, and patterns of behavior. As we have seen, this did not mean that all patients came to terms with their situation in an identical manner. Mediated by such factors as the nature and seriousness of their illnesses, their basic personality characteristics, their social backgrounds, and their life situations outside the hospital, different patients combined these patterned solutions in different ways. In short, the ways in which the patients of Ward F-Second adjusted to their situation varied— but not limitlessly.

The patterned similarities in their modes of adjusting had several kinds of social sources. The fact that the patients of Ward F-Second had common problems and a shared need for dealing with them was, of course, basic. Out of their like circumstances, partly through interaction with one another, patients gradually evolved group standards and forms of behavior for coping with their difficulties. Their ways of coming to terms were also significantly influenced by their relationship with the physicians of the Metabolic Group. The high degree of medical expertise and interest which patients developed and their strivings to attain the status of medical star grew partly out of their transference-induced need and desire to be like the physicians of the Metabolic Group and close to them. In turn, these ways of coming to terms were implemented and reinforced by the members of the Group, who dealt with their countertransference feelings about their patients—particularly their anxiety and guilt over not being able to make them better and experimenting on them—by furthering their medical education, and treating them as friends, colleagues, and medical celebrities.

Some of the other social factors which influenced the patterned ways in which F-Seconders came to terms were less specific to the ward and the hospital. They were connected with cultural values and institutions of American society. Most notably, the high valuation placed in our society upon medical science, and its status as front-page news, helped to make the phenomenon of medical stardom possible on Ward F-Second, and partly account for the fact that it seemed alluring and prestigious to many patients.

The importance placed upon activity and achievement in our society probably contributed to this form of excelling on the part of patients, as well as to their take-up-thy-bed credo and behavior. Illness had debarred the men of F-Second from work and other social activities that had once kept them busy and given them a sense of meaningful accomplishment.[20] In many cases, no matter how earnestly they might cooperate with their physicians in an effort to get well, patients could not expect ever to reattain sufficient health to engage fully and normally in those activities again. The fact that achieved success is a cardinal value in American society probably intensified the stress that F-Seconders experienced in the face of their inactivity, incapacity, and inability to get well. It may also have been one of the reasons for which many of the patients on Ward F-Second found nonsupine activities, the mastery of medical knowledge, and the attainment of stardom appropriate solutions for their problems.

The formation of an Adrenalectomy Club on Ward F-Second seems to represent a third respect in which the values and institutions of American society exerted some influence on F-Second's ways of coming to terms. Since the days of de Tocqueville,[21] it has often been noted that one of the unique features of our society is the extraordinary number of private associations that have been organized around special interests. The Adrenalectomy Club was an association of this kind. It was formed by patients on Ward F-Second who felt a strong sense of camaraderie as a result of having undergone the same radical experimental operation for their terminal conditions. The purposes of the Club were to "keep [members] in touch" with one another, and to inform and encourage other patients who might subsequently be candidates for this procedure.

Clubs formed by patients who have similar problems are not uniquely American. For example, we have already indicated that in the Swiss tuberculosis sanitorium which was the site of Thomas Mann's *The Magic Mountain*, a Half-Lung Club had been formed by patients who had undergone a pneumothorax. However, what is more specifically American about the existence of the Adrenalectomy Club on Ward F-Second is the larger pattern into which it fits. Many patient groupings of this sort exist in the United States. We ourselves have heard of the following: Alcoholics Anonymous, the Mended Hearts Club (for patients who have undergone cardiac surgery), the QT Clubs (made up of patients who have had ileostomies), the Polio Society, Courage, Inc. (a group of physically handicapped patients), and the Ulcer Club. Not only are there numerous patient clubs in the United States, but some of them have acquired a very large membership, developed an elaborate organization, been recognized by the medical profession, and even attained national prominence. For example, Alcoholics Anonymous is familiar to large sectors of the American public. The various QT groups of this country have recently launched a publication known as *The Ileostomy Quarterly*. The Mended Hearts Club (which was founded by a small group of patients on the Cardiac Service in the Hospital where Ward F-Second was located) has been incorporated into the American Heart Association. It now has an associate membership of interested relatives and friends. And when it held an annual meeting in June, 1955, 750 people attended, of whom "400 were veterans of cardiac surgery, ranging in age from 9 to 64."[22] It is our guess that such patient groups are more pervasive and elaborate and have more prestige in the United States than in other societies. Their social origins and implications merit study as an interesting and important example of the proliferation of voluntary special-interest groups in American society.

In sum: the patterned ways of coming to terms exhibited by the patients of Ward F-Second grew directly out of their common predicament, and their deep connection with one another and with their physicians. In addition, they seem also to have been more indirectly influenced by three general characteristics of American society: our cultural emphasis on activity and achievement, the high valuation we place on science, and our tendency to form associations around special interests.

In this review of the problems of the physicians and patients of Ward F-Second, and their ways of meeting these problems, we come finally to their most general significance: their implications for the social psychology of human stress. Seen in the broadest possible perspective, what we observed in the conference room, laboratory, and on the ward were two groups of men who were faced with common stresses of magnitude: great uncertainty, limitation, hazards, and death. Through a process of interaction with members of their own group and with one another, physicians and patients arrived at comparable ways of dealing with their stresses. The grim joke and impious wager occurred in both groups. Each derived support and guidance from the tight-knit group to which they belonged, and also from their intimate contact and close identification with one another. Psychiatrists and psychologists would call the joking and wagering of physicians and patients counterphobic defense mechanisms; the identification of patients with their physicians, each other, and the hospital, manifestations of transference and secondary gain; and the personal, colleague-like relationship of physicians with patients, indications of countertransference. They would be inclined to view these as personality-determined modes of adjustment, which individual physicians and patients independently evolved in order to cope with the emotional challenges of their common situation. However, our observations have demonstrated that these ways of coming to terms were as much sociogenic as they were psychogenic. They gradually emerged as a group product from the interaction of physicians and patients in the problematic situation which they shared.[23]

The fact that physicians and patients came to terms in complementary and even identical ways suggests that to some extent, irrespective of differences in personality, in the statuses they occupy and in the substantive details of their problems, groups of men confronted with great uncertainty, limitation, danger, and death will tend to arrive at similar ways of adjusting to them. Some of the accounts of the ways in which soldiers in combat and persons involved in peacetime disasters reacted to stress provide evidence to support this view.[24] However, we need more systematic, detailed, *in situ* studies of how groups of individuals deal with life stresses of various sorts to determine whether in fact this is so, and to demonstrate specifically and precisely how social and psychological factors work together to shape their ways of coming to terms in such situations.

It is here that the most basic and general significance of this book about the physicians of the Metabolic Group and the patients of Ward F-Second probably lies. Their ways of thinking, feeling, and acting in the difficult situation they shared potentially link them with what we may come to know about other experiments perilous of which men are a living and dying part.

NOTES FOR CHAPTER VIII

1. McDermott, "A Consideration of the Present Ethics of Clinical Investigation."

2. Shimkin, "The Problems of Experimentation on Human Beings," p. 205.

3. Supported by a grant from Charles Pfizer & Co., Inc., and initiated by Joseph A. Precker, then Director of Market Research for Pfizer, the Bureau of Applied Social Research of Columbia University recently conducted a study to determine the ways in which physicians in practice make decisions to adopt new drugs. The physicians who were interviewed and whose prescription records were studied comprised 85 per cent of the general practitioners, internists, and pediatricians in four Midwestern cities ranging in population from 30,000 to 110,000. The findings of this study thus far published indicate that particularly during the first few months after a new drug becomes available, when there is still a great deal of uncertainty about its clinical properties, physicians in practice are very much influenced by the attitudes which their closest colleagues have toward the drug and toward using it. Thus, among those physicians who were relatively well integrated into the medical community, at first those who were advisors or discussion partners tended to introduce the new drug into their practice at the same time. Then it spread through the friendship network to doctors who were closely tied to the medical community. Furthermore, in each clique there seemed to be a few highly respected physicians, relatively conservative in their outlook, whose adoption of the new drug triggered off the almost simultaneous use of the drug by practically every other physician in that particular group. See Herbert Menzel

and Elihu Katz, "Social Relations and Innovation in the Medical Profession: The Epidemiology of a New Drug" (Publication No. A 190 of the Bureau of Applied Social Research of Columbia University), *Public Opinion Quarterly*, Vol. XIX, No. 4 (Winter, 1955-56), pp. 337-352; and James Coleman, Elihu Katz, and Herbert Menzel, "The Diffusion of an Innovation Among Physicians" (Publication No. 239 of the Bureau of Applied Social Research of Columbia University), *Sociometry*, Vol. 20, No. 4 (December, 1957), pp. 253-270.

4. Robert K. Merton, "Foreword" in Bernard Barber, *Science and the Social Order* (Glencoe, Illinois: The Free Press, 1952), p. xxii.

5. Conant, *Modern Science and Modern Man*, p. 67.

6. See Dorothy Freymeyer, "A Metabolic Unit at Work," *Nursing Outlook*, Vol. 4, No. 2 (February, 1956), pp. 85-86; Milton Lehman, "In Search of Medical Miracles," *The Saturday Evening Post* (March 31, 1956), pp. 34-35 and 103-104; James Howard Means, M.D., *Ward 4: The Mallinckrodt Research Ward of the Massachusetts General Hospital* (Cambridge, Massachusetts: Harvard University Press, 1958); and Ephraim Shorr, M.D., "Emergence of Psychological Problems in Patients Requiring Prolonged Hospitalization," in *Medical and Psychological Teamwork in the Care of the Chronically Ill*, ed. by Molly Harrower, Ph.D. (Springfield, Illinois: Charles C. Thomas, 1955), pp. 32-38.

A fifth publication about a metabolic ward in a small research hospital has recently appeared: William W. Schottstaedt, M.D., Ruth H. Pinsky, M.A., David Mackler, M.D., and Stewart Wolf, M.D., "Sociologic, Psychologic and Metabolic Observations on Patients in the Community of a Metabolic Ward," *The American Journal of Medicine*, Vol. XXV, No. 2 (August, 1958), pp. 248-257. This pilot study attempts to "appraise the effects of naturally occurring stressful situations on certain metabolic indicators among a group of patients" on a metabolic research ward. "Interpersonal difficulties" were found to be the "most common sources of stress . . . associated with metabolic deviations" in urinary excretion of water, sodium, potassium, calcium, nitrogen, and creatinine of patients who were on metabolic "balance" regimens. This article makes a precise and important contribution to knowledge about the interplay of social, psychological, and metabolic factors in situations which are experienced as stressful. However, because of its specialized focus, this article concentrates almost exclusively on stressful aspects of relations between patients on the ward and between patients and members of the medical staff, and only mentions in passing that "the atmosphere of the ward was usually a relaxed and pleasant one." Thus, this article does not contain detailed, empirical data about *non*-stressful aspects of the interpersonal relations on this ward with which our materials about the physicians of the Metabolic Group and the patients of Ward F-Second could be compared.

7. Freymeyer, "A Metabolic Unit at Work" and Shorr, "Emergence of Psychological Problems in Patients Requiring Prolonged Hospitalization."

8. Quoted from an unspecified article by Dr. Walter Bauer and Dr. Joseph C. Aub in Means, *Ward 4*, pp. 18-19.

9. Charles Sidney Burwell, M.D., "Foreword" in Means, *Ward 4*, p. xvii.

10. Means, *Ward 4*, p. 19.

11. *Ibid.*, p. 164.

12. "Charles Martell Shows the Way," Chapter IV in Means, *Ward 4*, pp. 32-41. See especially, pp. 32, 34, 35, 39, and 40.

13. Lehman, "In Search of Modern Miracles," p. 103.

14. Shorr, "Emergence of Psychological Problems," p. 35.

15. *Ibid.*, p. 36.

16. Malinowski, *Magic, Science, and Religion*, p. 70.

17. Merton, "Foreword," in Barber, *Science and the Social Order.*

18. The most important institution for clinical investigation which has been established in recent years is, of course, the Clinical Center of the National Institutes of Health in Bethesda, Maryland, which was opened in 1953, and is financed by Federal funds.

19. Rose Laub Coser, "The Role of a Patient in a Hospital Ward" (Unpublished Ph.D. dissertation, Columbia University, 1957).

20. Morse and Weiss, "The Function and Meaning of Work and the Job."

21. See Alexis de Tocqueville, *Democracy in America*, II (New York: Vintage Books, Alfred A. Knopf, Inc., 1954), 117-118.

22. "Mended Hearts," Editorial in *The New England Journal of Medicine*, Vol. 254, No. 13 (March 29, 1956), p. 626.

23. For an excellent general theory of the process of interaction through which a group of individuals with similar problems of adjustment gradually arrive at a common solution for their shared difficulties, see Albert K. Cohen, "A General Theory of Subcultures," Chapter III of *Delinquent Boys: The Culture of the Gang* (Glencoe, Illinois: The Free Press, 1955), pp. 49-72.

24. For example: it was reported in *The American Soldier* (two of the four volumes of *Studies in Social Psychology in World War II,* conducted by social scientists under the aegis of the Research Branch, Information and Education Division of the War Department) that among the factors which helped men to cope with the stresses of combat were the following: loyalty to buddies and pride in outfit; positive attitude (respect, loyalty, confidence, etc.) toward officers who were combat leaders; a code of masculinity, or "acting like a man" (displaying courage and aggressiveness, having knowledge of what to do, helping other men, cheering men by humorous remarks, etc.); prayer; magical or semimagical practices (carrying protective amulets, carrying out prebattle preparations in a fixed, ritual order, keeping articles of clothing or equipment associated with some past experience of escape from danger, avoiding actions regarded as unlucky, etc.); a fatalistic philosophy; and "the bitter humor of the front." See M. Brewster Smith, "Combat Motivations Among Ground Troops," Chapter 3 in Samuel A. Stouffer *et al., The American Soldier: Combat and Its Aftermath,* II (Princeton, New Jersey: Princeton University Press, 1949), 105-191.

Based on material collected from peacetime disasters in the United States (brought together by the Committee of Disaster Studies of the National Research Council), Martha Wolfenstein has written a book-length essay on how people react to disastrous events: *Disaster: A Psychological Essay* (Glencoe, Illinois: The Free Press, 1957). Here again, some of the attitudes and patterns of behavior that characterized large groups of individuals faced with catastrophe and possible death and helped them to cope with it, are remarkably like those of the physicians and patients of Ward F-Second. For example, many individuals reacted to disaster by engaging in strenuous activity, particularly rescue work; good will and kindly behavior toward others was widespread; humor was often used as a defense against stress; a group of persons who shared the same storm cellar during a number of tornadoes formed a "Tornado Club"; "when the toll of a disaster [was] reckoned up afterward . . . the question of why such a thing should have happened . . . why some survived and others perished . . . [came] up repeatedly" (p. 200); and "most recurrent of all [was] the view of disaster as the great equalizer . . . [that] in the face of overwhelming danger and imminent death all men are equal" (p. 220).

For a critical survey of published social science literature on "how people feel, think, and behave at times when they are facing the threat of pain, serious injury, or death," see Irving L. Janis, *Psychological Stress: Psychoanalytic and Behavioral Studies of Surgical Patients* (New York: John Wiley & Sons, Inc., 1958), pp. vii-32. These published studies about stress behavior include controlled laboratory experiments, field studies of major disasters, and a few psychoanalytic studies. Dr. Janis found that all these studies have serious methodological shortcomings, and that seen as a whole, they "yield only a very meager list . . . of warranted scientific generalizations" (p. vii).

Epilogue: Forty-Five Years as a Participant Observer of Patient-Oriented Clinical Research

THE INVITATION to deliver the 1995 Foundation of Medical Sciences Lecture (on which this epilogue is based) led me to review the almost 45-year-long relationship that I have had as a sociologist of medicine with what is presently termed patient-oriented clinical research. (By patient-oriented research I mean the sort of investigation that entails moving back and forth, in both directions, between the clinical bedside and the laboratory bench; that involves patients as subjects; and that is directed toward finding more effective modes of diagnosing, treating, and preventing the diseases and disorders from which its patient-subjects suffer). My long relationship with this type of research encompasses my participant observation-based sociological studies of a metabolic research ward; of the education and socialization of medical students; of organ transplantation, the artificial kidney and dialysis, and the artificial heart; of young European physicians' post-World War II struggles to pursue careers as clinical researchers; and of the genesis, evolution, and significance of bioethics.

Reflecting on what I have experienced and learned from these firsthand inquiries turned my thoughts toward some of the worries about this type of research that are currently being expressed in medical circles and in the public sphere. Paramount among these are concerns about the intellectual demise of patient-oriented research; the dearth of young physicians willing to commit themselves to this sort of research career partly because, in the words of Harold Varmus, director of the U.S. National Institutes of Health, they are "choos[ing] molecules over medicine";[1] the complexity of the informed voluntary consent and benefit-risk issues, at once moral and interpersonal, that are involved in enlisting patients as human subjects; and the episodes of "sloppy science" and of scientific misconduct associated with certain research projects that have aroused media attention, the watchfulness of regulatory agencies, and dismayed anxiety among medical professionals.

Using my own itinerary as the narrative frame for this epilogue, and its primary source of data, I hope to provide a historical and sociological account of phenomena relevant to clinical investigation that I have directly observed, and that I think have bearing on present-day characteristics of this genre of medical research, and on some of the problems it now faces.

I

Let us start where it all began for me:

In a time-seasoned red brick building, set back a few hundred yards from a maze of trolley-car tracks and a big-city traffic circle, bounded and illumined by the famous medical school that flanks it, and situated at the end of a long hospital corridor—there existed a special community known as Ward F-Second. The windows of F-Second overlooked the laboratory. . . .

F-Second was an all-male, fifteen-bed metabolic research ward in a small but renowned teaching hospital, affiliated with a prominent medical school, located in one of the major hospitals of New England. A considerable number of the patients hospitalized on Ward F-Second were ill with diseases that are still not well understood and cannot be effectively controlled by present-day medical science. Partly as a consequence, many of these patients had agreed to act as research subjects for the . . . Metabolic Group of the hospital. This was a team of eleven young physicians: clinical investigators, whose dual responsibility was to care for the patients of F-Second and also to conduct research upon them.[2]

These are the opening paragraphs of *Experiment Perilous*, my first published book, based on the three years (from 1951 to 1954) that I spent at the Harvard Medical School-affiliated Peter Bent Brigham Hospital in Boston as a participant observer on its premier metabolic

research ward (F-2), and in the laboratory and conference room of its
Metabolic Group. This book centers on the entwined problems of the
patients and physicians of F-Second, their reciprocal stresses, and the
socially patterned ways they evolved for coming to terms with those
problems and stresses. Out of their common predicament of chronic
and terminal illness, high medical uncertainty and risk, severe therapeutic limitation, and constant closeness to death, and in response to
their dual, often conflicting roles of physician-investigators and patient-subjects, the men of F-Second created a tragicomic hospital community in which doctor and patient were collegially committed to medical research. I can still see the white, Greek temple-style building in
the Harvard Medical School quadrangle on which the back of the
hospital faced. Chiseled on its gleaming portico was the famous
Hippocratic aphorism: "Life is short, the art long, occasion instant,
decision difficult, experiment perilous" it read, like a cosmic sign-
board, conveying to me the essence of the world of F-Second. *Experiment Perilous* became the title of my book.

Path-making clinical research was being done by the Metabolic
Group, assaying the activity of newly synthesized steroids (ACTH,
cortisone, and Compound F), administering these compounds experimentally to patients with a wide array of clinical conditions, trying
various modes of administering them, and studying their biochemical,
biological, and clinical effects. The advent of ACTH and cortisone had
opened a new chapter in the clinical management of Addison's disease,
which until this time had been incapacitating and, in many instances,
fatal. The synthesis of cortisone and other adrenal cortical steroids had
also made it possible to remove the adrenal glands of patients, and to
maintain them post-operatively on substitution therapy. In collaboration with the Surgery and Renal Groups of the hospital, the Metabolic
Group was investigating the effects of total adrenalectomy on patients
with advanced hypertensive vascular disease, reactivated cancer of the
prostate, and hyperadrenalism. In conjunction with the Surgery Group,
the Metabolic Group was studying the body water and electrolyte problems of patients who had undergone a finger-fracture valvuloplasty, an
operation for mitral stenosis developed by a Brigham cardiac surgeon
(Dwight E. Harken) that had just become possible. With the Renal
Group, they were conducting studies on patients in acute renal failure
and with chronic kidney disease—particularly patients with severe

edema and those in renal shutdown who underwent hemodialysis on the artificial kidney machine. (Dialysis was in its infancy; the Renal Group was working with an improved model of one of Willem Kolff's original dialysis machines, which he had donated to the hospital; and chronic intermittent dialysis was not yet possible). Finally, under the joint aegis of the Medicine, Surgery, and Pathology Departments, the Metabolic, Renal, and Surgery Groups were engaged in what was known as the "Homologous Transplantation of Tissues and Organs" project, out of which came the world's first successful human kidney transplant, between identical twins, performed by Joseph E. Murray in 1954.

It was the golden era of clinical medical research—the epitome of Claude Bernard's conception of the symbiotic relationship between the laboratory and the bedside. "But if I had to deal with beginners [in medicine]," Claude Bernard wrote at the turn of the century:

I would first say to them, go to the hospital, that is the first thing to know. For, how can one analyze by means of experimentation, illnesses that one does not know? I do not say substitute the laboratory for the hospital. On the contrary, I say go first to the hospital, but that is not sufficient to achieve a scientific or experimental medicine: we must go into the laboratory to *analyze* experimentally what we have noted through clinical observation.[3]

This Bernard-ian view of experimental medicine was combined with the post-World War II paradigm of clinical research that the United States National Institutes of Health (NIH) exemplified. The NIH's institutionalization of disease-focused, patient-oriented research conducted by physician-scientists had begun in 1944 when the U.S. Congress created the National Cancer Center. This notion of medical research flourished throughout the thirteen-year period (1955 to 1968) that James A. Shannon was NIH's director. During that era, the NIH received enthusiastic and generous support from the Congress; its annual budget grew from $80 million to $1.4 billion; and the disease-specific institutes under its aegis proliferated.[4]

[C]linical investigation in American medicine was at its zenith. . . . [T]he war on disease was advancing on all fronts. The infrastructure of biomedical research had been put in place; clinical research centers had been built into the teaching hospitals of the major academic medical schools, and all the brightest young men—there were few women in medicine then, much less in medical research—were being recruited for federally funded post-doctoral positions.[5]

Modern Western medicine was in the midst of a biological and therapeutic revolution. Anatomy, pathology, and bacteriology, the pre-World War II reigning medical sciences, were giving way to physiology, cellular biology, virology, immunology, biochemistry, biophysics, molecular biology, and genetics. And on the clinical level, a continuous stream of pharmacological, surgical, and technological advances that had been occurring since the 1940s had catapulted medicine out of its prior, infectious disease era, when it could do little for most illnesses other than diagnose them, vigilantly follow their course, treat them with hands-on nursing care, and try to anticipate their outcome. At the center of this vortex, physiology, which during that period was focused on organ systems and their functions, was the integrative discipline that played a pivotal role in linking the basic scientist and the clinical investigator, the laboratory bench and the hospital bed.

Catalyzed by scientific progress, and facilitated by organizational reform and financial backing, this exuberant development of medicine and medical research was also fostered by strong moral and political convictions that grew out of World War II. These convictions were resoundingly stated and legislatively implemented in the International Health and Research Act of 1959, popularly known as the "Health for Peace" bill, that was passed by the U.S. Congress. In the words of this joint congressional resolution, the purpose of the act was:

To establish in the Department of Health, Education and Welfare the National Advisory Council for International Medical Research, and to establish in the Public Health Service the National Institute for Medical Research, in order to help mobilize the efforts of medical scientists, research workers, technologists, teachers, and members of the health professions generally, in the United States and abroad, for assault upon disease, disability and the impairments of man and for the improvement of the health of man through international cooperation in research, research training, and research planning.[6]

A view of disease and disability as "the common enemies of all nations and peoples" underlay this act, along with an evangelical commitment to "the full utilization of all possible resources, wherever they may be, in mankind's research effort against [them]."[7]

Peter Bent Brigham Hospital and its Ward F-Second incarnated these developments. It was also a setting in which clinical research of great audacity was conducted—some of it what Francis D. Moore (who was the surgeon-in-chief of the hospital during the time of my study) might now consider to fall in the realm of what he has called "desperate remedies for desperate patients" with "desperate[ly] hopeless" conditions.[8] Not only did the physician-investigators of F-2 and the Brigham dare greatly in some of the major forms of trail-blazing research that they conducted with patients, but in so doing, they incurred high mortality rates, both because of the very sick state of the patients who were their initial subjects, and because of the experimental nature of the surgical and medical treatments that they essayed. A heroic Brigham tradition underlay these undertakings. In the founding years of the hospital's history, for example, in the early 1900s, Harvey Cushing's brain tumor operations epitomized such daring ventures. In the 1920s, Eliot Cutler's attempts to operate on the mitral valve of the heart were comparably bold and risk-ridden. In the 1950s (the period of my F2/Brigham research), the human kidney transplantations and the total bilateral adrenalectomies that were launched, and also the experimentation with very high doses (up to 500 milligrams a day) of newly synthesized ACTH and cortisone, fell in the same intrepid (and at the time, highly controversial) pioneering category. Looking back at this period in the hospital's and the metabolic ward's history from his own perspective as a zealously path-making transplantation surgeon, Thomas E. Starzl wrote in 1984 (on the thirtieth anniversary of the Brigham's first successful renal transplant):

If gold medals and prizes were awarded to institutions instead of individuals, the Peter Bent Brigham Hospital of 30 years ago would have qualified. The ruling board and administrative structure of the hospital did not falter in their support of the quixotic objective of treating end-stage renal disease despite the long list of tragic failures that resulted from those early efforts, leavened only by occasional encouraging notations.[9]

The Brigham, Starzl went on to say, was "a unique world resource for that moment in history."[10]

The hospital was indeed a "world resource" in that era, in ways that extended beyond the part that it played in transplantation. It was a center and a crossroads of clinical research training for a stream of gifted, aspiring young physician-investigators who came to its portals from all over the United States, Canada, and Western Europe. For many of these physicians, the choice of a career in clinical research was closely tied to their wartime experiences. Whether they had been in combat during the war, members of a resistance movement in an occupied country, or insulated from it by their youthful ineligibility for service, the neutrality of their native land, or by emigration, medical research seemed to them the antithesis of the physical and moral destruction, and the death that World War II had brought in its wake. Among the deeper things that the physicians of F-2 and the Brigham shared was a war-borne sense of the kind of affirmation and engagement their involvement in medical research represented. For many of them, it was a constructive and expectant way to build a new life, and to contribute something meaningful to the future understanding of human disease, its prevention and its cure, at a historical juncture when (in the words of Nobel Laureate François Jacob), "one could feel the earth trembling" in biology and medicine, and the approach of "momentous events" in the laboratory.[11]

The small size of the hospital (250 beds), and the even smaller microcosm of Ward F-2 and the Metabolic Group within it helped to create a collective identity and an intimate atmosphere that fostered and facilitated the clinical research that took place within its walls. Physicians who trained or did their initial work at the Brigham in this era, as house officers, post-doctoral fellows, assistants, or associates, still remember what they describe as the "family spirit" of the hospital. It was "like a house," they said, in which "everybody knew everybody"—a "cohesive house" that "was always pulsating with excitement."[12]

More than size and ambience were involved. Certain organizational and structural features of the Brigham contributed to the close, face-to-face relations, and what was felt to be its "exhilarating . . . milieu of inquiry."[13] The hospital had a definite status hierarchy, topped by the physician-in-chief (George W. Thorn), the surgeon-in-chief (Francis D. Moore), and the pathologist-in-chief (Merrill Sosman), each of whom also occupied a prestigious Harvard Medical School chair. It was understood that the physician-in-chief had the most senior status. But at the same time, a collegial spirit and a great commonality of interests existed between the three chiefs, which enabled them and their services to work together in collaborative and creatively interdisciplinary ways. This was epitomized by the hospital's kidney transplantation project, which entailed long-term, multifaceted cooperation between medicine, surgery, and pathology, and drew upon the scientific and clinical competencies and talents of numerous persons in each of these divisions. The teamwork involved, Francis Moore has written, was like that of "a small orchestra."[14]

Horizontal and vertical bridging mechanisms interconnected the various levels of the physician hierarchy. The most pivotal of them was the intermediary of what might be termed "junior/senior" and "senior/junior" status roles. Under the authority and close supervision of the senior staff, the bright younger physicians, with at least several years of research training, who filled these positions acted as a sort of junior faculty, and were also responsible for running the daily activities of clinical research teams and their facilities, like the Metabolic Group, its Ward F-Second, and its laboratories.

The physical layout of Ward F-Second and the way that it was built into the hospital facilitated the kind of clinical research in which it was involved. It optimized the conditions under which patients' dietary intake could be carefully controlled and all their body excretions accurately measured. The existence of a specially constructed, combined research and clinical laboratory immediately adjacent to the ward reified Claude Bernard's dictum about the importance that navigating between the hospital and the laboratory had for achieving "a scientific or experimental medicine." It also helped to forge fruitful working relationships between basic scientists, clinical investigators, and clinicians.

In 1991, in the midst of an oral history conference on the development of clinical research, some very senior physician alumni of the Brigham described these aspects of what the hospital was like in the era when I did my *Experiment Perilous* research. Afterward, a younger associate professor of medicine exclaimed:

I envy the time in which there was movement back and forth from the wards to the laboratory and back again, [and] when clinical research was something that was visible to medical students and house staff and junior faculty. It's not now. Research is something that goes on somewhere [else] on the . . . campus . . . [and we] have gone from a small, intimate department to a large corporation. If you look at the budget sheets of most major departments of medicine, they are up there, and the chairman has become a CEO. The chairman and the senior faculty are not on the wards talking and looking.[15]

While scrupulously trying to avoid the pitfalls of retrospectively romanticizing the past, or the "goldenness" of "the great golden years" of clinical investigation, the participants in this conference all agreed that many of the organizational attributes of the Brigham that were once so valuable in promoting patient-oriented clinical research, were now largely "gone."[16]

The effervescent atmosphere notwithstanding, during the 1951-1954 period when I made my study, the Metabolic Group and its collaborators were passing through the characteristic "black years"[17] of very early clinical trials with patient-subjects. Successful outcomes with the radical new therapies tried were few and ephemeral. Unknown and uncontrolled factors abounded. Serious, unexpected, and inexplicable adverse side-effects frequently occurred. And many of the already gravely ill patient-subjects died as a result of their end-stage illnesses, complicated still further by experimental procedures. Some of the patients receiving high doses of ACTH or cortisone experienced psychotic episodes, as did a number of the first patients successfully operated on for mitral stenosis. Those persons in chronic renal failure who were put on the artificial kidney machine relapsed into the terminal state from which they were momentarily rescued, because there was no chronic intermittent dialysis to sustain them. In this period which antedated the development of immunosuppressive chemotherapy to forestall the inexorable rejection reaction that grafts of other people's tissues or organs set off in a recipient's body, the patients who received kidney transplants were treated with a crude form of whole-body radiation that usually accelerated the predicted fatal outcome of their medical conditions. And one after another, the patients with severe advanced hypertensive vascular disease or advanced cancer of the prostate on whom total adrenalectomies were carried out died enigmatic deaths that seemed to be related to their "adrenal-less" state as well as to their grave illnesses. The added suffering and risk to which these path-making clinical trials often subjected patient-subjects, and their dismal, death-ridden results triggered dismayed comments and vociferous criticism throughout the hospital. Eventually, a quietly declared clinical moratorium was called on the performance of total bilateral adrenalectomies, although for a while, in his annual reports, the hospital's physician-in-chief continued to refer to the results of the adrenalectomies as "encouraging."[18] The trials with mitral valve surgery, the artificial kidney machine, and with human kidney transplants went forward, though, in spite of the overwhelming mortality rates that accompanied them, and the acute ethical questions they raised.

Institutional review boards, hospital ethics committees, and ethics consult services did not yet exist; and it was not until fifteen years later that the field of inquiry and action known as bioethics would emerge. But at the close of each day, at the evening rounds that the Metabolic Group held in a conference room next to Ward F-Second and its laboratory, these physician-researchers did more than report on the clinical course of each of their patients and summarize the data forthcoming from their laboratory. Through collective debate, lamentation, gallows-humor joking, and also through the "game of chance" in which they engaged—their ironic, protesting, self-mocking, yet hopeful ritual of taking bets on how their experiments would turn out—the physicians of the Metabolic Group wrestled with the problems that they faced of being clinical investigators, expressed their feelings about them, and tried to deal with them. Particularly troublesome to them in what they termed "this laboratory life" that they had elected to lead were the high level of uncertainty with which all their endeavors were surrounded; the severe therapeutic limitations under which they labored, which curtailed their ability to improve their patients' clinical conditions, arrest the relentless course of their diseases, or, in many instances, prevent their deaths; and the numerous ways in which their responsibilities as clinicians and as investigators conflicted. Because the physicians of the Metabolic Group were not solely, and sometimes not predominantly, oriented to benefiting patients, they often felt morally uncertain about how they reconciled the dualistic requirements of their professional role. On the one hand, it was possible that they had unnecessarily impeded an experiment because they had been too concerned about the welfare of their patient-subject; on the other hand, they might have exposed a patient to an undue amount of risk and suffering because they had been too avid about the research they were conducting. In this latter regard, they felt especially uneasy about temporarily withdrawing patients from needed medications, or administering placebos to them as part of a research design. "There are times when this business makes me feel like a Dr. Jekyll and a Mr. Hyde," one of the members of the Metabolic Group commented. When something went wrong with an experiment, when their subjects who were also their patients grew sicker, and especially when they died, the physician-investigators felt more like Dr. Jekylls.[19]

On F-Second, inside the ward community they formed around their common predicament, patients lived out and discussed the same issues of clinical research that their physicians pondered. Many F-Seconders had become experts in their own diseases and in the experiments to which they had consented. Some of the studies they agreed to undergo were pertinent to their medical conditions and gave them the hope that through the research to which they contributed, treatments for their illnesses might be developed. Among those patients who had been told that this was not probable and that their prospects for recovery were slight, there were some for whom acting as a research subject was a way of "not giving up." In both groups of patient-subjects, the desire to do something "for the good of medical science, and for the humane benefit of others in the future" was prevalent. Some patients achieved prominence—what the ward called "stardom"—as research subjects, both in the eyes of their fellow-patients and the physicians of the Metabolic Group. They were especially likely to be viewed as "collaborators" and "colleagues" in the research for which they served as subjects. Patients who were among the first to have successful cardiac surgery even founded a Mended Hearts Club of their own; and those who underwent adrenalectomies created a comparably select Adrenalectomy Club, with a president, vice president, and secretary-treasurer who were the first, second, and third respectively to have their adrenal glands removed. (When the president of the Adrenalectomy Club died, by tacit consent, his office was left vacant.)

Although in the social world and the value system of Ward F-Second patients viewed becoming a research subject as an effective, rewarding, and admirable way of coping with their situation, they did not consider it either wholly beneficial or uncontroversial. The drawbacks and dangers that it entailed, as well as the assets and virtues it represented, were continually weighed by the men of F-Second. In their ongoing argumentation, Leo Angelico, a 40-year old patient with undiagnosable paraplegia of his legs and flaccid paralysis of his left arm, who was a "permanent," in-hospital subject for an array of the

Metabolic Group's studies, and 28-year old Paul O'Brian, dying of Hodgkin's disease, who was fiercely determined not to surrender to the centripetal pull of the hospital or the seduction of the role of research subject, became morality play-like figures for the ward. Around their persons and the antithetic positions they took, F-Second's eternal debate about what was the best adjustment to their situation raged.[20]

I do not mean to portray this Ward F-Second/Metabolic Group/ Peter Bent Brigham Hospital universe as a patient-oriented clinical research utopia. Experiments were launched in that setting, such as total bilateral adrenalectomies for the treatment of severe hypertension, that perhaps never should have been undertaken (although in Chicago, Charles Huggins was demonstrating a favorable response to adrenalectomy in patients with advanced hormonal-dependent prostate and breast cancer). Nor was engaging some of the patients who sacrificially contributed to the early development of dialysis and organ transplantation unquestionably justifiable: for example, the patients with end-stage renal disease whose one or two dialyses on the Kolff-model artificial kidney machine could not be repeated; or the "kidney-less" patients, whose single kidney had been removed because of injury or, even worse, because of mistaken identity, who underwent renal transplants from unrelated, unmatched donors, and without immunosuppressive therapy. Unbridled enthusiasm, optimistic bias, and the desperate desire to save otherwise doomed patients sometimes led to experimental excesses. But by and large, the research carried out in this setting, at that time, under the medical-scientific, historical, and social circumstances I have described, was done competently, thoughtfully, and ethically, with the full knowledge and close mutual supervision of junior and senior physician-investigators, the informed consent of the patient-subjects, and with a dedication to this sort of research that has become increasingly rare.

II

From the Brigham I went on to Columbia University to become the chief field-worker for a sociological research project that was involved in studying the education and socialization of medical students.[21] For the next four years, once again as a participant observer, this time at Cornell University Medical College in New York City, I followed the entwined processes of scientific, clinical, and attitude learning through which medical students were progressively transformed into physicians. My prior immersion in a hospital-based clinical research world, pervaded by medical uncertainty, made me more aware than I otherwise might have been of what I identified as the training for uncertainty sequence through which medical students passed.[22] It consisted of a flow of medical school experiences that successively and cumulatively taught students to perceive medical uncertainty, to recognize and acknowledge some of its implications for the role of physician and for the well-being and security of patients, and to develop shared, patterned ways of coping with its meaning and consequences, as well as its de facto existence. Students were confronted with three basic types of uncertainty as they advanced from one phase of the curriculum to another: the uncertainties that originated in their incomplete mastery of the huge and rapidly growing body of knowledge and skills that modern Western medicine encompasses; the uncertainties that stemmed from the gaps, limitations, and ambiguities that also characterize this corpus of medical knowledge and technique; and the uncertainties that grew out of difficulties in distinguishing between personal ignorance and ineptitude, and the intrinsically imperfect and tentative properties of medicine itself. Some of the collective ways of coming to terms with these forms of uncertainty that medical students developed were junior versions of the coping mechanisms that the physicians of the Metabolic Group had employed. Although medical school curricula have undergone many revisions and numerous reforms since the mid-1950s when I made these observations, it is notable how important this training for uncertainty continues to be. For example, in the testimony given by medical students about the impact that Harvard Medical School's New Pathway program is currently having upon them, they cite "learn[ing] that medicine is filled with uncertainty—indeed, that uncertainty rather than certainty tends to be the norm," and the "process of wrestling with [it]" as the most "impressive . . . achievement" of the curriculum.[23]

III

U.S. medical schools in the 1950s were relatively small-scale institutions in which students, house staff, and fellows had continuous contact with even the most senior faculty, whom they could watch carry out their triple, interconnected roles of teaching, caring for patients, and doing research. Describing what his daily round was like at the time that he was professor of medicine and physician-in-chief, George Thorn said that he "assumed" he was "a mentor for a good many people." "I don't think," he remarked, that it involved

anything else except to start rounds at seven-thirty or eight o'clock in the morning with students, and be with them, with . . . patients. You [didn't] get to your office administratively until one o'clock or so in the afternoon, and what [you did] in the meantime with your research group [was] to hope you [could] stimulate them. You [did] things yourself in the first few years and then you count[ed] on these bright young people that join[ed] you later to keep it going, and you provided the glue and the finances.[24]

The clinical research in which faculty were largely engaged in that era was patient-oriented, emanating at the bedside, on the hospital wards, and in the medical chart record rooms, before it was transposed to the laboratory. This meant that medical students and young physicians had ample first-hand opportunities to watch this sort of research unfold, and, if they chose, to participate and become competent in it.

One of the ironies of this 1950s period was that as a consequence of the veritable outpouring of funds that became available to medical schools at that time, especially through National Institutes of Health research and training grants, departments grew larger and larger; and as they did, the responsibility of operating and managing them began to take chairmen and senior faculty further and further away from the bedside, the patient side, the student side, and from the laboratory. Here is how Paul Beeson, renowned clinician, teacher, and clinical investigator, portrays that metamorphosis:[25]

In 1952, I went to Yale and stayed there for 13 years. 1952 was really the heyday—the money was just rolling in—and Congress was giving medical research more than it was asking for. When I went to Yale, the Department of Medicine had 18 full-time people. I thought it was a huge department. . . . But it grew . . . steadily. You couldn't stop it. The money was there. All of our division people wanted to enlarge their labs and to bring in more fellows. . . . By the time I left, . . . we had about 65 full-time people. . . . I enjoyed the expansion and the excitement and the training of new people, but I found by 1965 that I was no longer doing much teaching of students, and I was no longer seeing patients . . . regularly, [or] doing . . . research. . . . I was sitting in my office, and someone was coming in to see me every 15 minutes about this or that.

The scale of full-time U.S. medical school faculty has continued to grow since then. The Yale Department of Medicine now has more than 250 faculty members; and in the 126 accredited U.S. medical schools taken as an aggregate, faculty increased about 25 percent between the academic years of 1989-1990 and 1993-1994. No matter what their status, most faculty are now on "soft money," which means they must devote considerable time and energy to generating income for their salaries and the ongoing of the big departments to which they belong, chiefly from patient fees or research grants. Partly as a consequence, face-to-face, in situ teaching of medical students, house staff, and other junior physicians in which members of this enormously expanded faculty currently engage has progressively diminished.

What is more, the nature of the research in which faculty are involved has changed dramatically since the 1950s. With the advent and ascendancy of molecular biology, organ system-oriented pathophysiological research that comes from observation on patients in clinical settings has given way to molecular-based research that is confined to the laboratory. "Going down" to the molecule has triggered an explosion of reductionistic new knowledge that disaggregates biological systems by breaking them into smaller and smaller parts. Once the clock has been taken apart, so to speak, it will have to be put back together again. But at this juncture, an integrating paradigm does not yet exist that enables physicians to think about patients in molecular detail when such knowledge is crucial for diagnosis, prevention, or therapy, without being encumbered by a myriad of micro-facts that impede clinical analysis and decision. This intellectual gap between "medicine and molecule"[26] is reflected in the research presently conducted by an increasing number of faculty in the clinical as well as the science departments of medical schools.

IV

At Cornell University Medical College and its associated New York Hospital, as had been the case at the Peter Bent Brigham, and also at the Massachusetts General Hospital where I had done some sociological research on the psychiatric service, I met a number of talented European physicians who had come to the United States to prepare themselves for clinical research careers in academic medicine. I not only became interested in why they had selected the United States for their postdoctoral training, but why many of them were apprehensively uncertain about whether they would be able to pursue their research or their careers when they returned home. Much more seemed to be involved than the material difficulties they anticipated in obtaining the ample research funds and equipment to which they had become accustomed in the United States. What worried these physicians was how they, their professional outlook, and their work would be received in what they termed the "old Europe" milieux from which they came. They were not even sure that the biomedical phenomena and questions in which they were absorbed, and the scientific concepts, language, and techniques they used, would be understood and accepted by the powerful, gatekeeping professors of medicine under whose aegis their careers would obligatorily unfold.

At the end of the 1950s, throughout a significant part of Europe, with the notable exceptions of England and the Scandinavian countries, a good deal of medical research was housed, sociologically as well as architecturally, in "ancient buildings [which were] remnants of a glorious past."[27] "Like ruined, *grands seigneurs* we have preserved the old 'châteaus' and furnishings of another age," proclaimed professor of medicine Raoul Kourilsky, in the *Leçon inaugurale* that he delivered in 1958, when he assumed his chair at the University of Paris. "The great sacrifice has been research," he continued. "We have watched from afar the triumphant ascent of biology."[28] The university-affiliated research units that existed in Continental Europe at that time were typically headed by one full professor, with the power, authority, and the style of a *grand patron*. Generally, all the other members of the research group were juniors, and greatly subordinate to him in status. Positions like research assistant and research associate, assistant professor and associate professor did not exist. Within this very hierarchical structure (described by one Belgian research physician whom I interviewed, "like a building in which the ground and top floors have been constructed, but in which they haven't gotten around yet to putting in the floors in between"), aspiring young clinical investigators occupied impermanent, often untitled, and sometimes unpaid positions that depended solely on the good will of the *patron*, and what monies he had at his disposal to support research. The "high professor," patriarchal ambiance of these European settings did not encourage young physicians to express their ideas, or to take the initiative of translating them into scientific inquiry. In contrast, such young physicians testified, the atmosphere surrounding medical research in the U.S. medical centers to which they came for postgraduate training was "a striking departure" from what they had known in Europe. They were "amazed" they said, and "delighted" that senior professors and scientists invited them to formulate questions, listened with respect and interest to what they had to say, and allowed, even asked them to develop research around the most promising of their ideas.

In the summer of 1959, I made a trip to Belgium, England, France, and Switzerland with the intent of learning more directly and in greater detail about the research conditions and problems that European physicians whom I had come to know at Harvard and Cornell had described. That first journey rapidly led to a study of the social, cultural, and historical factors that affected clinical research and research careers in Belgium, which became the microcosm where I explored distinctly Belgian versions of general European patterns. In turn, that inquiry developed into a study of Belgium through the windows of its medical laboratories; and eventually, it transported me to Zaire—the former Belgian Congo—where I did first-hand sociological research as well.

But this is a saga of almost 35 years' duration, spanning 1959 to 1993, which came to a close with the publication in 1994 of my most recent book, *In the Belgian Château*, whose scope falls outside the orbit of this epilogue.[29] The specific pertinence of my questing in Belgium to the examination of clinical research in which we are engaged here, resides in the issues with which that prolonged study began. The "case" of Belgium, seen in relationship to other Continental European countries and the United States in the late 1950s and the early 1960s, throws into bas-relief the role that social structure and social institutions, cultural attitudes and values, and historical tradition play in shaping, facilitating, and hindering the ongoing of scientific research (be it medical or otherwise), and the ideas, efforts, and accomplishments of those who participate in it.

V

I seem to have a penchant for spending many years, even decades, in pursuit of the topics and themes to which I have devoted my research. Certainly that is true of my involvement as a participant observer and chronicler of the development of organ transplantation, the artificial kidney, and the artificial heart. In 1968, fourteen years after I had witnessed the pioneering clinical trials with dialysis and renal transplantation at the Peter Bent Brigham Hospital, I began what became a 24-year long collaboration with historian of medicine and science Judith P. Swazey, studying the evolution of organ replacement—chiefly in (U.S.) American society, but with side trips to explore particular phenomena and events in Hawaii, Majuro (the Marshall Islands), Canada, Europe, and China. During this period, from transplanting the kidney, the field has expanded to encompass the transplantation of virtually every solid organ in the human body, and many sorts of tissues and bones as well. Procedures for multiple-organ transplants have been devised and put into practice; and increasing numbers of successive organ transplants have come to be performed. The artificial kidney machine has been technologically advanced. Chronic intermittent dialysis has become feasible, and progressively more streamlined. Peritoneal dialysis has been introduced. And in the wake of the meteoric rise and fall of the Jarvik-7 artificial heart, research on temporary, bridge-to-transplant ventricular assist devices has been undertaken, along with undeterred attempts to design an effective, permanently implantable, total artificial heart.

This evolution has been undergirded and galvanized by what Judith Swazey and I have termed the "courage to fail" ethos[30] of the physician-researchers who have pushed forward the frontiers of organ replacement through their pioneering roles in the development and clinical trials of the technology, procedures, and immunosuppressive compounds that the process of organ transplantation and the deployment of artificial organs entail. Their bellicose, heroic, and indomitably optimistic outlook—with its "death is the enemy," "dare greatly," "climb every mountain," "we shall overcome," "accentuate the positive," "you've got to believe," "rescue" components—has strengthened their commitment to the field of organ replacement, reinforced their medical and moral rationale for the daring research and therapeutic innovation in which they have engaged, and helped them to persevere in the face of engulfing uncertainty, high risk, daunting obstacles, and tragic clinical outcomes. But this same "courage to fail" ideology has also led to distortions of professional judgment and experimental and therapeutic excesses, such as over-enthusiasm about the immunosuppressive drugs cyclosporine and tacrolimus; premature expectations about a breakthrough in organ xenografts; the performance of multivisceral, "cluster" transplants in dying children; and an open-ended willingness to carry out one transplant after another in patients whose bodies continually and acceleratingly reject the organs they receive. The over-determined optimism and defiance of limits which empowered these physicians, helped them to cope with the challenging, stress-ridden situations they faced, and enabled them to assist patients who could benefit from transplants or artificial organs, have also subjected such patients to added jeopardy and suffering. These patterns, their double-edged nature, and the dilemmas they pose are not confined to the sphere of organ replacement. They were endemic to the range of "experiment[s] perilous" conducted on Ward F-Second; and they seem to play an important role in the dynamics of patient-oriented clinical research, particularly in its early phases, and especially in the context of American medicine.

One of the recurrent forms of the "ritualized optimism"[31] clinical investigators display, which I have repeatedly observed, is embedded in what I call "the therapeutic innovation cycle."[32] In the case of organ transplantation, I have watched it happen again and again as one new immunosuppressive agent after another has emerged from the laboratory and experimentation on animals, and been taken to clinical trials on human patients. This occurred in a particularly flamboyant way in connection with the appearance of cyclosporine on the scene. At the end of the 1970s and throughout the early 1980s, clinical investigators and prominent transplanters exuberantly hailed the "advent" of cyclosporine. Hundreds of medical journal articles described it as the most "important," "unique," "interesting," "remarkable," "exciting," "powerful," "effective," "superior" agent yet discovered in the effort to combat rejection. The fervor with which it was embraced precipitated the dramatic rise in the number of organ transplantations that were carried out during the 1980s, a development which was reported no less enthusiastically in the professional literature than in the mass media. As the 1980s unfolded, numerous toxic side effects of cyclosporine

were progressively cited in the literature. At first, they were characterized as "unforeseen" and "surprising," and largely attributed to inexpe-
rience in the clinical management of the drug—its modes of administration and dosage—or to the complications of the "lethal diseases"
from which the patients receiving it suffered, rather than to the intrinsic properties of a fungal metabolite like cyclosporine, or to generic
responses of the human organism. Slowly and regretfully, the generalized tendency to extol cyclosporine, and to explain away or play down
its limitations and iatrogenic dangers, gave way to more balanced statements about its drawbacks as well as its positive attributes. By this
time, another new immunosuppressive drug, known by the code name
of FK 506 (tacrolimus), was entering early clinical trials, and was
being greeted with enthusiastic expectancy.[33]

As I have written, there are no intrinsic biological or pharmacological reasons why recognition of the beneficial properties of a new agent
should precede identification of its limitations and unwanted side effects, or why clinical investigators should be "surprised" or "disappointed" when they encounter them. Underlying these patterns is a
nonscientific, utopian belief in the existence of an all-therapeutic,
"magic-bullet" kind of medical treatment and a "necessity to hope"
outlook that are intensified by the desire of research physicians to
effectively care for, and prolong the lives of the gravely ill patients
who are also their research subjects.[34]

One of the areas of modern medicine in which this kind of scientific magic most frequently surfaces is the field of oncology. Periodically, it is announced that an agent has been discovered that has the
potential capacity to eliminate primary tumors, and to slow the growth
and prevent the spread of metastatic tumors. These initial reports are
invariably followed by more cautiously phrased and soberly toned publications, which dispel the claim that at last a "solution to cancer" has
been found. Nevertheless, such a solution continues to be hoped for,
and to be sought; and this sets into motion once more, the same therapeutic innovation cycle.

VI

Spare Parts, the second co-authored book on organ replacement that
Judith Swazey and I published (in 1992), contained within it an exten-

sive, first-hand study of the Jarvik-7 artificial heart experiment.[35] (Taking our cue from Act IV, scene iii, of Shakespeare's *Hamlet*, we termed the device a "desperate appliance.") I will not attempt to summarize the dramatic and ultimately tragic history of the Jarvik-7, or present our analytic interpretation of its very public rise and fall. But there are several aspects of the Jarvik-7 story, and the larger issues about patient-oriented clinical research which they raise, that I would like to briefly discuss as I bring my epilogue to a close.

Our research revealed that knowledgeable onlookers had serious questions and strong doubts about the readiness of the Jarvik-7 for human use at the time that the University of Utah artificial heart team decided to implant it into Dr. Barney Clark, the first terminally ill patient-subject with Class IV cardiomyopathy who was selected to receive it. Furthermore, through our observations, interviews, and examination of relevant documents, we learned that the principal investigator of the Jarvik-7 experiment had little prior experience or trained expertise in designing or conducting patient-oriented clinical research; that he submitted several scientifically inadequate drafts of a research protocol for the clinical trials of the device to the Institutional Review Board (IRB) of the University of Utah Medical Center; and that the IRB was so concerned about the deficiencies of the protocol, that they overstepped their role and helped the investigator to rewrite the proposal and turn it into an acceptable scientific plan. Around the four successive patients whom he implanted with the device (three patients at Humana Hospital in Louisville, Kentucky, following Dr. Clark's implant and death), the principal investigator engaged in what some of those working with him described as highly empirical, unfocused, trial-and-error research that entailed the omnivorous collection of reams of computerized data, which were only occasionally and crudely analyzed, and in the end, resulted in very few publications. All of this, and other questionable features of the Jarvik-7 clinical trials, took place under the supposedly watchful eyes of a wide range of relevant "gatekeepers," including institutional officials and members of the IRB at the University of Utah and the Humana Hospital Audubon; the Food and Drug Administration's (FDA) Division of Cardiovascular Devices, and its advisory panel; senior officials of the National Institutes of Health (NIH), the National Heart, Lung, and Blood Institute, and its artificial heart program; the wider professional community of cardiovascular and cardiac surgeons, especially those involved in cardiac replacement; patients and their families who consented to an artificial heart implant and their referring physicians; members of the artificial heart implant teams; non-physician experts in areas such as medical ethics and health law; the print and electronic media; and professional journals, their staff, and peer reviewers. Despite all the potential social control and regulatory agents that surrounded the Jarvik-7 trials, and the extraordinary amount of media scrutiny and coverage that was centered on them, questions about their medical scientific rationale, about the merits of the research protocol on which they were based, and about the qualifications of their chief investigator were not openly or authoritatively asked.

The result was that the experiment went forward until January 1990 when the FDA withdrew the agency's approval for the investigational use of the Jarvik-7 heart. Deficiencies in the manufacturing quality control of the device, in monitoring the research sites, in the training of personnel, and in the studies being conducted were cited by the FDA as the reasons for their recall motion, along with the adverse patient reactions that had occurred. On balance, the FDA concluded, "the risks to patients were outweighing the benefits." No explicit mention was made of whether the clinical trials should have been launched in the first place, or whether the principal investigator had the competence to properly design and run them. It was not conceivable that this "desperate appliance" could serve as a life-saving, "desperate remedy" for Barney Clark, William Schroeder, Murray Haydon, and Jack Burcham, the four patient-subjects in whom it was implanted. (They died 112, 620, 488, and 10 days respectively after their implants, of thromboemboli, biomaterial-related sepsis, rampant infections, and other complications.) The only justification for the trials was the contribution they might make to clinically relevant biomedical knowledge and technology. From its inception, however, this project and its chief surgeon-implanter-investigator failed to meet the standards of scientific excellence that might have made such contributions possible. In my view, this is one of the major reasons why the Jarvik-7 "experiment perilous" was fundamentally unethical.

When it comes to clinical trials, Richard Peto, Oxford University's renowned expert on the subject, has stated, "ignorance is the biggest form of misconduct."[36] By this he meant two things: first, that he believes flawed medical research, conducted by physicians who are inadequately trained in scientific reasoning and in the basics of clinical trial design and execution, occurs more frequently than practices like falsifying, fabricating, or plagiarizing data; and second, that he considers such slipshod research along with fraudulence in science to be morally as well as intellectually egregious. What we uncovered through our exploration of the Jarvik-7 story has not only come to exemplify for me the wrongdoing and damage that incompetent clinical research entails, but also how difficult it is to erect and enforce systematic surveillance and oversight of that research. This monitoring problem is greatly magnified in the case of very large-scale clinical trials, such as those carried out under the aegis of the National Institutes of Health— for example, the National Cancer Institute's National Surgical Adjuvant Breast and Bowel Project (NSABP), which conducts and coordinates surgical and drug treatments for breast and bowel cancers; involves tens of thousands of subjects, and more than 400 collaborating centers across North America; and has been headed and administered for many years by one investigator, the renowned University of Pittsburgh surgeon and cancer researcher, Bernard Fisher, with the assistance of a single deputy. In 1995, several of the major studies run by the NSABP were found to be contaminated with falsified data, on the one hand, and beset with serious problems of randomization, on the other. Independently of the participating physicians' integrity, their understanding of, and respect for the scientific process, and their methodological and technical competence, or of the clinical and experimental stature and the management skill of the project's director, such aberrations and defects seem inevitable to a social scientist like myself, unless an entire new social system is invented that is more appropriate for directing clinical trials of this magnitude and dispersion. For example, having a single physician-researcher, located in Pittsburgh, who is responsible for running a project like this seems to me to be analogous to assuming that medical research can still be carried out by solo investigators, working in their own laboratories, equipped only with test tubes, glass beakers, syringes, pipettes, casseroles, simple microscopes, and notebooks, as was the case in the anatomo-pathological and bacteriological eras of medicine.

VII

Chris Feudtner, a young physician and historian of medicine and science, who kindly read and critiqued the text for this introduction, told me he was particularly struck by the fact that both the "clock" of biological knowledge and the "clock" of social relationships that once integrated and sustained patient-oriented clinical research have been disassembled by scientific, historical, and sociological developments that have ensued since the 1950s. Especially notable is the way that the processes of molecularization, on the one hand, and the expansion of scale and scope, on the other, have converged to diminish the ranks of physician-investigators, and move them away from the bedside, the patients, and the students. If this line of analysis is valid (as I believe it is), then it will take more than the increased and stabilized funding, improved training, and greater respect currently being recommended by the American Federation of Clinical Research[37] and the U.S. Institute of Medicine[38] to reinfuse patient-oriented clinical research with the creative vitality and competence, and the relevance to the diagnosis, treatment, and prevention of human disease that previously characterized it.

NOTES

This epilogue was originally delivered as the Foundations of Medical Science Distinguished Lecture, before the McGill University Faculty of Medicine, in Montreal, Canada, on March 8, 1995. It later appeared as an article in the Winter 1996 issue of *Perspectives in Biology and Medicine* 39, no. 2: 206–26.

I am grateful to Nicholas A. Christakis, Willy De Craemer, and Chris Feudtner for their careful reading of the article, their thoughtful responses to it, and for the suggestions they made to improve it.

1. M. Frase-Blunt, "Choosing Medicine Over Molecules," *AAMC Reporter* 4 (December 1994): 1 and 3.

2. R.C. Fox, *Experiment Perilous: Physicians and Patients Facing the Unknown* (New Brunswick, NJ: Transaction Publishers, 1997), 13.

3. L. Binet, ed., *Esquisses et Notes de Travail Inédites de Claude Bernard* (Paris: Masson & Cie., 1952), 105 (my translation).

4. B. Culliton, "NIH Begins Year-Long 100th Birthday Party," *Science* 234 (7 November 1986): 662-63.

5. G. N. Gill, "The End of the Physician-Scientist?" *The American Scholar* 53 (Summer 1984): 353-68.

6. 86th Congress, 1st Session, S.J. RES. 41, in the Senate of the United States (2 February 1959).

7. H. A. Rusk, "'Health for Peace' Gains," *N.Y. Times* (13 March 1960): 61.

8. F. D. Moore, "The Desperate Case: CARE (Costs, Applicability, Research, Ethics)," *JAMA* 261 (10 March 1989): 1483-84.

9. T. E. Starzl, "Landmark Identical Twin Case," *JAMA* 251(18 May 1984): 2572-73.

10. Ibid.

11. F. Jacob, *La Statue intérieure* (Paris: Seuil [Éditions Odile], 1987), 264 (my translation).

12. R. C. Fox, J. P. Swazey, and J. C. Watkins, eds., *The Study of the Sick: Proceedings of an Oral History Conference on the Development of Clinical Research* (Philadelphia: Medical College of Pennsylvania, 1992), 39.

13. Ibid., 40.

14. F. D. Moore, report of the surgeon-in chief, in the *Thirty-Seventh Annual Report of the Peter Bent Brigham Hospital, for the Year 1950*, p. 60.

15. Fox, Swazey, and Watkins, eds., *The Study of the Sick,* 65.

16. Fox, Swazey, and Watkins, eds., *The Study of the Sick,* 39.

17. F. D. Moore, "Medical Responsibility for the Prolongation of Life," *JAMA* 206 (7 October 1968): 384-86.

18. G. W. Thorn, report of the physician-in chief, in the *Thirty-Ninth Annual Report of the Peter Bent Brigham Hospital, for the Year* 1952, pp. 56-58.

19. Fox, *Experiment Perilous,* p. 62.

20. Ibid., 191-205.

21. R. K. Merton, "Some Preliminaries to a Sociology of Medical Education." In *The Student-Physician: Introductory Studies in the Sociology of Medical Education,* edited by R. K. Merton, G. Reader, and P. L. Kendall (Cambridge: Harvard University Press, 1957), 3-79.

22. R. C. Fox, "Training for Uncertainty." In *The Student-Physician,* edited by Merton, Reader, and Kendall, 207-41.

23. M. T. Silver, "The Student Experience." In *New Pathways to Medical Education: Learning to Learn at Harvard Medical School,* edited by D. C. Tosteson, S. J. Adelstein, and S. T. Carver (Cambridge: Harvard University Press, 1994), 126-28.

24. Fox, Swazey, and Watkins, eds, *The Study of the Sick,* 15.

25. Ibid., 64-65.

26. Frase-Blunt, "Choosing Medicine Over Molecules."

27. D. M. Gates, "Basic Research in Europe," *Science* 128, 3318 (1958): 227-35.

28. R. Kourilsky, "Leçon inaugurale," *L'Expansion scientifique française* (1958) (my translation).

29. R. C. Fox, *In the Belgian Château: The Spirit and Culture of a European Society in an Age of Change* (Chicago: Ivan R. Dee, 1994). R.C. Fox, *Le Château des Belges: Un peuple se retrouve,* translated by Christine Pagnoulle and edited by Yves Winkin (Louvain-la-Neuve, Belgium: Duculot, 1997).

30. R. C. Fox and J. P. Swazey, *The Courage to Fail: A Social View of Organ Transplants and Dialysis* (Chicago: University of Chicago Press, 1974).

31. B. Malinowski, *Magic, Science, and Religion, and Other Essays* (Glencoe, Ill.: Free Press, 1948).

32. R. C. Fox, J. P. Swazey, and E. M. Cameron, "Social and Ethical Problems in the Treatment of End-Stage Renal Disease Patients." In *Controversies in Nephrology and Hypertension,* edited by R.G. Narins (New York: Churchill Livingstone, 1984), 46-53.

33. R. C. Fox and J. P. Swazey, *Spare Parts: Organ Replacement in American Society* (New York: Oxford University Press, 1992), 154-69, 199.

34. T. E. Starzl, *The Puzzle People: Memoirs of a Transplant Surgeon* (Pittsburgh: University of Pittsburgh Press, 1992).

35. Fox and Swazey, *Spare Parts,* 95-193.

36. Quoted in R. Nowak, "Problems in Clinical Trials Go Beyond Misconduct," *Science* 264 (10 June 1994): 1538.

37. E. Marshall, "Clinicians Catch Top NIH Officials' Attention," *Science* 267 (January 1995): 448.

38. W. N. Kelley and M. A. Randolph, eds., *Careers in Clinical Research: Obstacles and Opportunities* (Washington, D.C.: National Academy Press, 1994).

Index

(Note: patients' names are given in quotation marks.)

Achievement: patients', 140-141, 151, 165, 251; social valuation of, 147, 253. *See also* Success

ACTH (adrenocorticotrophic hormone): study and importance of, 16-19, 30, 51, 92, 93, 94-95; and Addison's disease, 69-71; test, 120, 121; psychotic reaction to, 129-30. *See also* Steroid compounds

Addison's disease, 17, 22, 31, 40, 45, 57, 69-71, 151, 153-154, 157, 159, 162-164, 212, 233; with diabetes, 23, 32, 44, 72-73, 74, 102; with mitral stenosis, 38-39, 51-52; and water test, 52-53

Adrenalectomy, 102, 142, 180; study of, 17, 18, 32, 34, 35, 36, 41, 42, 44, 54, 56, 61; and hypertensive disease, 58-60, 72, 126, 136, 137, 138, 139-140, 141-142, 151, 153-154, 160, 167, 211, 213; uncertainties, 60, 127-128; and Addison's disease, 70-71, 151; in news stories, 93-94

Adrenalectomy Club, 141, 148, 160, 184, 188, 189, 213, 217, 251-252

Ages: of Metabolic Group physicians 19; of F-Second patients, 21, 22

Aldosterone, 30, 36-37. *See also* Steroid compounds

Alexander, Leo, cited, 66, 112-113

Amphenone, experimental use, 51, 53-54. *See also* Steroid compounds "Angelico, Leo," 21, 68, 72, 126, 132, 173, 184, 185-186, 187, 188, 216, 217, 219, 220, 222, 235; case, 49-50, 53-54, 196-202, 206, 207; and amphenone treatment, 53-54, 55; praise for, 92, 93; and "Paul

O'Brian," 202-204, 208-209, 248; other patients' reactions to, 204-205; reaction to sociologist, 214

Aub, Joseph C., cited, 255

Barber, Bernard, cited, 255; and Elinor G., cited, 65

"Barber, William," 39, 94-95, 150

Bauer, Walter, cited, 255

"Baum, Bob," 58-59

Bean, W. B., cited, 66

Beaumont, William, cited, 67-68

Bendix, Reinhard, cited, 235

Bernard, Claude, 43, 66

Bets, betting. *See* "Game of chance" behavior

"Bontadini, Louis," 94, 146, 199

Bowen, Elenore Smith (pseud.), cited, 235, 236

Burwell, Charles Sidney, cited, 255

Cancer of the prostate, 17, 18, 23, 32, 54, 128; and adrenalectomy, 35-36, 42. *See also* Diseases

Cannon, Walter B., cited, 65

"Celebration" of patients, 92-95, 97, 227, 251. *See also* "Stardom"

Chronic disorders. *See* Diseases

Clinical care: postoperative management, 18, 19, 34-36; and physicians' uncertainties, 37-39; versus medical research, 43-56, 60, 68, 75, 87, 241-242; and physicians' humor, 79; and privileges for patients, 89; quality of, 96, 104, 105; and patient's submission to physicians, 119, 248; and lack of recovery, 130-131. *See also* Therapy Clubs, formed by patients, 145, 188, 252-253, 256. *See also* Adrenalectomy Club